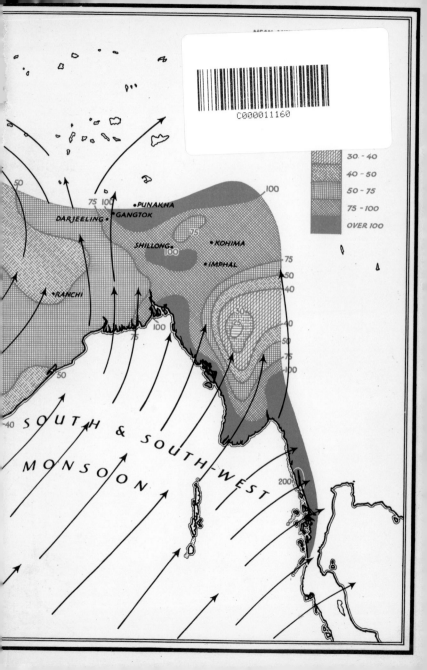

30 - 40
40 - 50
50 - 75
75 - 100
OVER 100

•PUNAKHA
100
DARJEELING• •GANGTOK
SHILLONG• 75 •KOHIMA
100
•IMPHAL
75
50
40
•RANCHI
100
50
75
25
40
50
75
100
50

40

S O U T H   &   S O U T H - W E S T

M O N S O O N

200

INDIAN HILL BIRDS

INDIAN
HILL BIRDS

By
SÁLIM ALI

Illustrated by
G. M. HENRY

DELHI
OXFORD UNIVERSITY PRESS
BOMBAY CALCUTTA MADRAS

Oxford University Press, Walton Street, Oxford OX2 6DP

Oxford   New York
Athens Auckland Bangkok Bombay
Calcutta Cape Town Dar es Salaam Delhi
Florence Hong Kong Istanbul Karachi
Kuala Lumpur Madras Madrid Melbourne
Mexico City Nairobi Paris Singapore
Taipei Tokyo Toronto

and associates in
Berlin Ibadan

First published 1949
Second impression (with new preface) 1979
Sixth impression 1994

ISBN 0 19 561170 5

Text printed by Rekha Printers Pvt. Ltd., New Delhi 110020
and plates by Indraprastha Press (CBT), New Delhi 110 002
and published by Neil O'Brien, Oxford University Press,
YMCA Library Building, Jai Singh Road, New Delhi 110001

PREFACE TO THE 1979 REPRINT

INDIAN HILL BIRDS went out of print in 1974. The growing cult of mountaineering and mountain trekking in the country, and of international nature tourism, has within recent years generated an unprecedented and urgent demand for such a book. To meet this demand the publishers have decided to reprint the book in its original form as an interim measure, pending the preparation of a revised second edition incorporating the changes in the taxonomy that have become necessary as well as the accretions to our knowledge of distribution, ecology, etc. that have occurred since the book was published nearly thirty years ago.

Perhaps the most significant changes to affect the casual user of the book are the territorial names, thanks to the subsequent reorganization of the states of the Indian Union and the creation of several new ones. These changes may cause some confusion in the matter of the geographical distribution as given for various species. To help reconcile the difficulty the following note is provided:

ANDHRA PRADESH. Until 1953 the northern half of Madras State including most of the former Hyderabad State, the deltas of the Krishna and Godavari rivers, and the arid hills of the Eastern Ghats.

ARUNACHAL PRADESH. 'The Province of the Dawn'. The Himalayas east of Bhutan including the Dafla, Abor, Miri and Mishmi hills. Before 1972 this area was the North-East Frontier Agency (NEFA) comprising the Kameng, Subansiri, Siang and Luhit frontier divisions.

ASSAM. Before 1947 the province included Arunachal Pradesh, Meghalaya, Mizoram and Nagaland (qq.v.); since 1972 it is restricted to the Brahmaputra Valley.

BANGLADESH. Constituted in 1971, formerly East Pakistan. Besides the Brahmaputra plains it includes the Chittagong Hill Tracts in the south.

BENGAL. Prior to 1947 the Ganges-Brahmaputra delta area; later divided into Bangladesh (q.v.) and West Bengal.

GUJARAT. The northern part of the former Bombay State separated from Maharashtra in 1960, including Saurashtra (q.v.).

HARYANA. The fertile plains area north and west of Delhi, formerly part of the Punjab (q.v.).

HIMACHAL PRADESH. 'The Snowy Province'. The Himalayan hill states were united under this name in 1948, and in 1966 the area was enlarged by the hill regions of the Punjab.

KARNATAKA. The official name of Mysore since 1973.

KERALA. Constituted in 1956 to include the former states of Travancore and Cochin together with the district of Malabar.

LAKSHADWEEP. The official name of the Laccadive Islands since 1973.

MADHYA PRADESH. A part of the former Central Provinces together with the former central Indian states of Gwalior, Bhopal, Indore, etc.

MAHARASHTRA. The southern part of the former Bombay State, separated from Gujarat in 1960, together with an adjoining part of the former Central Provinces.

MEGHALAYA. 'Cloud Land'. The Garo, Jaintia, Khasi and Cachar hill districts of former Assam, constituted a separate state in 1972.

MIZORAM. The Lushai or Mizo Hills area, constituted a separate state in 1972.

NAGALAND. The Naga Hills area, constituted a separate state in 1962.

NEFA. Now Arunachal Pradesh (q.v.).

OUDH (= Awadh). The eastern Gangetic plains, now part of Uttar Pradesh ('Northern Province'), the name given in 1950 to the United Provinces of Agra and Oudh.

PAKISTAN. Sind, Baluchistan, Punjab (q.v.), the North-West Frontier Province and Bahawalpur.

PUNJAB. Prior to 1947 the whole of the northern plains area watered by the Indus and its five tributaries namely Jhelum, Chenab, Ravi, Beas and Sutlej; divided in 1947 into West Punjab (Pakistan) and East Punjab (India). In 1966 East Punjab was further divided into Punjab, Haryana and Himachal Pradesh (qq.v.).

SAURASHTRA. The union of Kathiawar states was merged with Bombay in 1956, and since 1960 has been part of Gujarat (q.v.).

SRI LANKA. The official name of Ceylon since May 1972.

TAMIL NADU. The name given to Madras State in 1969.

Information about more Himalayan birds can be obtained from *Field Guide to the Birds of the Eastern Himalayas* (Sálim Ali, 1978) and from the ten-volume *Handbook of The Birds of India and Pakistan* (Sálim Ali & Dillon Ripley, 1968–74) published by Oxford University Press.

Bombay   Sálim Ali

PREFACE

HOLIDAY VISITORS to the hills have constantly felt the want of a handy book that would tell them by simple word and picture something of the birds they meet about their hotels and bungalows, and in the course of their excursions and treks. Many of these visitors are sophisticated townsfolk, hard-boiled professional or business men, who in their workaday lives have seldom bothered themselves about such 'puerile' and unremunerative pursuits as bird-watching. But here, in spite of the round of cinemas and dances, and of cabarets, cocktails and bridge, a modicum of time has still hung heavy on their hands and they have deigned to turn to birds, perhaps more in the nature of self-defence—as an antidote to boredom—than for any other reason.

I know some such people: they started off on bird-watching when thus driven, and ended by becoming quite knowledgeable enthusiasts. But I know a lot more who began with the best will in the world but who soon gave up because they could find no simple bird book to guide them: to tell them what they wanted to know in a way that they could understand.

At first, Douglas Dewar's *Birds of the Indian Hills*, and latterly, Hugh Whistler's *Popular Handbook of Indian Birds*, went a long way towards supplying the deficiency. But the former carries no pictures, while the latter—though it is partly illustrated—contains a large number of birds that are not likely to be met with in the hills. Many of its illustrations, moreover, are uncoloured and, as such, of little help to the novice. For it is a fact that colour, perhaps even more than song, is what first attracts the attention of a layman towards a bird and impresses it upon his mind. Therefore, in order that a complete beginner, or one who is only casually interested, may be enabled to recognize a bird he sees without undue effort on his part he must be provided with simple keys and coloured illustrations. To people who have a flair for solving cross-word puzzles, identification keys possess a special fascination. If keys are suitably devised and so linked with the coloured pictures and descriptions that with cross-references and a certain amount of fiddling about, they lead to a satisfactory recognition of the bird, it helps to sharpen and sustain their interest.

This books sets out, first and foremost, to meet the wants of the average visitor to the hills. Obviously, to illustrate and describe *every* bird *ever* likely to be found at or around *every* hill-station in India, and yet keep the volume within reasonable limits of size and cost, would be an impossibility. The alternative was to make a representative selection of the commoner birds—such as anyone could hope to come ac   at one time or another in the Indian hills. The latter course has bee adopted, but the selection has not been easy and opinions are boun to differ greatly on what species should have been included and wh left out. Unfortunately, this criticism cannot altogether be avoided in ny pocket book that aspires to deal in a comprehensive way with the birds of such diverse and far-flung areas as our Indian hills. It is suggested, however, that if used in conjunction with Whistler's *Popular Handbook of Indian Birds*, and with my own *Book of Indian Birds*, a great many of the omissions will be rectified.

The beautiful colour plates have been specially painted for this work by Mr G. M. Henry, the well-known artist of the album of the *Birds of Ceylon*. Many of the species, as far as I am aware, have never been depicted before, and certainly never published anywhere. It is unfortunate that due to the high cost of colour-printing it has not been practicable to illustrate every species described, as was our original plan.

As in *The Book of Indian Birds*, it has been considered advisable to employ common and familiar birds as standards for comparison of size rather than indicate this in inches. The success which has, on the whole, attended this method clearly justifies its adoption. The standards used are again the same as before, namely:

A	Sparrow (6″)	G	Crow (17″)
B	Quail (7–8″)	H	Kite (24″)
C	Bulbul (8″)	I	Duck (24″)
D	Myna (9″)	J	Village hen (18–30″)
E	Pigeon (13″)	K	Vulture (36″)
F	Partridge (13″)		

The keys for field identification are based on the points that arrest the observer's attention on his first meeting with a bird—some peculiarity in the length or shape of its bill, tail, or crest; or some salient feature in its colouration. There is nothing scientific or rigidly consistent about them, and they will not bear critical scrutiny. For instance, it is obvious that under section 5e (sober BROWN birds) there are a number of species jumbled together that might just as well have fitted in a different category. But it is hoped that a working familiarity with the keys will provide a convenient scheme and offer leading suggestions for satisfactory determination in the majority of cases.

A work of this type has of necessity to be largely a compilation of the scattered notes of many observers. Excellent piecemeal observations have been recorded from time to time in the Journal of the Bombay Natural History Society during the last sixty-two years. I have sifted and freely drawn on these, and others, wherever desirable in order to supplement my own observations. It has been impossible to indicate the source in each case, but I take this opportunity of acknowledging my indebtedness to all the contributors, jointly and severally. Our knowledge of the life histories of Indian birds, meagre as it is, derives largely from the pieced-together, and often haphazard, observations of amateurs. It is to be hoped that one of the objects this book will serve will be to swell the ranks of competent bird-watchers and give a fillip to their activities.

To the ornithologist, the Indian Empire connotes the territory of the Indian Union, Pakistan, Burma and Ceylon. The author has followed this convention and his references to the Indian Empire are without any political significance.

S. A.

BOMBAY
8 *June* 1948

CONCERNING HILL BIRDS

ONE OF THE THINGS that make trekking in the Himalayas so particularly delightful is surely the constant change in the character of the plants and birds that one meets as one climbs higher and higher, and passes from one zone of altitude into another.

It is well known that the character of any vegetation is largely determined by climate, which means a combination of temperature, rainfall and humidity. As a mountain is ascended, temperature drops at the rate of 3·22 degrees Fahrenheit for every thousand feet. In other words, a temperature that is 80° F. at sea-level will become 65° at 4,500 feet (the elevation of Mahableshwar), 60° at 6,000 feet (that of Mussooree), and fall to 13° below zero on the summit of Mt. Everest.

Thus it is that on a lofty mountain chain like the Himalayas we find climates ranging upward from tropical at their base, through subtropical, warm and cool temperate to alpine and arctic. Changes in climate are accompanied by corresponding changes in vegetation. Upon this latter, directly or indirectly, depends the character of the bird life inhabiting the various altitudinal belts—or 'Life Zones' as they are called. These changes are often so clear-cut that, after a little experience, it is frequently possible to guess the approximate elevation of any spot that one is passing through with tolerable accuracy.

Vertical zonation of the above kind is most striking on mountains standing in the tropics. Here the transition from a tropical to a temperate flora becomes far more abrupt in a few thousand feet of ascent than in the many hundreds of miles of latitude required to compensate for the fall in temperature experienced in the ascent. It may be said that conditions on the sides of a high mountain are a syncopated or telescoped replica of those that obtain elsewhere over much greater distances of latitude. The alpine and arctic conditions encountered in the higher Himalayan zones, for example, are not repeated till one reaches the northerly latitudes of Asia, quite two thousand miles away.

There is a well-recognized natural axiom, known as Bergmann's Rule, that among warm-blooded animals which inhabit an extensive geographical range, those occupying the colder portions grow to a larger size than their fellows of the warmer portions. Thus, in the northern hemisphere, animals of the temperate regions average larger than their representatives in the tropics. And this same rule is also found to apply as between forms occupying higher and lower life zones on mountains. Side by side with the increase in size go certain correlated and adaptive modifications in the structure to meet the specialized life conditions.

2

Among other things, for example, warm-blooded dwellers at high elevations possess a larger lung capacity than their fellows of the plains, in order to cope with the paucity of oxygen in the rarefied air. For high altitude involves not only a steep fall in temperature, but also in the pressure of the atmosphere. The air pressure, which is 14·7 lb. per square inch at sea-level, is reduced to half at 18,000 feet.

Typical high-altitude birds also exhibit this increased lung capacity. Other points that seem to characterize them are that they seek their food on the ground while hopping about, and fly little—habits doubtless of some survival value on exposed hillsides subject to violent gales and blizzards. Of necessity also, they roost and nest on protected ledges, or in holes in cliffs.

Birds, however, are perhaps the class of animals least affected directly by its climatic surroundings. On the whole, they exhibit far less specialization for a high-altitude life in their make-up than mammals. Their power of flight enables them to overcome barriers that restrict the movement of mammals and subject them to distributional isolation.

But just as many birds inhabiting the bleak northern lands are obliged to migrate to warmer countries nearer the Equator in order to escape the rigours of winter—shortening hours of daylight, and difficulty of procuring food when the ground is shrouded in snow and all water frozen—so are the birds of the high life zones forced to lower levels in winter. This seasonal altitudinal, or up-and-down, movement is migration in its strictest sense. It involves the crucial rhythm—a periodically alternating swing between two areas that provide optimum living conditions at respective seasons. Snow-line in the Himalayas, which in summer is between 15,000 and 18,000 feet, descends in winter to 8,000 or 9,000 feet. Many birds of the higher zones, such as the Wall-Creeper, are then forced down to the elevation of our popular Himalayan hill-stations, whence they are completely absent during the summer months.

As spring turns to summer the snow-line recedes, and with it the birds reascend to populate the areas they had evacuated. Even on the lower slopes of the Himalayas where snow-line does not come into the picture at all, and also in the hill ranges of peninsular India where winter conditions are comparatively mild, considerable altitudinal movement takes place among the resident birds. Many Himalayan Laughing-Thrushes that are found in summer up to 8,000 or 9,000 feet, descend to less than half those levels in winter, and even down into the foothills. In the Nilgiris and adjacent hills a similar altitudinal movement is also observed among the Laughing-Thrushes, and many other birds.

Another distinct type of seasonal movement, also of a truly migratory character, is noticeable among hill birds. Instead of shifting merely from a higher to a lower level in winter, and vice versa in spring, certain strong flying species migrate over many degrees of latitude to reach analogous life zones on mountains situated in warmer regions. Familiar examples of such 'mountain-top migrants' among our Indian birds are the Woodcock (p. 182), the Indian Blue-Chat (p. 54) and the Pied Ground-Thrush (p. 67). These birds have their home in the Himalayas in the sense that they breed only there, but they habitually spend the winter in the Nilgiris and associated hills of south-west India. From the fact that they are so rarely met with in the intervening country, it is evident that they must normally perform their journeys between the Himalayas and their winter quarters in a single hop covering from twelve to fifteen hundred miles.

While birds that reside permanently at very high altitudes doubtless do derive some advantage from adaptive adjustments in their internal structure, it is obvious that for short periods, at any rate, even unspecialized birds can withstand the intense cold and attenuated air of the higher levels without apparent discomfort. I have watched Turkestan Rock-Pigeons coming up from below and merrily picking the votive grain sprinkled by pious pilgrims at the head of Dolma La Pass, 18,700 feet, in W. Tibet. One of the Everest Expeditions observed Lämmergeiers sailing along at 24,000 to 25,000 feet up, while Choughs followed the climbers effortlessly up to 27,000 feet. More recently a scientist in photographing the sun at Dehra Dun accidentally obtained a picture of unsuspected geese flying across the orb at a height reliably estimated as about 29,000 feet, or almost five and a half miles! This, and the effortless flight of birds—even sailing and hovering—at heights where the supporting power of the atmosphere is reduced to half, or one-third, shows that even species that are not especially equipped for high-altitude life are not appreciably handicapped by the abnormal conditions prevailing there. Indeed, it is inconceivable that any birds would ascend to these heights if they suffered the least discomfort, since there is ostensibly no pressing need for them to do so.

The controlling effect of mountain chains and hill ranges on local climate and vegetation, and therefore on the distribution of animal life, is well known. The Himalayas stretch across our northern frontier like a gigantic wall, cutting off the Indian plains from the high plateau of Tibet and Central Asia. They bar the northward passage of the moisture-laden wind currents, driven up seasonally from the south-west through the Arabian Sea and the Bay of Bengal, to the lands beyond. This high mountain barrier also serves to insulate the plains of India alike from the icy northern gales of winter and from the dry scorching winds of summer, thus making our climate less severe than it would otherwise be. The arid upland steppes of Tibet, with their low humidity and bleak winters, and analogous elevations on the southern aspect of the Himalayan range (under the influence of the SW. Monsoon) present marked contrasts in their climate and vegetation. The Himalayas constitute the boundary between two of the six Zoo-geographical Regions into which scientists have divided the earth, namely, between the *Palaearctic* (which includes all Europe and North Africa and stretches across northern Asia) and the *Oriental*, south of this, which is again sub-divided into the Indian, Indo-Chinese and Indo-Malayan sub-regions.

The areas of heaviest rainfall on the western side of India are those sections of the Sahyadri Range (or Western Ghats) that lie directly across the path of the SW. Monsoon currents. Here again, the heavily vapour-charged winds from the Arabian Sea strike the mountain barrier along the coast and are forced upwards. The ascensional movement into the higher and cooler atmospheric strata enveloping the higher mountain-sides causes the vapour to condense and fall in the form of rain. Only a small proportion of the moisture-laden winds is able to get across the Ghats, thus resulting in a remarkable disparity in the rainfall between the seaward and landward aspects of the hills.

A specific example of what this means is provided by Mahableshwar, situated at an elevation of 4,500 feet, some forty miles south of Poona. The average rainfall at this delightful hill-station, between June and October, is over 300 inches. At Panchgani, another popular resort with about the same altitude and only twelve miles away to lee, the annual average drops to 60 inches, while at Wai, twelve miles or so farther inland, at the foot of the Ghats and on the edge of the Deccan Plateau (c. 2,000 feet), the average annual precipitation is only 30 inches. The great local divergences in the vegetation and bird life within this restricted area of the Ghats are so striking that they cannot escape even a casual observer. They afford an outstanding example of the rôle that mountain ranges play in the character and local distribution of our animal life in general, and also of our birds.

The contrast between the avifauna of the slopes exposed to the rain-bearing influences of the SW. Monsoon on the Nilgiris, Palnis and adjacent hills of SW. India, and that of the protected side—of the 'rain shadow' as it is termed—is equally remarkable. It is these divergences, and the causes that bring them about, that makes the study of Indian hill birds so fascinating.

Botanists have long remarked upon the general similarity of the flora of the higher slopes of such widely separated mountain ranges as the Himalayas, the Nilgiris and other hills of SW. India, the central mountains of Ceylon, the Khasi and associated hills of Assam; and even the mountains of Java, Sumatra and the Philippines.

No less remarkable is the general similarity in the pattern of the bird fauna inhabiting analogous altitudinal zones on these far-flung mountains. Several outstanding examples spring to mind, but one must suffice. The Laughing-Thrushes of the genus *Trochalopteron* are prolific both in species and individuals throughout the lower Himalayas from extreme west to extreme east, and they also inhabit the mountains of Assam, Burma and Malaysia. They are resident birds, subject only to a restricted altitudinal movement which does not call for strong or sustained flight.

Laughing-Thrushes are not found in peninsular India, until, after an intervening gap of 1,000 to 1,500 miles, two endemic species reappear in the mountain zone of the south-west. Here they occur side by side with the Himalayan plant genus *Rubus* (Wild Raspberry), whose geographical distribution presents a strikingly parallel discontinuity. In the hills of south-western India—the Malabar section of the Sahyadri Range, or Western Ghats—*Rubus* is met with roughly from elevations of about 3,500 feet up. And curiously enough, with the reappearance of *Rubus*, *Trochalopteron* also reappears on the scene!

The parallel conditions of temperature and environment obtaining in analogous life zones on mountains, more especially in the tropics, would seem sufficient to account for the existing similarity in the bird life of widely separated hill regions. But how are we to account for the *origin* of the isolated communities of such sedentary and weak-flying birds as the Laughing-Thrushes? Several ways have been suggested, one or more of which may have operated, and may be required to explain individual instances. In the case of our Laughing-Thrushes, it seems plausible that at one time the genus *Trochalopteron* was distributed over the entire country that spans its present ranges. The intervening population went under in competition with more virile or better adapted forms. Or it disappeared with the wearing away of the elevated country that may once have stretched unbroken between its present far-flung habitats. The Himalayan and South Indian communities of Laughing-Thrushes do strongly suggest that they are relic colonies of a once continuous population.

In the case of somewhat stronger fliers, it is conceivable that the birds may have wandered from mountain-top to mountain-top seeking analogous life conditions, and then become marooned on widely separated mountains by the disappearance of some of the intermediate steps due to subsidence or other earth-breaking causes. It may also be that these steps became uninhabitable for the species owing to some adverse changes in ecological conditions.

WHERE THE BIRDS DESCRIBED IN THIS BOOK ARE FOUND

(Asterisk denotes occurrence)

Explanation of abbreviations used:

Ar. Mt. Abu; Aravalli Hills.

As. Assam hills [Garo, Jaintia, Khasi (Shillong), Lushai, and others].

B Burmese hills (Pegu and Arakan Yomas, Chin and Karen Hills, Tenasserim ranges, etc.)

C Ceylon (Central Hill Zone).

EG Eastern Ghats (Vizagapatam ghats, Nallamalai, Seshachalam, Palkonda, Chitteri, Javadi, Shevaroy, and other hills).

EH Eastern Himalayas [outer ranges from Nepal to extreme East Assam (Darjeeling, etc.)].

K Kashmir (Gulmarg, Sonamarg, Pahalgam, etc.).

N Nilgiri Hills (Ootacamund, Coonoor, Kotagiri, etc.); Brahmagiris and Wynaad hills.

NW Hills of NW. Frontier Province, Sind, Baluchistan [Khirthar, Suleiman (Quetta, Sandeman, Fort Ziarat, etc.)], Punjab Salt Range.

P Palni Hills (Kodaikanal), and south-western section of Western Ghats embracing Annamalai, Cardamom, and associated hills of Travancore and Cochin.

PI Peninsular Indian hills [Vindhya and Satpura Ranges, Mahadeo Hills (Pachmarhi), Maikal, Kaimur, Ajanta, and other hills)].

WG Western Ghats or Sahyadris from Khandesh and the Surat Dangs (south of Tapti River), south to and including the hills of Mysore and Coorg (Khandala, Lonavla, Panchgani, Mahableshwar, Matheran, etc.).

WH Western Himalayas (outer ranges from Punjab to Nepal, Murree, Dalhousie, Dharamsala, Kulu, Simla, Mussooree, Chakrata, Naini Tal, Ranikhet, Almora, etc.), embracing the Siwalik Range.

DISTRIBUTION OF THE BIRDS DESCRIBED—(contd.)

3

xxiv

xxv

Plains and Foothills

DISTRIBUTION OF THE BIRDS DESCRIBED—(contd.)

HOW TO RECOGNIZE BIRDS IN THE FIELD

1. Birds with prominent TAILS

SIZE*	LENGTH AND DESCRIPTION OF TAIL	PREDOMINANT COLOURS OF BIRD	SPECIES	PAGE
A	3″ – ; fan shaped	Sooty brown; white	White-throated Fantail-Flycatcher (5e)	88
A	3″ – ; fan shaped	Sooty brown; white	White-spotted Fantail-Flycatcher (5e)	88
A	3″ – ; fan shaped	Sooty brown; white	White-browed Fantail-Flycatcher (5e)	88
A	7″; wire-like outermost feathers	Glistening steel-blue; white; chestnut (cap)	Wire-tailed Swallow (5c)	115
C–	6″ – ; forked with out-curving tips	Glistening metallic black	Bronzed Drongo (5a)	92
C–	4″ +; loose, graduated with dark spotted white tips	Streaked brown; fulvous white	Brown Hill-Warbler (5e)	99
C	6″; graduated	Black, chestnut; white	Shama (4e)	64
C	10–15″; double ribbons	Silvery white; metallic black	Paradise Flycatcher, adult male (5b)	85
C	10–15″; double ribbons	Chestnut; greyish-white; metallic black	Paradise Flycatcher, young male (5e)	85
C	7″ – ; forked with out-curving tips	Slaty black; slaty grey	Grey Drongo (5a), (5d)	92
C	7″ – ; forked with out-curving tips	Glistening jet black	Black Drongo (5a)	92
C	5″ +; forked with out-curving tips	Glossy indigo; white	White-bellied Drongo (5d)	92

I. Birds with prominent TAILS—(contd.)

SIZE*	LENGTH AND DESCRIPTION OF TAIL	PREDOMINANT COLOURS OF BIRD	SPECIES	PAGE
C–D	6″+; deeply forked	Pied black and white	Spotted Forktail (5c)	57
C–D	6″; square, with outer ends twisted and upturned	Glistening metallic black	Hair-crested Drongo (5a)	92
D	12″; graduated	Greyish-brown; black	Himalayan Tree-Pie (5e)	5
D	12″; graduated	Chestnut-brown or rufous; grey; black	Indian Tree-Pie (5e)	5
D	20″–; double wire-like spatula-tipped streamers	Glistening metallic black	Racket-tailed Drongo (5a), (3)	92
D	9″–; pointed, white-tipped	Grass green; bluish-pink (plum colour)	Blossom-headed Parakeet (4a)	145
D	9″–; pointed, yellowish tipped	Bluish-green; pinkish grey	Blue-winged Parakeet (4a)	146
D+	10″–; pointed, yellow-tipped	Grass green; slaty	Slaty-headed Parakeet (4a)	145
E	15–17″; graduated, with double streamers	Pale blue; black; white	Red-billed Blue Magpie	3
E	15–17″; graduated, with double streamers	Pale blue; black; white	Yellow-billed Blue Magpie	4
E	9″–; pointed, parakeet-like	Yellowish-green; pinkish-orange; yellow	Pin-tailed Green Pigeon	168
J+	20″+; long, narrow, pointed; barred buff and black	Mottled and barred cinnamon, buff, rufous, black. Scarlet round eyes	Cheer Pheasant (5e)	176

* SIZES: A=Sparrow; C=Bulbul; D=Myna; E=Pigeon; J=Village hen; –=Smaller; +=Bigger

* SIZES: A = Sparrow;

SIZE*	LENGTH AND DESCRIPTION Source of BILL	PREDOMINANT COLOURS OF BIRD	SPECIES	PAGE
A ±	1" – ; curved, slender, blackish	Mottled dark brown, smoky brown/white	Himalayan Tree-Creeper (5e)	49
A'	1¼"; curved, slender, blackish	Olive-green; yellow	Little Spider-Hunter	131
A – C	2"–; curved, slender, blackish	Dark-streaked olive-green and yellow	Indian Streaked Spider-Hunter	131
C – D	1¾"±; curved, yellow	Dark brown; white	Scimitar-Babbler (5e)	34
C – D	1"±; curved, yellowish-horny	Olive-brown; dark slaty	Slaty-headed Scimitar-Babbler (5e)	35
D +	Very heavy, conical	Bright yellow; black	Black-and-Yellow Grosbeak, male (4b)	104
D –	Very heavy, conical	Dull ashy, fulvous grey	Black-and-Yellow Grosbeak, female	104
D	1½"; curved, yellowish-horny	Olive-brown; rusty; white	Rusty-cheeked Scimitar-Babbler (5e)	35
F	3"; slender, straight, snipe-like; brown	Mottled, streaked and barred brown, black, rufous, whitish	Woodcock (5e)	180
H	4½"; heavy, horn-shaped, with casque; white and black	Brownish-grey; whitish-grey	Common Grey Hornbill (5d)	148
H – D	4"±; heavy, horn-shaped without casque; horny-yellow and blackish	Slaty-grey; ashy-grey	Malabar Grey Hornbill (5d)	148
H – K	7"±; heavy, horn-shaped, with casque; yellow and black	Pied black and white	Indian Pied Hornbill, Malabar Pied Hornbill	148

2. Birds with prominent BILLS—(contd.)

SIZE*	LENGTH AND DESCRIPTION OF BILL	PREDOMINANT COLOURS OF BIRD	SPECIES	PAGE
K	11", heavy, horn-shaped, with casque; yellow and black.	Pied black and white	Great Hornbill (5c)	148

* SIZES: A = Sparrow; C = Bulbul; D = Myna; F = Partridge; H = Kite; K = Vulture; − = Smaller; + = Bigger

3. Birds with prominent CRESTS

SIZE	PREDOMINANT COLOURS OF BIRD	ASSOCIATED COLOURS	SPECIES	PAGE
A	Blackish-slaty	Chestnut; white	Black Tit (5a)	14
A	Blackish-slaty	Chestnut; white	Crested Black Tit (5a)	14
A	Greyish-brown	Whitish	Brown Crested Tit (5e)	15
A	Yellow; black	White	Yellow-cheeked Tit (4b)	16
A+	Black; chestnut-red		Crested Bunting (5a)	112
C	Earth-brown	White; sulphur-yellow	White-cheeked Bulbul (5e)	47
C	Earth-brown	White; crimson; black	Red-whiskered Bulbul (5e)	47
C	Snow-white	Metallic black	Paradise Flycatcher, adult male (1) (5b)	85
C	Chestnut; greyish-white	Metallic black	Paradise Flycatcher, adult female and young male (1) (5b)	85
D	Glistening metallic black		Racket-tailed Drongo (1), (5a)	92
D	Rusty red	Black	Black-headed Sibia (5a)	39
D	Dark slate	Red bill and legs	Black Bulbul (5a)	45
H+	Brown; white		Crested Hawk-Eagle (5e)	166
J	Reddish-brown; whitish	Bare scarlet facial skin	White-crested Kaleej Pheasant, female (5e)	175

3. Birds with prominent CRESTS—(contd.)

SIZE*	PREDOMINANT COLOURS OF BIRD	ASSOCIATED COLOURS	SPECIES	PAGE
J	Mottled black, brown, buff	White (throat)	Koklas Pheasant, female (5e)	175
J+	Glistening black; brownish grey	White; bare scarlet facial skin	White-crested Kaleej Pheasant (5a)	175
J+	Grey; chestnut	Reddish-brown; metallic green (head and 'horns')	Koklas Pheasant, male (5e)	175
J+	Brilliant metallic green and purple; velvety black; cinnamon	White	Monal Pheasant, male (3)	176

* SIZES: A=Sparrow; C=Bulbul; D=Myna; H=Kite; J=Village hen; —=Smaller; +=Bigger

4. BRIGHTLY Coloured Birds — (a) Chiefly GREEN or GREENISH

SIZE	PREDOMINANT COLOUR	ASSOCIATED COLOURS	SPECIES	PAGE
A—	Dull olive-green	Greyish-white	Nilgiri Flowerpecker	133
A—	Yellowish olive-green	Black; whitish	Spotted Piculet	139
C	Grass green	Deep orange; black	Orange-bellied Chloropsis	43
C	Grass green	Golden-yellow; black; purple	Gold-fronted Chloropsis	43
D	Grass green	Crimson; black; blue	Blue-throated Barbet	140
D	Grass green	Dark brown	Small Green Barbet	141
D	Grass green	Bluish-red (plum); maroon red	Blossom-headed Parakeet, male (1)	145
D	Bluish-green	Blue; pinkish grey	Blue-winged Parakeet, male (1)	146
D	Grass green	Light blue; buff	Blue-bearded Bee-Eater	147
D+	Dull green	Yellow; crimson; black	Little Scaly-bellied Green Woodpecker	135

4. BRIGHTLY Coloured Birds — (a) Chiefly GREEN or GREENISH—(contd.)

SIZE*	PREDOMINANT COLOUR	ASSOCIATED COLOURS	SPECIES	PAGE
D+	Grass green	Brownish; bright yellow orbital skin	Green Barbet	142
D+	Grass green	Brownish; deep yellow orbital skin	Lineated Barbet	142
D+	Grass green	Slaty; maroon-red	Slaty-headed Parakeet (1)	145
D+	Glistening bronze-green	Brownish-pink; grey; white	Emerald or Bronze-winged Dove	171
E−	Yellowish-green	Maroon-chestnut; grey.	Grey-fronted Green Pigeon	168
E	Dull green	Yellow; crimson	Scaly-bellied Green Woodpecker	135
E	Dull green	Yellow; crimson; black	Black-naped Green Woodpecker	135
E	Yellowish-green	Maroon; orange-pink; yellow	Kokla or Wedge-tailed Green Pigeon	168
E	Yellowish-green	Pinkish-orange; yellow; cinnamon	Pin-tailed Green Pigeon (1)	168
E	Yellowish-green	Lilac; blue-grey; yellow	Common Green Pigeon	168
E+	Metallic bronze-green	Greyish-pink	Green Imperial Pigeon	171

* SIZES: A=Sparrow; C=Bulbul; D=Myna; E=Pigeon; − =Smaller; + =Bigger

4. BRIGHTLY Coloured Birds — (b) Largely YELLOW

SIZE*	PREDOMINANT COLOUR	ASSOCIATED COLOURS	SPECIES	PAGE
A−	Orange-yellow	Black	Black-and-Orange Flycatcher, male	82
A−	Bright yellow; ashy grey	Greenish-yellow	Grey-headed Flycatcher	83
A−	Bright yellow; greyish brown	Yellowish-green; white	Grey-headed Flycatcher-Warbler	97
A−	Greenish-yellow; bright yellow	Greyish	White-eye	127

4. BRIGHTLY Coloured Birds — (b) Largely YELLOW—(contd.)

SIZE*	PREDOMINANT COLOURS	ASSOCIATED COLOURS	SPECIES	PAGE
A	Yellowish-green; black	Bright yellow; white	Green-backed Tit	13
A	Bright yellow; black	White	Yellow-cheeked Tit (3)	16
A	Bright yellow; black	Greenish-brown	Himalayan Greenfinch	108
A	Lemon yellow; black	Grey	Yellow-headed and other Yellow Wagtails	119
A – C	Bright yellow; crimson	Olive-green; orange; black	Red-billed Leiothrix or 'Pekin Robin'	40
C –	Bright yellow; crimson	Slaty-green; black	Silver-eared Mesia	44
C –	Bright yellow; olive yellow	——	Yellow-browed Bulbul	48
C –	Bright yellow; grey; black	——	Short-billed Minivet, female (4c)	90
C –	Bright yellow; grey; black	——	Scarlet Minivet, female (4c)	91
C –	Bright yellow; grey; black	——	Orange Minivet, female (4c)	91
D –	Bright yellow; black	——	Black-and-Yellow Grosbeak (2)	104
D	Bright yellow; black	——	Golden Oriole	101
D	Bright yellow; black	——	Black-headed Oriole	102

* SIZES: A=Sparrow; C=Bulbul; D=Myna; — =Smaller; + =Bigger

4. BRIGHTLY Coloured Birds — (c) Largely RED

SIZE*	PREDOMINANT COLOURS	ASSOCIATED COLOURS	SPECIES	PAGE
A –	Crimson-scarlet	Metallic green, purple, etc.; yellow	Yellow-backed Sunbirds (several species)	128
A –	Scarlet-crimson; black; buff	——	Scarlet-backed Flower-pecker	132
A +	Crimson-pink	Brown	Rosefinch, male	106
A – C	Brilliant scarlet	Blackish	Scarletfinch, male	106

4. BRIGHTLY Coloured Birds — (c) Largely RED—(contd.)

SIZE*	PREDOMINANT COLOURS	ASSOCIATED COLOURS	SPECIES	PAGE
C	Scarlet; black	—	Short-billed Minivet, male (4b)	90
C	Scarlet; black	—	Scarlet Minivet, male (4b)	91
C	Orange-scarlet; black	—	Orange Minivet, male (4b)	91
D	Crimson-pink; yellowish-brown	Blackish-brown; blue bill	Malabar Trogon, male (5e)	150
D	Deep crimson; rusty brown	Light crimson	Red-headed Trogon, male	150
D	Crimson; dull orange-brown	—	Red-headed Trogon, female	150
E—	Brick red or rufous; grey	Black; whitish	Kestrel	163

* SIZES: A=Sparrow; C=Bulbul; D=Myna; E=Pigeon; —=Smaller; +=Bigger

4. BRIGHTLY Coloured Birds — (d) Largely BLUE

SIZE*	PREDOMINANT COLOURS	ASSOCIATED COLOURS	SPECIES	PAGE
A—	Purplish-blue; ashy-white; chestnut	—	Red-flanked Bush-Robin, male (5e)	63
A—	Blue; white	Blue-black	White-browed Blue Flycatcher, male	76
A—	Slaty-blue; greyish-white	—	Slaty-blue Flycatcher	76
A—	Purplish-blue; ashy	Purple	Small Niltava, male (5e)	84
A	Slaty-blue; chestnut	White (supercilium)	Indian Blue Chat, male (5e)	54
A	Dark indigo blue; white	—	White-bellied Blue Flycatcher, male (5e)	78
A	Dark blue; rusty red; white	—	Blue-throated Flycatcher, male (5e)	78
A	Dark blue; rusty red; white	—	Tickell's Red-breasted Blue Flycatcher	78
A	Bright blue-green	Black	Verditer Flycatcher	79

4. BRIGHTLY Coloured Birds — (d) Largely BLUE—(contd.)

SIZE*	PREDOMINANT COLOURS	ASSOCIATED COLOURS	SPECIES	PAGE
A	Bright blue-green	White	Nilgiri Verditer Flycatcher	79
A+	Brilliant dark blue; bright chestnut	Black	Rufous-bellied Niltava, male (5e)	84
A+	Azure blue; whitish	Black	Black-naped Blue Flycatcher	87
A–C	Dark blue; slaty blue; white	Chestnut	Shortwing	52
A–C	Slaty-blue; white; chestnut	—	Hodgson's Shortwing, male (5e)	52
D+	Glistening ultramarine blue; deep black	—	Fairy Bluebird, male	100
D+	Blue-brown, or peacock-blue; black	—	Fairy Bluebird, female	100

* SIZES: A=Sparrow; C=Bulbul; D=Myna; ⌐=Smaller; +=Bigger

4. BRIGHTLY Coloured Birds — (e) With several BRIGHT Colours in plumage

SIZE*	COLOURS	SPECIES	PAGE
A–	Crimson-scarlet; metallic purple, green, violet; yellow	Yellow-backed Sunbirds (several species) (4c)	128
A–	Scarlet-maroon; lilac; metallic green, etc., yellow	Small Sunbird	129
A–	Metallic bluish-green; buff; bright crimson	Fire-breasted Flowerpecker	132
A–	Scarlet-crimson; buff; black	Scarlet-backed Flowerpecker	132
A	Sandy; golden-yellow; bright crimson; black; white	Himalayan Goldfinch	107
A	Dull blue; bright blue; chestnut	Blue-fronted Redstart, male (5e)	60
A	Greyish-black; chestnut	Common Redstart, male (5e)	60

4. BRIGHTLY Coloured Birds — (e) With several BRIGHT Colours in plumage—*(contd.)*

SIZE*	COLOURS	SPECIES	PAGE
A – C	Ashy-grey; crimson-pink; white	Wall-Creeper	50
A +	Black; deep chestnut; white	White-capped Redstart	59
B	Olive-brown, streaked and mottled white and black; red bill and legs; chestnut	Painted Bush-Quail, male	177
C	Black; chestnut; white	Shama (1)	64
C	Blue; black; chestnut; white	Blue-headed Rock-Thrush, male	70
C	Blue; chestnut-maroon	Chestnut-bellied Rock-Thrush, male	70
D	Bluish-grey; orange-chestnut	Ground-Thrush	67
D	Grey; black; white; chestnut	Red-winged Shrike-Babbler, male	42
D	Olive-greenish and yellowish; bluish-grey; buff	Red-winged Shrike-Babbler, female	42
D – E	Pinkish-brown (fawn); grey; black; vivid blue	Black-throated Jay	6
D – E	Pinkish-brown (fawn); grey; black; vivid blue	Himalayan Red-crowned Jay	8
D – E	Golden yellow; black; white; crimson	Golden-backed Woodpecker	138
D – E	Green; violet blue-back; scarlet; blue; yellow	Great Himalayan Barbet	140
E	Golden olive; black; white; crimson	Malherbe's Golden-backed Woodpecker	137
F	Olive-brown mottled black and chestnut; grey; black; crimson orbital skin	Common Hill-Partridge	179
F	Olive-brown; rufous; slaty; black; chestnut; grey; crimson orbital skin	Rufous-throated Hill-Partridge	179
J +	Brilliant metallic green and purple; cinnamon; velvety black; white	Monal Pheasant, male (3)	176

* SIZES: A=Sparrow; B=Quail; C=Bulbul; D=Myna; E=Pigeon; F=Partridge; J=Village hen; +=Bigger; —=Smaller; +=Bigger;

xliii

5. SOBER Coloured Birds—(a) Wholly or largely BLACK or BLACKISH

SIZE*	COLOURS	SPECIES	PAGE
A	Slaty black; white; chestnut	Black Tit (3)	14
A	Slaty black; white; chestnut	Crested Black Tit (3)	14
A+	Glistening black; chestnut red	Crested Bunting (3)	112
C−	Glistening metallic black	Bronzed Drongo (1)	92
C	Slaty-black, slaty-grey	Grey Drongo (1), (5d)	92
C	Glistening jet black	Black Drongo (1)	92
C−D	Glistening metallic black	Hair-crested Drongo (1)	92
D	Glistening metallic black	Racket-tailed Drongo (1), (3)	92
D	Dark slate; red bill and legs	Black Bulbul (3)	45
D	Black; grey; yellow legs, bill, eyelids	Grey-winged Blackbird, male	65
D	Black; white; yellow legs, bill, eyelids	White-collared Blackbird	66
D−E	Blue-black; glistening blue	Whistling-Thrush	71
D−E	Glistening jet black; yellow legs, bill and head-wattles	Grackle or Hill Myna	103
E	Black; grey	Jackdaw	2
E+	Blackish-slate; lilac	Ceylon Wood-Pigeon	170
G	Glistening jet black	Red-billed Chough	10
G	Glistening jet black	Yellow-billed Chough	10
G+	Glistening jet black	Jungle Crow	1
G+	Glistening jet black	Carrion Crow	1
H	Glistening jet black	Raven	1
H+	Brownish-black; bright yellow legs and cere	Black Eagle	166
J+	Glistening black; white; brownish-grey; scarlet facial skin	White-crested Kaleej Pheasant, male (3)	175

* SIZES: A=Sparrow; C=Bulbul; D=Myna; E=Pigeon; G=Crow; H=Kite; J=Village hen; −=Smaller; +=Bigger

xliv

5. SOBER Coloured Birds — (b) Wholly or largely WHITE

SIZE*	COLOURS	SPECIES	PAGE
C	Pure silvery white; metallic black	Paradise Flycatcher, adult male (1), (3)	85
E	White; brown; dark slaty-grey	White-bellied or Snow-Pigeon	172
H	White; black	Neophron or Scavenger Vulture, adult	161
K +	Creamy or buffy white; blackish brown	Himalayan Griffon Vulture	159

* SIZES: C=Bulbul; E=Pigeon; H=Kite; K=Vulture; – =Smaller; + =Bigger

5. SOBER Coloured Birds — (c) General effect PIED BLACK AND WHITE

SIZE*	COLOURS	SPECIES	PAGE
A	—	Pied Bush-Chat, male (5e)	55
A	Orange-brown breast	Collared Bush-Chat, male (5e)	55
A	—	House-Martin	114
A	Chestnut (cap)	Wire-tailed Swallow (1)	115
A	—	Hodgson's Pied Wagtail	117
A	—	Common House-Swift	152
A	Scarlet	Pigmy Woodpecker	139
A+	—	Little Forktail	57
C –	—	Blyth's White-rumped Swift	152
C	—	Large Pied Wagtail	118
C–D	—	Spotted Forktail (1)	57
C–D	Scarlet; brownish-yellow	Mahratta or Yellow-fronted Pied Wood-pecker	136
D	Crimson	Himalayan Pied Woodpecker	136
D	Crimson; golden brown	Brown-fronted Pied Woodpecker	136
D	Fulvous; crimson	Fulvous-breasted Pied Woodpecker	136
G	Crimson	Great Black Woodpecker	137
K	Yellow tinge on white portions	Great Hornbill (2)	148

* SIZES: A=Sparrow; C=Bulbul; D=Myna; G=Crow; K=Vulture; – =Smaller; + =Bigger

5. SOBER Coloured Birds —(d) General effect largely ASHY GREY, BLUE GREY or SLATY

SIZE*	COLOURS	SPECIES	PAGE
A –	Grey; pale rusty; chestnut; white	Red-headed Tit	17
A –	Purplish-blue; pale lilac-grey; black	Velvet-fronted Nuthatch	20
A –	Greyish; olive-green; whitish	Large Crowned Willow-Warbler	96
A	Grey; black; white	Grey Tit	11
A	Grey; chestnut; fulvous; white	White-tailed Nuthatch	19
A	Grey; chestnut; fulvous; white	Brooks's or Kashmir Nuthatch	19
A	Grey; black; white	White-cheeked Nuthatch	19
A	Grey; pinkish-fulvous	Rock Nuthatch	19
A	Grey; deep chestnut	Chestnut-bellied Nuthatch	19
A	Ashy-grey; black; white	Dark Grey Bush-Chat, male (5e)	56
A	Bluish-slate; bright chestnut	Plumbeous Redstart, male (5e)	60
A	Ashy-slate; white; crimson; black	Himalayan Rubythroat, male (5e)	61
A	Grey; white; black	White Wagtail	118
B – F	Grey; sandy; orange-yellow legs and bill	Seesee Partridge	180
C	Leaden blue	Blue Rock-Thrush	70
C	Slaty; grey	Grey Drongo (1), (5a)	92
C	Glossy indigo; white	White-bellied Drongo (1)	92
C – D	Grey; rufous; whitish; black	Rufous-backed Shrike	89
E –	Slaty-grey; white; rufous	Central Asian Hobby	162
E –	Slaty-grey; black; rusty-red	Indian Hobby	163
E	Ashy; brownish-ashy; white; black (barring)	Cuckoo (several species)	143
E	Bluish-grey; black; glistening green and magenta tints	Blue Rock-Pigeon	172
E	Pale bluish-grey; ashy-grey; metallic green and magenta tints	Turkestan Rock-Pigeon	173

xlvi

5. SOBER Coloured Birds — (d) General effect largely ASHY GREY, BLUE GREY or SLATY—(contd.)

SIZE*	COLOURS	SPECIES	PAGE
F+	Pinkish grey-brown; buff; black; chestnut; crimson legs and bill	Chukor Partridge	180
G+	Slaty-blue; black; rusty red	Shahin Falcon	162
G+	Slaty-grey; white; rufous	Eastern Peregrine Falcon	162
H	Brownish-grey; whitish grey	Common Grey Hornbill (2)	148
H	Slaty-grey; ashy-grey	Malabar Grey Hornbill (2)	148

* SIZES: A = Sparrow; B = Quail; C = Bulbul; D = Myna; E = Pigeon; F = Partridge; G = Crow; H = Kite; − = Smaller; + = Bigger

5. SOBER Coloured Birds — (e) Largely BROWN

SIZE	COLOURS	SPECIES	PAGE
A−	Dark brown mottled whitish; smoky brown; white	Himalayan Tree-Creeper	49
A−	Streaked brown; whitish; bright chestnut	Red-headed Fantail-Warbler	93
A−	Streaked brown; whitish	Streaked Fantail-Warbler	94
A−	Olive-brown; bright yellow	Tickell's Willow-Warbler	95
A−	Sooty brown	Sooty Flycatcher	74
A−	Brown; black; white; orange chestnut	Red-breasted Flycatcher	75
A−	Fulvous olive-brown; chestnut; blue	Small Niltava, female (4d)	84
A	Sooty-brown; white	White-browed Fantail-Flycatcher	88
A	Bright cinnamon-rufous; pale yellow	Cinnamon Tree-Sparrow	109
A	Sooty-brown	Crag-Martin	113
A	Streaked brown and/or black; whitish	Pipit (several species)	120
A	Streaked brown; whitish	Skylark	125
A	Brown; whitish; chestnut; bright blue	Bluethroat	62
A	Olive-brown; orange-chestnut; whitish; deep blue	Red-flanked Bush-Robin, female (4d)	63

xlvii

5. SOBER Coloured Birds — (e) Largely BROWN—(contd.)

1

5. SOBER Coloured Birds — (e) Largely BROWN—(contd.)

li

5. SOBER Coloured Birds — (e) Largely BROWN—(contd.)

SIZE*	COLOURS	SPECIES	PAGE
K+	Chocolate-brown to sandy-white; black	Himalayan Griffon Vulture	159
K+	Cinnamon-brown; black	Indian Griffon Vulture	159
K+	Silver-grey; fulvous; black	Lämmergeier or Bearded Vulture	160

* SIZES: A=Sparrow; C=Bulbul; D=Myna; E=Pigeon; F=Partridge; G=Crow H=Kite;
  J=Village hen; K=Vulture; −=Smaller; +=Bigger

LIST OF PLATES

COLOURED

7   liii

MONOCHROME

THE JUNGLE CROW

Corvus macrorhynchos Wagler

PLATES I AND 7I

SIZE : Larger than the familiar House Crow of the plains.

FIELD CHARACTERS : A uniformly jet black crow with purplish sheen, and heavy bill. Its cawing differs from the House Crow's in being hoarser and deeper. Sexes alike. More or less replaces the House Crow at all our hill-stations.

The Carrion Crow (*Corvus corone orientalis*)—indistinguishable from this species in the field—is found in north-eastern Kashmir (Ladakh, Baltistan, etc.), and possibly also in other parts of the Western Himalayas. The 'Jungle Crows' of Mussooree, for example, have a very unorthodox call—more raucous and of the bell-like quality of the Raven's. In overhead flight their tail presents a distinctly wedge-shaped outline. In the hand the intenser blackness of its plumage and the stiffer, glossier feathers of the hindneck, with distinct glistening shafts, differentiate it from the Jungle Crow. These crows need to be closely investigated.

The Raven (*C. corax*), an enlarged edition of the Jungle Crow, almost the size of the Kite, is usually seen at high altitudes along the various Himalayan trade routes to Central Asia, and by sheep *chaupōans*. It has a variety of hoarse bell-like calls, *prūk*, *prūk*, or *kreeūk*, often uttered as a pair indulges in its remarkable aerobatics around some precipitous cliff.

DISTRIBUTION : Western and Eastern Himalayas (up to 15,000 feet in summer); Assam hills; Mt. Abu; Vindhya and Satpura Hills; Western and Eastern Ghats; Nilgiris; Palnis; Mysore and Travancore hills (generally up to the highest human habitations). Also practically throughout the low country in India, Burma and Ceylon.

Four geographical races are recognized within this range, differing chiefly in size of wing and bill.

HABITS : The Jungle Crow replaces the House Crow as a scavenger at the hill-stations all over the country. Here it is usually found in smaller numbers than its cousin in the plains. In the Himalayas, particularly, it moves up and down the heights a great deal according to season—higher in summer, lower in winter. It is omnivorous in diet and lives on any scraps it can pick up around kitchens and municipal refuse dumps and picnic grounds, or in the vicinity of cooly barracks or outlying shepherds' encampments. Everywhere it is as cheeky and bold as ever, and as wary. While entering a verandah and sidling up to carry off a titbit from the breakfast table, it keeps an ever watchful eye on the exit ready to make

I

a hurried withdrawal on the first scent of suspicion. It is destructive to fruits in hill orchards and responsible for considerable casualties among the eggs and young of many birds.

NESTING: The normal breeding season in tne hills—Himalayas, as well as the peninsular and South Indian hills—is chiefly March to May. The nest is of the usual crow type—an untidy platform of twigs lined with soft roots and fibres. It is placed at heights between 20 and 60 feet from the ground in some large tree standing near a village or outlying homestead. In the Himalayas deodars are much favoured. A normal clutch is of 4–6 eggs, pale blue-green, spotted and blotched with brown all over and more densely at the broad end.

Both sexes share in the building work, incubation and feeding the young.

THE JACKDAW

Corvus monedula Linnaeus

PLATE I

SIZE: Smaller than the House Crow; about that of the Pigeon (13-inch).
FIELD CHARACTERS: A dainty, small-sized crow, distinguished by its silver-grey sides of head and neck forming a broad grey collar, rather short neck and small crow-like bill. At close quarters the greyish-white, or 'wall' eye is a feature. Sexes alike. Flocks on meadows, camping grounds, cliffs and trees.

Alongside with this species may sometimes be founa the Rook (*Corvus frugilegus*), a purplish blue-black bird like the Jungle Crow, with a bare unfeathered face. Flocks on pasture land.

DISTRIBUTION: Resident in Kashmir, Ladakh and Eastern Tibet. In winter wandering into the plains, principally in the Punjab sub-Himalayan districts. In Kashmir it does not ordinarily occur above about 9,000 feet. The range of our Eastern race—*soemmeringi*—extends westward through Afghanistan and Iran into Turkey and the Balkans.

HABITS: Few summer visitors to Srinagar, Gulmarg, Pahalgam, Sonamarg, and other holiday camping resorts in the Sind, and other delightful valleys of Kashmir, fail to strike up an early acquaintance with this pretty little 'crow with the golden voice'. It is perhaps commoner about Srinagar than elsewhere. Its caw is very different from the raucous note that one is accustomed to wake up with in the plains. It is a rather high-pitched, short and pleasant *tschak*—sometimes a double note. The bird is of a highly social disposition and is seldom seen except in flocks, which may number from twelve or twenty to anything up to a hundred individuals. In winter the flocks are particularly large. The birds are commonly seen stalking jauntily about the meadows in company with choughs and starlings, digging up earthworms and crickets, or picking up crumbs around camp and picnic sites. They are usually tame and fearless, and freely enter the precincts of villages and towns. Large numbers collect to roost at night in the magnificent old chenars in and about the various *Baghs* near Srinagar, and also in the reed-beds and willow trees about the Wular and Dal Lakes. Great noise prevails before the birds settle down to sleep. The flight is less leisurely than a crow's and rather reminiscent of the pigeon's. The aerial contortions and aerobatics of a flock of Jackdaws disporting themselves high up in the heavens, as they frequently do, is delightful to watch.

The Jackdaw is not particular as to what it eats. Grain, fruits, insects, mice, eggs and nestling birds are equally welcome; and the litter of untidy holiday-makers is not despised.

NESTING: The principal breeding month in Kashmir is May, but eggs may be found in April as well as June. The nest is an untidy collection of twigs lined with rags, hair, wool, grass and other rubbish. It is built in the roofs of houses, holes in walls and hollows in the trunks and boughs of ancient willow and chenar trees. A large hollow chenar may sometimes hold half a dozen nests. The eggs—four to seven—are a pale bluish sea-green, sparsely spotted and speckled with dark brown and purple. Both sexes share in building the nest and feeding the young, possibly also in incubation. The incubation period is said to be 17–18 days.

THE RED-BILLED BLUE MAGPIE

Urocissa erythrorhyncha Boddaert

PLATE 2

SIZE: About that of the Pigeon, with the two central feathers of the long graduated tail 15 to 17 inches long.

FIELD CHARACTERS: A conspicuous long-tailed blue bird unmistakably related to the Tree-Pie of the plains. Head, neck and breast black; underparts greyish-white. Tail feathers tipped white. Bill and legs crimson. Sexes alike. Pairs or parties in Himalayan hill forests.

An allied species, *Urocissa flavirostris*, distinguished by a wax-yellow bill instead of red, is found side by side over the greater part of its range. In Darjeeling it appears largely, or almost entirely, to replace the Red-billed species.

DISTRIBUTION: Throughout the Himalayas, from Kashmir to extreme east Assam and the Burmese hills, normally at altitudes between 5 and 10,000 feet in summer. In winter at much lower elevations. Three races are recognized on minor differences. The one that mainly concerns us is the NW. Himalayan *occipitalis*.

HABITS: The Red-billed Blue Magpie is a common bird at all the West Himalayan hill-stations. Pairs, or family parties of 5 to 7—sometimes two or more such parties banded together—are usually seen flying from tree to tree in follow-my-leader fashion, hunting among the branches of hill oaks, rhododendrons and pines for food. They are mainly arboreal, but frequently descend to the ground, where they hop among the fallen leaves with the tail partly cocked and held well off the floor. They are noisy birds and have a variety of loud, harsh, creaking and chattering calls. Some of these are strongly reminiscent of the 'scolding' of the large jungle squirrel (*Ratufa*); others are almost identical with those of the Black-throated Jay which often inhabits the same localities. They are good mimics: I have heard them imitating to perfection the call of the Pied Crested Cuckoo—*piu . . piu . . . piu–piu–piu* and so on—the Drongo-like challenging cries of the Shikra hawk, and the high-pitched screaming whistle—*kek–kek–kek–keee*—uttered by the Crested Serpent Eagle as it circles above the forest. Their diet is omnivorous. Fruits, insects and caterpillars are normally eaten. They seldom miss a chance of joining the miscellaneous mob of birds in the slaughter of winged ants emerging from the ground. I have seen Blue Magpies hopping about near bunga-lows, picking up kitchen scraps; and like their cousins the Tree-Pies, they are habitual robbers of the eggs and nest-young of small birds. The flight, rather noisy, is slow and undulating—a few wing beats followed by a glide. The long tail is spread, and a party on the wing makes a charming spectacle.

NESTING: The season generally is from April to June, but the principal month for eggs seems to be May. The nest is a smallish, flimsy, shallow, rough cup of twigs, leaves and coarse roots. It is usually placed 10 to 20 feet up—sometimes higher—in trees either on forested slopes or in opener country near hill cultivation. The normal clutch consists of five to six eggs. They are clay- or stone-coloured, boldly marked with blotches of dark brown or reddish-brown, often dense and forming a ring round the broad end.

PLATE 1
1 THE SOUTHERN JUNGLE CROW (*see* page 1)
2 THE JACKDAW (*see* page 2)
About 1/5 Nat. Size

PLATE 2
THE RED-BILLED BLUE MAGPIE (*see* page 3)
About 1/4 Nat. Size

THE HIMALAYAN TREE-PIE

Dendrocitta formosae Swinhoe

PLATE 3

SIZE: That of the Myna, with a tail 12 inches long.

FIELD CHARACTERS: A long-tailed, greyish-brown bird with black crown. Hindneck and most of underparts ashy. A conspicuous white spot in wing. The brown throat and a small chestnut patch under root of tail provide further clues. Longest tail feathers ashy with broad black tips. In flight the tail appears rather spatulate at the tip, and the bird looks somewhat smaller and slenderer than the Tree-Pie of the plains. Sexes alike. Pairs or parties in hill forest.

The Indian Tree-Pie (*D. vagabunda*) takes the place of this bird at most non-Himalayan hill resorts. It is similar in general appearance, but chestnut-brown with sooty head and neck. Greyish-white patches on its wings, and the long black-tipped grey tail, are particularly conspicuous in flight. Its habits closely resemble those of its Himalayan cousin.

In the hills of the wet zone of SW. India (Travancore, Mysore, etc.), is met the Southern Tree-Pie (*D. leucogastra*). It is chestnut-bay above, white below. Hindneck, hindcrown and rump, white. Forecrown, foreneck and breast black. Wings black with a large white patch. Tail grey and black.

DISTRIBUTION: Throughout the Himalayas from Afghanistan to eastern Assam, and down through the Burmese hills into Tenasserim. Four geographical races are recognized on minor differences. The two that mainly concern us are (1) the West Himalayan, *occidentalis*, and (2) the East Himalayan, *himalayensis*, which are most common between 2,000 and 7,000 feet elevation. The newly rediscovered peninsular race —named *sarkari*—smaller than the Himalayan bird and with a shorter bill, is apparently common in the Vizagapatam section of the Eastern Ghats, about 3,000 feet elevation.

HABITS: The Himalayan Tree-Pie is a bird of more or less thick forest and is seldom found away from it. In this respect, therefore, it differs markedly from its cousin of the plains and peninsular hills which frequents open wooded country often in the neighbourhood of villages and cultivation. It is largely arboreal, but sometimes descends into low bushes, and even the ground, in search of food. The birds are commonly present amongst the mixed avian hunting parties that rove the hill-forests of oak, rhododendron and other broad-leaved trees. Striated and

White-throated Laughing-Thrushes are amongst their usual associates. At lower elevations, among the foothills, sal forest forms a suitable habitat. They go about in pairs or parties which keep up a noisy conversation in harsh, rather metallic notes. Some of the calls, however, are quite melodious. The flight is undulating, consisting of a few rapid flaps followed by a short glide. Especially when flying from one treetop to another the birds seem to rocket down in a curious way at a steepish angle on each undulation. Its food consists chiefly of fruits and insects, but like its cousin of the plains it also destroys large numbers of eggs and nest-young of small birds. It is likewise very fond of flower nectar; Silk Cotton and Rhododendron blossoms are regularly visited in season.

NESTING: Throughout its Himalayan range this Tree-Pie breeds at elevations between two and five thousand feet, and sometimes up to seven thousand feet. April to July are the months most favoured. The nest is of the crow type, a flimsy platform of thin twigs, coarse roots, tendrils, etc.: the shallow depression for eggs in the centre is lined with finer material. It is usually built between eight and twenty feet up on saplings growing in forest or in the neighbourhood of scrub-covered ravines. The eggs—three to five—range from pale bluish or yellowish-stone colour to rich yellowish cream. They are boldly blotched with dark or reddish-brown, more numerously at the broad end. The texture is fine and glossy.

THE BLACK-THROATED JAY

Garrulus lanceolatus Vigors

SIZE: Between the Myna and the Pigeon.

FIELD CHARACTERS: A pinkish-brown and grey bird, rather like the Myna in shape except for the somewhat longer tail, which is a vivid blue, cross-barred with black. The wing feathers are black, barred with bright blue, in keeping with the tail. The head wears a black rounded tuft after the pattern of the Red-vented Bulbul. The throat and foreneck are black streaked with white, and there is a conspicuous white patch in the wing. Sexes alike. Pairs or parties, in trees or on the ground.

The true jays are purely Himalayan and have no representatives in the peninsular hills. The Indian Roller, commonly called 'Blue Jay', belongs to an entirely different natural order. It has nothing to do with the Crows, with which jays are closely related.

DISTRIBUTION: Western Himalayas from Chitral, Hazara and Kashmir to Nepal, between four and nine thousand feet. It is extremely common round many hill-stations like Kulu. Dalhousie, Murree, Simla, Mussooree, Naini Tal.

HABITS: The Black-throated Jay is a common bird in the more open West Himalayan forests at elevations of between 5,000 and 7,000 feet in summer. The birds are also frequently met with about outlying homesteads and hillmen's cultivation on hillsides covered with sparse scrub and dotted with small trees. In winter a slight movement to lower elevation is noticeable, but the birds are mainly resident. They go about in noisy pairs or small parties of four or five. In autumn and winter these may enlarge to twenty or more individuals. Jays are very inquisitive birds and often quite bold. They have the same habit as crows of collecting and raising a hue and cry when one of their number has come to grief. In flight, and in their actions generally, their relationship with the crows is evident. They have harsh monosyllabic calls, some very like those of the Tree-Pie. Others are strongly reminiscent of the screeching 'Snake alert' of the Common Myna. Their food consists of insects, reptiles, the eggs and young of small birds, and anything else that can be conveniently had. I have seen them feeding on kitchen scraps near bungalows at hill-stations. They are destructive to fruits in hill orchards. In autumn large parties may be observed hopping amongst the outside twigs and foliage of *Banj* oaks and plucking the ripe acorns. The acorn is held under foot and the kernel hacked out by repeated hammer blows of the short, strong bill and swallowed. Windfalls are either carried off to a branch or dealt with on the ground.

NESTING: The season is April to June. The nest is a deep, untidy, loosely-built cup of twigs, lined with roots, fibres and grass stems. It is usually placed in the top of an oak sapling—15 to 20 feet up—in open forest on a hillside. The eggs—three to five—are olive-brown to olive-green, minutely freckled and thinly blotched with brown. The markings coalesce to form a ring or cap at the broad end, where there usually are also some twisted black lines.

THE HIMALAYAN RED-CROWNED JAY

Garrulus bispecularis Vigors

PLATE 4

SIZE: Same as the preceding.

FIELD CHARACTERS: Differs from the Black-throated Jay in having the head and crest pinkish-brown or fawn like the back and underparts, and a black tail. A broad black band or patch on cheeks. Thighs, and root of tail both above and below, white. Close-barred black and bright blue pattern on wings as in previous species. In flight the black tail, white rump and fawn-coloured back are good clues to its identity. Sexes alike. Pairs or parties in trees, and sometimes in bushes or on the ground.

DISTRIBUTION: Himalayas, from Kashmir to Sikkim, and through the Khasi and Naga Hills of Assam down into the Chin and Kachin Hills of Burma. Four races are recognized chiefly on differences in shades of colouration, viz., the Western Himalayan *bispecularis*, the Sikkim *interstinctus*, the Khasi Hills *persaturatus*, and the Chin Hills race *haringtoni*.

HABITS: The Red-crowned Jay inhabits more or less the same type of thin hill forest of oak, rhododendron and other species, evergreen as well as deciduous, as does its Black-throated cousin. The elevation most congenial to it appears to be between three and seven thousand feet, or slightly higher. There is a slight up and down movement in summer and winter, but the species is, on the whole, resident. In the Western Himalayas the range of the two jays overlaps, and the birds may often be found side by side in the same patch of jungle, though perhaps this is less common everywhere than the Black-throated Jay.

In its voice, food and general habits, it does not differ markedly from the Black-throated Jay.

NESTING: The breeding season is from April to June. The nest is sometimes like that of the Black-throated Jay, but usually it is characteristic in being much more neatly and compactly built of twigs mixed with green moss, and lined with roots. The site selected is in forest of mixed oak, chestnut, firs and other trees. It is placed among the topmost branches of saplings—mostly under 20 feet from the ground. The eggs are similar in colour and markings to those described. Both sexes share in the duties of incubation, and presumably also in feeding the young.

THE HIMALAYAN NUTCRACKER

Nucifraga caryocatactes Linnaeus

PLATE 5
SIZE: About that of the House Crow.

FIELD CHARACTERS: A chocolate brown and umber brown bird, spotted with white above and below. Stout and wedge-shaped, woodpecker-like bill. Tail chiefly white with a little black. Undertail coverts pure white. In flight the white tail and white undercoverts are a conspicuous feature. Sexes alike. Singly or separated pairs—sometimes small parties—on trees in pine forest.

DISTRIBUTION: The race *hemispila* is resident throughout the Himalayas from the extreme north-west, through Kulu and the Punjab Himalayas, Kashmir, Kumaon, Simla States, Garhwal, Nepal, Sikkim, Bhutan, into S. Tibet.

An allied species, the Large-spotted Nutcracker (*N. multipunctata*) inhabits more or less the same range of mountainous country. It is much more profusely spotted with white all over, especially on the underparts which look almost white. The rump and upper tailcoverts are also marked with white as against the plain chocolate brown of the Himalayan species.

HABITS: This Nutcracker is a dweller in pine, spruce, fir and deodar forests, normally at elevations between 6,000 and 12,000 or 13,000 feet in summer. In winter it is sometimes met with down to 3,000 feet. It is usually seen singly or in widely separated pairs, but family parties of five or six are occasional. They feed largely on the seeds of the spruce (*Picea morinda*) and various species of pine (*Pinus*) found at these altitudes. The seeds are extracted, before the cones open naturally and scatter them on the ground. For this the Nutcracker has perfected a technique of his own. The stout, pointed bill is wedged in from below between the cracks in the seed-chamber of the cone. The crack is forced asunder by the opening of the mandibles, allowing the loose seed to escape and drop into the open gape of the bird. They also eat other seeds, fruits, nuts and insects. In the case of walnuts, it is probable that only those with very thin shells are tackled, or those partly cracked or gnawed by rodents. Nutcrackers are very noisy birds and their native forests resound with their loud, guttural *kraak, kraak, kraak,* etc., which immediately suggests their relationship with the crows. These calls are usually preceded by a nasal bleat as that of a young goat kid. The flight is straight and direct, achieved by rather deliberate flapping of the wings as in the crow, but

9

with a curious 'delayed action' effect between one flap and the next. When alarmed or suspicious, as for instance when their nest is approached, the birds become fussy and noisy, flying about from tree to tree in the vicinity and uttering their harsh *kraaks*.

NESTING: The season appears to be from about March to June. The nest is rather like the crow's—a platform of twigs—but more neatly built, and with sometimes a little lichen mixed on the outside. It is lined with grass and pine-needles. The site selected is usually in mixed forest on a steep hillside. The nest is placed in the horizontal branch of a deodar or some other large tree near the stem, between 20 and 50 feet from the ground. The normal clutch is of four eggs, pale bluish-white with a few blotches and numerous specks of dull brown and inky brown scattered all over the surface, but rather more densely at the broad end. Both sexes evidently incubate.

THE RED-BILLED CHOUGH

Pyrrhocorax pyrrhocorax Linnaeus

PLATE 6

SIZE: That of the House Crow; slightly slenderer.

FIELD CHARACTERS: An unmistakable cousin of the crow, glossy jet black all over with bright red legs and red, rather slender curved bill. Sexes alike. Flocks about cliffs and meadows at high elevations in the Himalayas.

The Yellow-billed Chough (*Pyrrhocorax graculus*) generally speaking, a bird of higher altitudes, is found over the same section of the Himalayas. The Everest Expedition of 1924 found it up to 27,000 feet. It differs in having a shorter *yellow* bill although its legs are also red. Its call is a shrill loud *chirp*; also a *cree cree* and a very Jackdaw-like cry which is almost indistinguishable from that of the Red-billed species.

DISTRIBUTION: From extreme NW. Himalayas, right across to E. Tibet. Outside Indian limits it is found in N. Africa, Europe and N. Asia.

HABITS: To the trekker, camper or climber at high elevations, around and beyond the more frequented summer resorts in Kashmir, Kulu and other parts of the Himalayas (from Quetta to Darjeeling), the Red-billed Chough soon becomes a familiar object both by its soft musical Jackdaw-like calls and by the remarkable aerial contortions it is wont to indulge in around and about precipices. It is a resident at high altitudes—anything between 8,000 and 16,000 feet in summer, but in winter may sometimes be found as low as 5,000 feet. This Chough is essentially a bird of open, steep pasture-lands beyond the limits of tree forests, and wild precipitous country with lofty jagged peaks and crags standing out here and there. It is usually seen in flocks of twenty or thirty, and even up to a hundred birds. Sometimes they associate with Yellow-billed Choughs, Blue Rock-Pigeons and Ravens to feed on ripening grain in the scanty terraced cultivation. They also feed on ripe fruits and berries. On the various favourite camping grounds in Kashmir—e.g. Sonamarg and Thajiwas—the birds may commonly be seen sauntering about the grassy meadows in amongst the grazing sheep and pack animals, digging up grubs, earthworms and crickets. They are usually present round about the sheep and cattle *chaupans* of the nomadic herdsmen in the mountains. Their flight and general behaviour is crow-like, but the birds are characteristically fond of disporting themselves high up in the air, especially during the middle of the day, when a whole flock may be seen floating on motionless wings in graceful circles or vieing with one another in nose-diving, tumbling, turning and twisting, and performing a series of the most spectacular aerobatics. The birds utter a shrill, rather musical cawing *chiaow, chiaow,* which, when heard faintly in the distance, has often reminded me curiously of the Pied Crested Cuckoo.

NESTING: The principal breeding months are March, April and May. The nest is built of sticks and twigs and lined with wool. It is sometimes placed in the holes and fissures of inaccessible cliffs. Sometimes in holes in walls of disused or inhabited houses in a high mountain village. Several nests may occasionally be found close to one another. The eggs, three or four, are white or pale greenish-, bluish-, or pinkish-white blotched with light reddish-brown or umber to dark brown. There are fainter lavender or inky-grey marks scattered thickly over the whole surface.

THE GREY TIT

Parus major Linnaeus

PLATE 7

SIZE: That of the Sparrow.

FIELD CHARACTERS: An active sparrow-like bird with glossy black crestless head and throat, and a broad black band down the centre of the breast. White cheek-patches, grey back and whitish underparts, are further aids to recognition. Sexes alike. Pairs or small parties, on trees in fairly wooded open country, commonly about hill-stations.

DISTRIBUTION: In summer up to 7,000 feet (and often to 12,000 feet) in the Himalayas from Baluchistan through Kashmir, Garhwal, etc., across into Assam and Burma. There is a marked downward movement from the higher hills to lower elevations in winter. Also resident at Mt. Abu, in the Satpura and Vindhya Hills, Western and Eastern Ghats, Nilgiris and other peninsular hills. In the plains and foothills practically all over India, Burma and Ceylon. Six races are recognized on slight differences of size, shades of colouration, and the relative extent of black, white and grey in the tail feathers. Its abundance varies from place to place. For instance, it is common in the foothills below Darjeeling, but apparently does not ascend to the station.

HABITS: The Grey Tit inhabits well-wooded localities. It avoids heavy evergreen forest though it may haunt its outskirts and where intermingled with the deciduous type. Pairs or small flocks are met with, either by themselves or in the mixed roving bands of small insectivorous birds. They scatter about the trees keeping in touch with one another by means of joyous cheeping or twittering notes. The birds spend their time hunting on the trunk and branches, or amongst the foliage—clinging to the sprigs and flowering stems upside down, sideways, and in all manner of acrobatic positions—peering under leaves, probing into flowers, and also searching the lichens and crevices in the bark for insects. They destroy large quantities of noxious insects, and their eggs and larvæ, and are thus welcome in orchards in spite of some little damage they may do to fruits and fruit buds. They also eat seeds and berries. To get at the kernel of hard-shelled nuts the bird holds the nut down under one foot and hacks it with repeated hammer blows of its strong conical bill.

In the breeding season the male utters a loud clear whistling song: *whee-chi-chi . . . whee-chi-chi . . . whee-chi-chi*, etc. In different localities the song may vary considerably within the limits of the constant pattern of the species. The variation commonly heard in the W. Himalayan stations, for instance, goes: *wittychi, wittychi, wittich . . . wittychi, wittychi, wittychi*, and so on, repeated three or four times; then a break of four or five seconds—repeat—break—repeat, for many minutes, as the bird hunts among the foliage with its mate somewhere near at hand.

NESTING: In Kashmir and the rest of its Himalayan range, the season is principally between March and June; in the Nilgiris and other peninsular hills, February to June. Sometimes two broods are reared. The nest is a thick pad of moss, grass, feathers and wool, etc., placed in hollows in tree stumps, or in deserted woodpecker or barbet holes 5–15

PLATE 3
THE HIMALAYAN TREE-PIE (*see* page 5)
About 1/4 Nat. Size

PLATE 4
THE HIMALAYAN RED-CROWNED JAY (*see* page 8)
About 1/3 Nat. Size

PLATE 5
THE HIMALAYAN NUTCRACKER (*see* page 9)
About 3/8 Nat. Size

PLATE 6
THE RED-BILLED CHOUGH (*see* page 10)
About 1/4 Nat. Size

feet high. Also in holes and crevices in banks, and walls of buildings, etc. The birds readily take to nest-boxes. The eggs—four to six—are white or pinkish-white in colour, spotted and speckled with reddish-brown.

Both sexes share in building, incubation and care of the young.

THE GREEN-BACKED TIT

Parus monticolus Vigors

PLATE 8

SIZE: That of the Sparrow.

FIELD CHARACTERS: Very like the Grey Tit in having the white cheeks, a glossy black crestless head, breast and broad ventral band down middle of abdomen. Differs from it in the back being yellowish-green instead of grey, and the underparts bright yellow instead of whitish. Sexes alike. Pairs or small parties in trees at Himalayan hill-stations.

DISTRIBUTION: Throughout the Himalayas between 4,000 and 10,000 feet, from the extreme NW. to the extreme NE. and down through the Assam hills into Manipur and Chin Hills. Two races are recognized on the basis of slight differences, viz., the Simla Green-backed Tit (*P. m. monticolus*), and the Eastern (*P. m. lepcharum*), which is found from E. Nepal and Sikkim eastwards. It is a purely Himalayan species.

HABITS: Though occurring in Kashmir only in small numbers, the Green-backed Tit is a very common and familiar bird in Murree and the rest of the Himalayan hill-stations lying to the east of it, and also in Shillong. They have the same restless and sprightly habits as the Grey Tit, and are usually seen hunting for insects among the foliage of trees growing in orchards and on hillsides often quite close to inhabited bungalows. They also keep largely with the mixed hunting parties, of which the most regular members here are Red-headed Tits, Grey-headed Flycatchers and several species of tree-warblers. By the middle or end of March most birds have paired off. At this season the male utters a clear, loud and pleasant whistling song: *whit-tee, whit-tee, whit-tee*, or *whee-tee, whee-tee, whee-tee*, repeated four to six times. Sometimes it is varied with *which-whichy, which-whichy, which-whichy, which* (or *which-which*), and so on. Its food consists of insects, their eggs and larvæ, and various berries, as well as fruit and flower buds.

NESTING: The principal season is from April to June, with a month on either side for early and late breeders. The nest is a pad of fur or

9   13

wool, with a quantity of moss, grass or feathers as foundation. It is placed in holes in tree stumps, posts or walls. A favourite site is the space between the ceiling and corrugated iron roof of a cottage. The proximity of human beings does not appear to worry them particularly; a pair will often enter a verandah and hop up boldly to a woollen floor-rug and tug with a will at strands for their nest, all under the very noses of the inmates. A normal clutch consists of five to eight eggs, very similar in appearance and markings to those of the Grey Tit. Like it, also, these birds readily adopt nest-boxes for rearing their families.

THE BLACK TIT

Lophophanes rufonuchalis Blyth

PLATE 8
SIZE : That of the Sparrow.
FIELD CHARACTERS : A dark coloured tit with upstanding pointed black crest, head and breast, and a broad black band down middle of abdomen. The white patch on the earcoverts, the white stripe from under eye down side of neck and the chestnut patch under tail are the points to look for. Sexes alike. Pairs or small parties in trees in high Himalayan forests.

The Crested Black Tit (*L. melanolophus*), found only in the W. Himalayas, is a rather similar looking bird and likely to be confused with it. It is slightly smaller and less dark; the conspicuous double row of rust-coloured spots on its wings always provides a very good distinguishing feature.

DISTRIBUTION : The Himalayas at high altitudes, 7,000 to 12,000 feet in summer; somewhat lower in winter; from Afghanistan through Kashmir, Kumaon, Garhwal, Nepal (presumably) and Sikkim to Tibet and W. China. Everywhere it is locally rather than generally common. Two races are recognized: the Simla or Western race (*rufonuchalis*) has the lower as well as the upper breast black; and the Sikkim or Eastern race (*beavani*) with the lower breast ashy-olive.

HABITS : Except that as a rule this tit resides at greater altitudes, there is nothing remarkably different in its general habits from the species already dealt with. In summer when the birds have paired off, the high juniper and pine forests on the mountain-sides ring with its penetrating merry calls. It is a musical double whistle, *whi-whee, whi-whee, whi-whee, whi-whee*, usually repeated four times, the first syllable short, the second long.

These tits are commonly met with amongst the mixed roving bands of *Phylloscopi* and other small insectivorous birds. They are said to have regular hammering places on boughs whither they take the berries to extract the seeds (presumably also the kernels from various small nuts).

NESTING: The principal months appear to be April and May. The nest is a pad of moss, fur and wool placed in a hollow in a tree stump fairly low down, in holes in a sloping bank or hillside, or under a stone or root. The normal clutch consists of six eggs, which in colour and markings are typical of the tits, and almost indistinguishable from those of the Grey Tit. Both parents feed the young.

THE BROWN CRESTED TIT

Lophophanes dichrous Blyth

PLATE 69

SIZE: That of the Sparrow.

FIELD CHARACTERS: A tit of the same general appearance as the Crested Black Tit, but with the upper parts greyish-brown and with the perky, erect, pointed crest also of the same colour. The white collar round the hindneck is a further clue to its identity. Sexes alike. Pairs and rarely small parties in high Himalayan forest.

DISTRIBUTION: South Kashmir, Garhwal, Nepal and Sikkim, at elevations between about 8,000 and 10,000 feet.

HABITS: This beautiful little tit is neither common nor abundant about any of the ordinarily visited Himalayan summer resorts, and as such, it does not perhaps rightly deserve a place in this book. It is being included for the reason that hikers or campers at higher elevations, where it is locally common, are quite likely to come across it and be left guessing its identity, as I myself was, on our first meeting many years ago. There is nothing on record about its habits which is in any way different from the others of its kind. I have not heard its call, neither does this seem to have been described.

NESTING: Nests have been taken rarely. The season is evidently April–May, and possibly June. The nest is a pad of moss copiously lined with fur or hair and a few feathers, placed in a hole in a branch or tree stump fairly low down. The normal clutch is of four or five eggs, pure white, rather thickly spotted with reddish, more numerously at the broad end.

In a nest found at Deoban c. 9,000 feet (above Chakrata) in oak and silver fir forest in the decaying basal portion of a tree stump which contained young on 20 May, 1936, I observed that both parents were bringing food—at the rate of one visit every two to three minutes. They usually flew out with the excreta of the young in their bill. If the cock was within the nest cavity when the hen arrived, she hopped about impatiently on the nearby branches uttering little beckoning chirrups, and entered as soon as he had left.

THE YELLOW-CHEEKED TIT

Machlolophus xanthogenys Vigors

PLATE 9
SIZE: That of the Sparrow.
FIELD CHARACTERS: A sprightly little black and yellow tit, with a prominent pointed black crest, a black stripe behind eye, and a broad black band running down middle of breast and abdomen. Yellow cheeks. Sexes alike in the Northern race, both male and female having black crest and black ventral band. In the Peninsular and Southern races the ventral band of the female is dull olive-green. The female of the latter race, moreover, is dimorphic—sometimes having the crown also olive-green. Pairs or parties in foliage of trees.

On a fleeting glimpse it is possible to confuse this with the Green-backed Tit (p. 13), often found side by side with it in the Himalayas. But the glistening white cheeks of the latter and its crestless head will settle all doubt.

DISTRIBUTION: W. Himalayas from about Murree through Simla Hills and Garhwal to Nepal and Sikkim, up to about 7,000 or 8,000 feet elevation, Mt. Abu, and all the peninsular hills, including the Satpuras, Vindhyas, Nilgiris, Eastern and Western Ghats. Also the Central India and Deccan plateau country.

Three races are recognized on minor differences of size and colouration, viz., the Northern (W. Himalayas), the Peninsular (Central India, Deccan, etc.), and the Southern (SW. Ghats). It is not found in Ceylon.

In the Eastern Himalayas, Assam hills and Burma, it is represented by an allied species, the Black-spotted Yellow Tit (*M. spilonotus*), distinguished by its bright yellow forehead.

HABITS: The Yellow-cheeked Tit is a resident of hill forests and well-

wooded plateau and foothills country throughout its range. It is usually
met with in pairs and family parties, restlessly hunting insects in the
leafy canopy of tall trees, often in company with the usual roving bands
of small insectivorous birds. The individuals keep up a joyous conversational *chee-chee* while in the quest. Insects, grubs and spiders comprise the
major part of their diet. Various fruits and berries are also eaten. Like
the Grey and other tits, they hop about the leaves and twigs, clinging
head downwards or completely upside down, prying into cracks and
crevices, and flitting from sprig to sprig. During the breeding season the
male utters a loud, clear whistling song: *cheewit-pretty-cheewit*, etc., or
local variations of the same. While singing the crest stands erect and the
wings droop at the sides.

NESTING: This tit breeds freely in the W. Himalayas between 4,000
and 7,000 feet elevation from March to June. Also at Mt. Abu, and
practically in all the other peninsular hills, between April and September,
according to local conditions. The nest is the usual pad of grass, moss,
wool, hair and feathers placed in a hole in a bough or tree stem 4 to 20
feet from the ground. Sometimes old barbet or woodpecker holes are
used. The site may be in forest as well as in gardens close to bungalows.
The normal clutch is of four to six eggs, very similar in appearance to
those of the Grey Tit—a glossless white or pinkish white, more or less
spotted and blotched with reddish- or purplish-brown. Both sexes share
in building, incubation and care of the young.

THE RED-HEADED TIT

Aegithaliscus concinnus Gould

PLATE 9

SIZE: Less than the Sparrow. About that of the Munia, or Sunbird.

FIELD CHARACTERS: A tiny, proportionately long-tailed tit, uncrested
but with a suggestion of a rounded tuft produced by the very long and
full feathers of the crown. Top of head chestnut. Upper parts bluish-grey,
lower pale rust-coloured or whitish. A broad white eyebrow, and some
white in the tail, seen chiefly when it is spread in alighting. Sexes alike.
Restless flocks, in trees and bushes. Purely Himalayan.

DISTRIBUTION: Western and Eastern Himalayas between 5,000 and
10,000 feet in summer; somewhat lower in winter. Assam hills down to
the Chin Hills. It also extends to the Shan States of Burma and to SW.

China. Four races are recognized, of which we are mainly concerned with two, viz., the Simla or West Himalayan race *iredalei*, and the Manipur or East Himalayan *manipurensis*. The latter differs from the former chiefly in having the eyebrow black-and-white instead of pure white.

HABITS: This dainty little tit, while not obtrusive in any way, is perhaps one of the commonest and most abundant birds to be met with in and about all the popular summer resorts of the W. Himalayas. It is usually seen in large flocks—often of twenty to thirty—almost invariably in association with other tits, flycatchers, warblers, white-eyes, and other small insectivorous birds. They are restless and untiring, and ever on the move, searching for insects among the leaves and flower buds and flitting from bush to bush, up and down the hillsides. They also eat berries of various kinds and are particularly fond of the wild raspberries (*Rubus*) that grow in such profusion everywhere. It is a pretty sight to see a number of these little birds clinging upside down or sideways on the bunches of the yellow berries engrossed in pecking away at them. They are usually tame and confiding and can be watched at close quarters. The note constantly heard as the birds go about their normal business is a shrill pleasant *tweet*, uttered both as they hop about from sprig to sprig or when the flock is flying across in loose disorderly fashion from one thicket to another some distance away.

NESTING: The season is early March to May. The nest is a remarkably beautiful little round or egg-shaped ball about 5 inches by 4 inches, made of green moss and lichens, fine roots, scraps of bark, spiders' egg cocoons, and a few small feathers bound together with cobwebs. It is thickly lined with feathers and some wool or vegetable down intermixed. The structure is either suspended between several twigs or wedged into a fork 3–6 feet up in stunted hill-oak bushes, or a bunch of deodar leaves on a low branch. It is well camouflaged in its surroundings and usually difficult to find. The eggs—three to six—are glossless, broad, blunt ovals, pure white to pale lilac-white or pinkish-white, with tiny freckles of pinkish-red scattered sparsely all over the surface, and in a dense ring round the broad end.

THE WHITE-TAILED NUTHATCH

Sitta himalayensis Jardine and Selby

PLATE 10

SIZE : About that of the Sparrow.

FIELD CHARACTERS: A short and square-tailed slaty-blue bird with fulvous and chestnut underparts and a longish, straight, pointed black bill. Distinguished from other similar nuthatches by a white patch above the base of the tail. In overhead flight a white patch on the otherwise blackish underwing, conspicuous. Female duller and paler. Pairs or family parties, scuttling up and along branches of trees.

Brooks's or the Kashmir Nuthatch (*S. kashmiriensis*) differs chiefly in having no white at base of tail, and the chestnut undertail coverts spotted with ashy. It inhabits the W. Himalayas from the Afghan border to Garhwal, being fairly common in mixed forests in Kashmir between 7,000 and 9,000 feet elevation.

In the White-cheeked Nuthatch (*S. leucopsis*) the upperparts are slaty-blue; the underparts fulvous white. The top and back of its head are glossy black; sides of head white. It is found from N. Kashmir to Garhwal between about 7,000 and 12,000 feet elevation.

The Rock Nuthatch (*S. tephronota*) is similar in appearance to the Kashmir Nuthatch: upperparts ashy-blue; underparts pale pinkish-fulvous. But both this and the White-cheeked species lack the white spots on the lateral tail feathers present in that bird. It lives on rocks just as its other congeners live on trees, and is common in the rocky valleys (*tangis*) about 3,000 and 8,000 feet elevation. Found in Afghanistan and Baluchistan.

The Chestnut-bellied Nuthatch (*S. castanea*), slaty-blue above, deep chestnut below, is found on most of the hill-stations and plateau country in peninsular India. It also occurs in the Himalayas from Murree to Assam, and down through Burma to Tenasserim.

DISTRIBUTION: Resident in the Himalayas between 5,000 and 11,000 feet from Kangra Valley across to NE. Assam.

HABITS: At elevations where it is commonest, i.e., between 6,000 and 8,000 feet (at which most of our popular W. Himalayan hill resorts approximately lie), the White-tailed Nuthatch inhabits the *Banj* oak and rhododendron forests that clothe the hillsides. Higher up it is also found among the pines, but on the whole, broad-leaved forest seems to be preferred. Pairs or scattered family parties are commonly seen creeping about on the moss and lichen covered branches of the lofty trees like little woodpeckers, or even like tree-mice. The birds move jerkily up, sideways, or down and around them, or cling to the bark upside down and along the undersurface in short spurts with surprising agility. They pry into the crevices and under the moss, and tap with their bills every now and again to dislodge lurking insects. Sometimes the birds descend into the undergrowth and work the thin branches methodically. The party keeps together by means of a high-pitched mousy *chi-chip*, etc. When one bird has finished its hunt it flies off to another tree, where it is presently joined by its companions one by one and the tireless search for food is resumed. Thus they move about from tree to tree and cover an extensive beat each day. They are frequently met with in the mixed bands of insectivorous birds that rove the forest, of which tits, flycatchers and tree-warblers are almost inseparable partners. Besides insects, grubs and spiders, Nuthatches, as their name implies, also eat a variety of nuts and hard-shelled seeds of forest trees. To extract the kernels, the nuts are firmly wedged into some crevice in a branch and pierced or hacked open by repeated hammer blows of the strong, pointed bill.

NESTING: The season is from March to May. The nest is placed in natural hollows in tree-trunks 15 to 25 feet up, and sometimes lower. The opening is plastered up with mud in the typical nuthatch manner, leaving a neat round entrance hole about 1½ inch in diameter. The site is in oak or mixed forest, and sometimes in more or less open country. Also on hillsides or within the straggling jungly compounds of hill-station bungalows. The eggs—five to seven—are white thickly blotched and spotted with dark red, more numerously at the broad end where they often form a ring.

THE VELVET-FRONTED NUTHATCH

Sitta frontalis Swainson

PLATE 10

SIZE: Smaller than the Sparrow.

FIELD CHARACTERS: A small purplish-blue nuthatch, with pale lilac-grey underparts. Velvety black forehead; coral red bill. The male has a black stripe above and behind eye; the female is without. Pairs or family parties on trunks and branches of trees in forest.

DISTRIBUTION: From the Kumaon Himalayas (i.e. about Naini Tal, Ranikhet and Almora) eastward to Assam. Nilgiris, Eastern and Western

PLATE 7
THE INDIAN GREY TIT (*see* page 11)
About 1/2 Nat. Size

PLATE 8
1 THE SIMLA BLACK TIT (*see* page 14)
2 THE GREEN-BACKED TIT (*see* page 13)
About 1/2 Nat. Size

PLATE 9
1 THE RED-HEADED TIT (*see* page 17)
2 THE SOUTHERN YELLOW-CHEEKED TIT (*see* page 16)
About 3/8 Nat. Size

PLATE 10
1 THE WHITE-TAILED NUTHATCH (*see* page 19)
2 THE VELVET-FRONTED NUTHATCH (*see* page 20)
About 1/2 Nat. Size

Ghats, and other hills of peninsular and South India, Burma and Ceylon.
HABITS : This lovely little nuthatch is essentially a bird of *sholas*, ever-green hill forest and well-wooded foothills country. It is met with in pairs or small family parties of four or five running up and down the moss-covered trunks and branches of trees—along and around them—searching with method and industry for insects and grubs lurking in the crevices of the bark. It may sometimes be seen clinging to the under-sides of small branches back downwards, and creeping along jerkily in this position, or even up moss-covered rocks like a Wall-Creeper or a Rock Nuthatch. This manner of hunting is typical of all nuthatches. Their feet are strongly developed for the purpose of clinging to the rough surface of the bark. The hind toe and claw are particularly large and powerful, while the inner toe and claw are dwarfed. In the adaptation of their feet for the purpose of climbing Nuthatches resemble the wood-peckers, but they possess short square tails without the elongated stiff central feathers which serve the woodpeckers as the third leg of a tripod.
NESTING : The season in N. India is April to June; in the Nilgiris and other S. Indian hills February to April, mostly between 2,500 and 6,000 feet elevation. The nest is the usual thick pad of moss, fur and feathers. It is placed in a natural hollow, or a disused barbet or woodpecker hole, in a branch 4 to 40 feet from ground, but mostly under 20 feet. Tiny holes requiring no treatment are usually selected, but larger ones are neatly plastered up with mud, leaving a small round entrance. The normal clutch in S. India is of three or four; in N. India four or five eggs. The eggs are white, spotted, speckled and blotched with red, and occasionally with pale purple. They are glossless and resemble tits' eggs.

In the Nuthatches as a family, incubation is said to take thirteen or fourteen days.

THE WHITE-CRESTED LAUGHING-THRUSH

Garrulax leucolophus Hardwicke

PLATE II

SIZE : About that of the Myna.

FIELD CHARACTERS : A dark olive-brown or olive-chestnut babbler-like bird with the crown, full rounded crest and upper breast white. A broad black streak from bill to earcoverts. Sexes alike. Noisy parties or 'sisterhoods' of six to ten in forest undergrowth and scrub-covered ravines.

DISTRIBUTION: The Himalayas mostly between 2,500 and 5,000 feet, from about Simla eastward to the Assam hills. Down through Burma into Tennasserim, Siam, etc. Four races are recognized on differences in the extent of white on the breast, grey in the crest, and other details. The two that concern us chiefly are the West Himalayan race *leucolophus* and the East Himalayan *hardwickii*.

HABITS: The White-crested Laughing-Thrush is a forest bird, inhabiting broken foothills country with Sal jungle, scrub-covered ravines and the like. It keeps in flocks or 'sisterhoods' of six to ten birds which rummage amongst the mulch on the ground, flicking aside or turning over the dry leaves in search of insects. They also clamber up into the undergrowth and the branches of trees. In many of their ways they are typical babblers. Their food consists of insects, but berries are also eaten. They are likewise fond of flower nectar. *Woodfordia* bushes, so characteristic of the steep-sided ravines they frequent, are in regular attendance when in blossom. The birds hop along the branches, and from branch to branch, probing into the flower tubes. They are noisy birds and keep up a continuous harsh cackling conversation. From time to time, especially when disturbed, the 'sisterhood' bursts into a chorus of the peculiar loud discordant laughter which has earned the family name. One bird begins, and then by ones and twos, the others quickly chime in until the forest resounds with the tumult of the discord. The birds dance around and flap their wings in accompaniment. In the distance the din does remotely suggest a chorus of human laughter, but to my ears it is more like the medley of a cackling hen about to lay, with the jumbled 'laughs' of the White-breasted Kingfisher and Golden-backed Woodpecker, and certain harsh calls of the Tree-Pie thrown in. Often two or more flocks join together and the cacophony then becomes particularly boisterous.

NESTING: The season is from April to June. The nest is a large, shallow cup of coarse grass and bamboo and other leaves, wound round with creepers and pliant twigs, and lined with fine roots. It is placed in shrubs and small trees, from a few inches to 20 feet off the ground—usually low down—in forested ravines, open bamboo jungle or in overgrown forest clearings. The normal clutch is four to six eggs. They are broad ovals, sometimes almost round in shape, pure china white, very glossy but finely pitted over the surface.

Both sexes share in incubation, which takes about fourteen days. The flocks do not break up even when nesting, but the breeding pairs detach themselves now and again for their domestic duties. When one bird is brooding the other keeps with the flock nearby.

THE WYNAAD LAUGHING-THRUSH

Garrulax delesserti Jerdon

PLATE 12
SIZE: About that of the Myna.

FIELD CHARACTERS: An uncrested babbler, chestnut-brown above, ashy-grey and chestnut below. Top of head, sides of neck and upper back deep slaty-grey. A broad black stripe from bill through eye to earcoverts. Chin, cheeks and throat, white. Tail black. Sexes alike. Flocks or 'sisterhoods' of six to ten birds in dense evergreen forest.

DISTRIBUTION: SW. India from about Castle Rock, in North Kanara, to Travancore inclusive.

HABITS: The Wynaad Laughing-Thrush is essentially a bird of the evergreen rain-forest areas of SW. India. It is found at all elevations from the plains and foothills country up to about 5,000 feet. Noisy flocks of six to ten birds or more may be met with in dank jungle among cane-brakes, rattan palms and evergreen undergrowth along the edge of forest footpaths and traces, and on the outskirts of cardamom clearings. The flocks rummage among the mulch and humus, turning over and flicking aside the dry leaves in search of insects. Their general habits are typical of the Laughing-Thrushes as described under the last species. They are great skulkers, and when alarmed will promptly scuttle away through the undergrowth or flit from thicket to thicket to escape, giving vent to a variety of squeaky shrieks. The birds also indulge in the characteristic chattering and cackling chorus. It starts with one bird calling; he is followed by the rest of the flock one by one, and ends up finally in a loud uproar of discordant 'laughter'. Sometimes they may also ascend small trees, but on the whole prefer the ground or low undergrowth. The food, as with others of the family, consists chiefly of insects, though berries are also commonly eaten.

NESTING: Curiously enough, this Laughing-Thrush nests at the height of the SW. Monsoon, June to August–September, and in areas where the seasonal rainfall is often 200 inches or more. The nest is a rough, untidy cup of fine twigs and roots in which grass and fibres are mixed. It is built in *Strobilanthes* plants and saplings, usually under 5 or 6 feet from the ground, in thick, damp forest. The normal clutch consists of three eggs, but sometimes up to six are found. They are unmarked white, roundish, smooth and glossy, and rather like many woodpeckers' eggs.

THE NECKLACED LAUGHING-THRUSH

Garrulax moniligera Hodgson

PLATE 13

SIZE: About that of the Myna; somewhat larger.

FIELD CHARACTERS: A large fulvous olive-brown Laughing-Thrush
with a bright fulvous collar on hindneck, whitish chin and throat, and
a broad black band or 'necklace' across breast. A narrow white line
above eye. Outer tail feathers with broad white tips, particularly noticeable in flight. Sexes alike. Noisy flocks or 'sisterhoods' in dense undergrowth in forest.

The Black-gorgeted Laughing-Thrush (*G. pectoralis*) found practically
over the entire range of the Necklaced species in identical habitats and
sometimes in close association with it, is slightly larger in size but otherwise of the same general appearance and easily confused with it. A black
cheek-stripe, starting backward from the gape and curving round the earcoverts to the upper part of the eye, is a good distinguishing feature. It
has a black patch on the wing-shoulder (primary coverts). Its irides are
reddish-brown as against orange-yellow in *moniligera*; its legs and feet
greyish instead of yellowish.

DISTRIBUTION: The Eastern Himalayas from Nepal to Assam and
down through Burma to Tenasserim and Siam. Two races are recognized:
the Indian *moniligera* and the Burmese *fuscata*. The latter differs from the
former in having buff tips to its tail feathers instead of white, and in
other minor details.

HABITS: The Necklaced Laughing-Thrush is, on the whole, a bird of
fairly low elevations. It is found in the plains country and foothills up to
2,500 feet, and only occasionally as high up as 4,500 feet. Flocks of six
to ten birds or more are usually met with, either by themselves or in
company with other Laughing-Thrushes. They keep to dense undergrowth in forest, but are also commonly seen in overgrown clearings for
cultivation, and in bamboo jungle near villages. Here they rummage
among the mulch for insects, or hunt among the stems of the bushes. They
are as noisy as their other congeners and indulge in the same sort of
cackling outbursts of choral laughter on the slightest provocation, the
members of the flock hopping about on the ground or in low bushes,
opening and closing their wings, bowing excitedly, and going through
a series of rather ludicrous antics.

NESTING: The principal months are April and May, but eggs may be
found a month or more on either side of these. The nest is a broad,

shallow, rather untidily built saucer of bamboo leaves mixed with roots, scraps of moss, bracken, etc., and lined with finer roots, tendrils and grass stems. It is placed in bushes high or low, or upon small trees and saplings from 2 to 20 feet. The site is often in the neighbourhood of bungalows and village houses. The normal clutch is of four or five eggs, deep blue, unmarked. They are oval in shape, of smooth texture, and with a slight gloss.

THE WHITE-THROATED LAUGHING-THRUSH

Garrulax albogularis Gould

PLATE 13

SIZE: Rather larger than the Myna.

FIELD CHARACTERS: A crestless olive-brown and rust-coloured (ferruginous) Laughing-Thrush with white cheeks and throat. It lacks the broad black breast band or 'necklace' of the previous species. Broad white terminal band to tail conspicuous in flight, especially when spread out for alighting. Sexes alike. Flocks or 'sisterhoods' of 8 to 10, usually in trees on well-wooded hillsides.

DISTRIBUTION: Throughout the W. Himalayas from the Afghan border to Garhwal. Also Nepal and Sikkim. Two races are recognized, viz., the darker *albogularis* of Nepal and Sikkim, and the paler and better known West Himalayan *whistleri*.

HABITS: The White-throated Laughing-Thrush is a common species at most of our West Himalayan hill-stations between about 4,000 and 9,000 feet elevation. Flocks of eight to ten birds are usually met with in hill oak forests with ringal undergrowth and on otherwise well-wooded hillsides, frequently in association with Himalayan Tree-Pies, Striated Laughing-Thrushes and others. They keep more to trees—hopping about from branch to branch in search of food—and are less addicted to rummaging on the ground than the White-crested species. The members of a flock keep in touch with one another by means of a peculiar short, rather high-pitched *ke, ke* note. When disturbed they explode into the typical laughing choruses, but the cacophony is shriller than that of the White-crested species with a mixture of peculiar hissing and squealing calls. The flocks keep together even in the breeding season. Their flight is, in a way, reminiscent of the Sirkeer Cuckoo's (*Taccocua*), and the likeness is heightened by the white terminal band to the broad graduated tail, which is also a feature of that bird.

NESTING: The season is mostly from about early April to the end of June. The nest varies from a deepish cup to a shallow saucer. It is made of coarse grass, creepers, dead leaves, moss, etc., sometimes unlined, at others lined with finer roots. It is placed in the horizontal fork of a branch in a small tree or shrub, 3 to 10 feet from the ground—occasionally between two upright stems of seedlings. The normal clutch consists of three eggs; exceptionally four. They are a lovely intense deep blue without any greenish tinge; long ovals in shape with a fine texture and beautiful gloss.

THE RED-HEADED LAUGHING-THRUSH

Trochalopteron erythrocephalum Vigors

PLATE 14

SIZE: About that of the Myna.

FIELD CHARACTERS: An uncrested olive-brown and fulvous Laughing-Thrush, with chestnut head and blackish face. Roundish black spots on sides of neck and upper back, and black crescent-shaped markings and white speckling on throat and breast producing a scale-like effect. Some golden yellow in wings and tail. Sexes alike. Flocks or 'sisterhoods' in thick undergrowth on hillsides. Essentially a forest bird.

DISTRIBUTION: The Himalayas from about SE. Kashmir through Nepal and Sikkim to easternmost Assam hills; down thence through Shan States and Burmese hills into Tenasserim. Over this wide range eight races are recognized mainly on differences of colouration and markings.

HABITS: The Red-headed Laughing-Thrush is a shy bird of oak, pine and silver fir forest and otherwise well-wooded hillsides between about 6,000 and 10,000 feet elevation in summer. In winter it descends to 4,000 feet or lower. It keeps largely to the ground and tangled undergrowth in forest and is fond of scrubby nullahs and brushwood, and thickets of ringal bamboo covering the steep hillsides here and there. It is a great skulker, scuttling away on the least alarm and seldom permitting a good view of itself. It is but rarely that one sees it up in a bush or tree and rarer still on the wing, since it invariably prefers to creep away through the undergrowth rather than leave cover and fly. When it does so, it is merely to shoot down the hillside and swing behind a thicket in order to escape observation.

While the flock is rummaging on the ground, turning or flicking over the dry leaves in search of insect food, the birds keep up what Whistler well describes as a 'curious low chuckling murmur' which gives away their presence in a thicket. The call is a clear musical double whistle, *pheeou-pheeou*, or *teew-teew*. Sometimes one long whistling note is followed by two short ones: *teew-ew-ew*. On the whole, they are silent and do not normally indulge in the boisterous laughing choruses which characterize some of their larger relations.

NESTING: The season extends from about April to August, but the principal months for eggs are June and July. The nest is a deep cup of dead leaves kept together with fern fronds and grass, and scantily lined with fine grass and roots. It is placed low down in bushes or small trees, usually between 4 and 20 feet from the ground, in oak, silver fir and rhododendron forest. The normal clutch consists of three eggs, sometimes only two. They are long ovals in shape, of a soft blue-green colour, boldly blotched and streaked with deep brown or black.

THE VARIEGATED LAUGHING-THRUSH

Trochalopteron variegatum Vigors

PLATE 14

SIZE: About that of the Myna.

FIELD CHARACTERS: An olive-brown and ashy-brown Laughing-Thrush with pale rusty underparts, much golden yellow in wings and tail, and black and white markings on face. Head dark ashy-grey with whitish forehead. Chin and throat black. Cheeks whitish, meeting underneath round the black throat. The broadly white- or grey-tipped tail is a conspicuous feature, especially in flight. Sexes alike. Flocks in undergrowth in Himalayan forest.

DISTRIBUTION: Himalayas from Chitral through Kashmir and Chamba to Nepal. Two races are recognized: the Eastern, *variegatum*, with flight feathers and tail largely golden yellow; and the Western, *simile*, with those parts chiefly slaty-blue. The boundary between the two races is about Dharmsala in Kangra District.

HABITS: The Variegated Laughing-Thrush is found at elevations between 8,000 and 12,000 feet in summer, but descends to as low as about 4,000 feet in winter. It inhabits rather open forests of silver fir, birch and horse-chestnut, preferably with plenty of undergrowth; also thickets of ringal bamboo in steep-sided nullahs and on hillsides. Noisy flocks of up to twenty birds may here be met with feeding on the ground amongst the fallen leaves or up in the bushes or branches of trees. Like others of their kind, they eat insects principally, but also fruits and berries. In quest of food, or when trying to escape observation, the birds hop energetically from branch to branch up a pine or deodar, always keeping close to the main trunk. They are of a garrulous disposition and keep up a running conversation as they feed, which gives away their presence in the undergrowth. The call note is a clear, loud whistling *p'tēe-whee, p'tēe-whee*, etc.

NESTING: The season ranges between May and July. The nest is a compact, rather shallow cup of coarse grass mixed with a few dead leaves and roots, lined with pine needles and finer grass. It is placed low down in bushes and saplings in thick undergrowth and overgrown nullahs in forests of oak, silver fir and deodar. The eggs, normally three, are the typical blue or blue-green, boldly blotched and spotted with reddish-brown or dark brown.

THE NILGIRI RUFOUS-BREASTED LAUGHING-THRUSH

Trochalopteron cachinnans Jerdon

SIZE: About that of the Myna.

FIELD CHARACTERS: An unmistakable cousin of the Jungle Babbler ('Seven Sisters'). Olive-brown, with bright rufous throat and breast. Crown and nape slaty-brown. A broad white stripe running from forehead back over the eye bordered above by a thin black line and below by another through the eye. Sexes alike. Noisy flocks or 'sisterhoods' in *sholas* and on well-wooded hillsides.

DISTRIBUTION: Nilgiri Hills of South India, from about 4,000 feet elevation to the highest peaks.

HABITS: This Laughing-Thrush is a common bird, and familiar to all residents of the several charming little hill-stations on the Nilgiris. It is invariably the first new bird to catch the eye of the visitor from the plains, even as the Mettupalaiyam bus that carries him splutters and pants laboriously uphill. Like its cousins of the Himalayas, it lives in flocks of a dozen or more birds. They spend their time searching for food either in the undergrowth among the dry leaves on the ground, or amongst the stems and branches of the trees. Although of a shy and retiring nature, it

VIEW PLATE THIS WAY

PLATE 11
THE WEST HIMALAYAN WHITE-CRESTED LAUGHING-THRUSH (*see* page 21)
About 1/2 Nat. Size

PLATE 12
1 THE PALNI LAUGHING-THRUSH (*see* page 29)
2 THE WYNAAD LAUGHING-THRUSH (*see* page 23)
About 3/8 Nat. Size

PLATE 13
1 THE INDIAN NECKLACED LAUGHING-THRUSH (*see* page 24)
2 THE WEST HIMALAYAN WHITE-THROATED LAUGHING-THRUSH (*see* page 25)
About 1/3 Nat. Size

PLATE 14
1 THE EASTERN VARIEGATED LAUGHING-THRUSH (*see* page 27)
2 THE RED-HEADED LAUGHING-THRUSH (*see* page 26)
About 1/3 Nat. Size

may commonly be met even within the Municipal limits of Ootacamund, Coonoor and Kotagiri, in gardens and orchards and near bungalows, as well as in the *sholas* nearby. Here it is commonly seen among the mixed parties of birds, hunting on the moss-covered trunks and branches of the trees, hopping up and along them with great agility. Some of its harsh conversational notes are almost identical with the *ke-ke-ke* of the Tree-Pie. The call, which is not unpleasant, is of the same general calibre as that of the White-breasted Laughing-Thrush to be described hereafter. While uttering the bill is raised more or less perpendicularly heavenwards and the tail depressed. Another member of the flock promptly responds with the *ke-ke-ke* notes. Its food consists of insects as well as fruits and berries. It is particularly fond of the Hill Guavas (*Rhodomyrtus tomentosa*) which grow in such profusion on the Nilgiri hillsides.

NESTING: The season normally is from February to May, and sometimes on till July. The nest is a neat, fairly large and deep cup made of grass roots, moss and lichen, and lined with roots and fibre. It is built in a bush or small tree between 3 and 15 feet from the ground, usually within a well-wooded *shola*. The normal clutch is of two or three eggs— pale blue with blotches, spots and speckles of pale reddish-brown and dark brown. In shape they are blunt ovals. The birds are not shy when brooding, and will sit very close when the nest is approached. Both sexes share in building the nest, and evidently also in incubation.

THE TRAVANCORE OR PALNI WHITE-BREASTED LAUGHING-THRUSH

Trochalopteron jerdoni Blyth

PLATE 12

SIZE: About that of the Myna.

FIELD CHARACTERS: A crestless olive-brown and rufous Laughing-Thrush with slaty-brown head. The white eyebrow with black lines above and below it is conspicuous. Differs from the Nilgiri species chiefly in having the breast grey instead of rufous. Sexes alike. Flocks or 'sisterhoods' around *sholas* and in forest undergrowth.

DISTRIBUTION: Confined to the Coorg, Wynaad, Travancore and Cochin hills in SW. India, between about 3,000 and 7,000 feet elevation. Within this limited range three races are recognized: the black-chinned *jerdoni* (Brahmagiris, Coorg, Wynaad); the grey-chinned *fairbanki* with white eyebrow extending behind eye (Palni Annamalai and N. Travancore hills); and the grey-chinned *meridionale* in which the short white eyebrow does not pass behind eye (Ashambu Hills, S. Travancore).

HABITS: The White-breasted Laughing-Thrush is perhaps less a bird of evergreen tree forest than its congener of the Nilgiris. It prefers the bush-dotted hillsides and the extensive patches of bracken usually found on the edge of *sholas*, and is almost inseparable from the dense scrub of tall bracken and wild raspberry which springs up along the banks of hill streams, even running through orderly well-kept tea plantations. Dense growth of eeta bamboo (*Ochlandra travancorica*) and secondary scrub bordering cardamom cultivation in the higher hills also form some of its favourite habitats. Flocks of six to a dozen birds are usually seen rummaging on the ground among the undergrowth, or in low bushes. The birds are great skulkers; on the least suspicion they creep away through the cover uttering a low *wit-wit-wit* as they disappear, only rarely giving a glimpse of themselves. Their squeaky shrieks of alarm are rather like those of the Jungle Babbler, but louder and shriller. Some of the call notes are quite pretty and mellow, and rather like an oriole's. Family parties call and reply to one another and keep in touch when separated by means of notes which Bates renders as *pee-koko*, *pee-koko*, etc. Call . . . answer . . . quiet. Call . . . answer . . . quiet, and so on. At the approach of the breeding season the male calls loudly from the topmost branches of a small tree. This Laughing-Thrush is very common at Kodaikanal, where it has become tame and confiding, haunting gardens within the station as well as the adjoining *sholas*. Its food consists of insects, fruits and berries. In the Palni Hills, the birds are said to do some damage to peaches and raspberries in orchards.

The Laughing-Thrushes of the genera *Garrulax* (one species) and *Trochalopteron* (two species) in the hills of SW. India present one of the most interesting cases of discontinuous geographical distribution of animals in India. They are strongly represented throughout the Himalayas, but completely absent in peninsular India. The occurrence again in the S. Indian hills of such sedentary forms, after a break of a thousand miles or more, is a remarkable circumstance.

NESTING: The season is February to May. March is evidently the best month for eggs. The nest is a compact cup of coarse grass and bracken leaves with an inner lining of fine grass. It is placed in the dense part of a bush or in thick bracken on hillsides, always well concealed. The eggs—two or three—are very like those of the Rufous-breasted Nilgiri species both in colour and markings.

THE STREAKED LAUGHING-THRUSH

Trochalopteron lineatum Vigors

PLATE 15

SIZE: Slightly smaller than the Myna.

FIELD CHARACTERS: A typical babbler, with ashy-grey head, rusty earcoverts and olive rufous body. The prominent shaft streaks to the feathers give it a striped or streaked effect. Longish, loose tail cross-rayed rufous, ending in a black band with terminal grey tips. No distinct eyebrow. Sexes alike. Squeaky pairs or parties in undergrowth on hillsides scuttling like rats.

DISTRIBUTION: The Himalayas from Baluchistan through Chitral, Kashmir, Garhwal, etc., east to Bhutan, between about 5,000 and 8,000 feet elevation. Five geographical races are recognized within this range, differing from one another in shades of colouration and other minor details.

HABITS: The Streaked Laughing-Thrush is one of the commonest and most familiar birds of all the West Himalayan hill-stations. It keeps largely to the ground in pairs or small parties of four or five birds, in gardens and shrubbery around the bungalows. It also affects the thickets of wild rose, raspberry and bracken dotted about the *khuds* and open hillsides, and is equally at home in hill forest wherever there is a sufficiency of low cover. The birds hop in and out of cover, or from branch to branch up a tree, bobbing, dipping, turning from side to side, jerking their wings and tail, and keeping up a shrill squeaky conversation amongst themselves. They are great skulkers and can seldom be induced to fly, preferring to scuttle away through the bushes on alarm. When forced to take wing, they merely shoot a few yards downhill to dive into the undergrowth, where they quickly thread their way through the tangles and disappear. As a rule they are not shy and can be observed at close quarters if one keeps silent and motionless. Their inquisitiveness and lively movements are a pleasure to watch. In the breeding season the males constantly clamber up to the exposed tops of bushes and sing their peculiar squeaky whistling song. Osmaston syllabifies this as *Its-so-difficult-to-see-me* rapidly repeated. Whistler renders the loud, clear whistle as *pitt-we-are* or *titty-titty-we-are.* which is perhaps more accurate. Their food consists of insects as well as berries.

NESTING: The breeding season is a long one, extending from about March to September. The nest is a deep circular cup of coarse grasses mixed with leaves and lined with finer grasses and rootlets. It is placed in thick bushes of wild raspberry or stunted rhododendron, deodar and the like, 4 to 8 feet from the ground, and usually well concealed. The site may be forest, open tree jungle, roadside thickets or garden bushes. The eggs—normally three—are unmarked greenish-blue, smooth and rather glossy. Evidently both sexes share in nest building and incubation. The brooding bird sits close and slips away quietly only when the observer is within a couple of feet of the nest. It hops about on the ground nearby in pretended unconcern, and returns immediately the observer has moved a few yards away.

THE STRIATED LAUGHING-THRUSH

Grammatoptila striata Vigors

PLATE 15

SIZE : Slightly larger than the Myna.

FIELD CHARACTERS: A large umber-brown Laughing-Thrush, covered all over with narrow white streaks or striations. Tail chestnut, partly white tipped. Short, stout black bill. Sexes alike. Noisy pairs or small parties in trees in Himalayan hill forest.

DISTRIBUTION: Himalayas between about 4,000 and 7,000 feet elevation from the Sutlej Valley eastward through Nepal and Bhutan to the Assam hills—Khasi, Naga, Mishmi, and others—and Chin Hills of Burma. Three races are recognized, viz., the Simla race *striata*, the Sikkim *sikkimensis*, and the Assam *austeni*. They differ from one another in details of colouration and markings.

HABITS: The Striated Laughing-Thrush is also one of the commoner birds of its kind all about the hill-stations within its range, and perhaps particularly so about Simla, Naini Tal and Darjeeling. It is met with in pairs or small parties of four or five birds, frequently in association with Himalayan Tree-Pies and other Laughing-Thrushes. There is nothing notably different in its habits from those already described, except that as a rule it frequents high forest and keeps more to the upper branches and crowns of trees than to undergrowth or the ground. Like its cousins also, it is a noisy bird and utters a large variety of discordant cackling or clucking notes. The loud lively whistling call, which one observer renders as *O see saw whitey — oh white*, resounds in the forest and is quite intriguing when heard for the first time. Its food consists of insects as well as berries and seeds.

NESTING: The season ranges from May to July. The nest is a large, rather shallow cup made of tendrils of creepers mixed with roots, moss and green ferns on the exterior, and lined with finer roots and fibres. It is usually placed high up in small trees in forest up to about 20 feet—but sometimes in thick bushes only 3 or 4 feet from the ground. The full clutch normally consists of two eggs—pale blue, unmarked. They have a fine and smooth texture but very little gloss. In shape they are long ovals, sometimes slightly pointed at the small end.

THE RUFOUS BABBLER

Argya subrufa Jerdon

PLATE 16

SIZE: Somewhat smaller than the Myna, or about same size.

FIELD CHARACTERS: An olive-brown and rufous babbler with deep grey forehead. Sexes alike. Squeaking flocks or 'sisterhoods' of six to eight in scrub undergrowth and bamboo jungle.

DISTRIBUTION: The Sahyadris or Western Ghats south of Khandala, Nilgiris, Palnis, and hills of Mysore, Cochin and Travancore. Foothills and up to about 3,500 feet elevation.

HABITS: The Rufous Babbler is a resident of the country which is intermediate in character between the humid evergreen rain-forests of SW. India and the deciduous, with a free intermingling of the two types of vegetation. It haunts dense scrub undergrowth in the foothills and up to moderate elevations, especially where mixed with tall coarse grass and bamboo brakes such as is found on the edge of forest clearings for cultivation and plantations. Through the vicious tangles of bamboo clumps—the spiky species *Bambusa arundinacea* being characteristic of its habitat—the birds scuttle in and out and hop up the stems with the agility of a rat. They keep up a continuous shrill whistling *tree . . . tree . . . tree* frequently without a break for quite ten seconds at a stretch. In quality and volume this is like the chirping of a large cricket, but it is punctuated now and again by one or two tell-tale harsher squeaks. Its harsh squeaky alarm notes uttered as the bird creeps away through the bushes and undergrowth is the unmistakable 'babbling' of its tribe. Its food consists of insects as well as *Lantana* and other berries. The 'sisterhoods' rummage among the fallen leaves, flicking them aside or turning them over to search for lurking insects. The nectar of *Erythrina, Bombax* and other flowers is also largely eaten. They are shy birds and not easy

33

to watch, since they seldom expose themselves and dive headlong into cover on the least suspicion.

NESTING: The season, as with many of their low country relations, is not well defined. Eggs may be found from February to May, and they have also been taken in August and November. But March and April appear to be the months when nesting activity is at its peak. The nest is a rough bulky cup of leaves and grass built in bushes and small trees in abandoned coffee clearings, etc. The normal clutch is of four eggs, blue in colour with no markings. They are fine-textured and smooth.

THE PENINSULAR INDIAN
SCIMITAR-BABBLER

Pomatorhinus horsfieldii Sykes

PLATE 17

SIZE: Between the Bulbul and the Myna.

FIELD CHARACTERS: A dark brown babbler with white throat and breast, a prominent white eyebrow, and curved pointed yellow bill. Sexes alike. Pairs or parties in scrub and secondary jungle. Calling and answering one another in mellow whistling notes.

DISTRIBUTION: Mount Abu, the Western and Eastern Ghats, and all the foothills and hill-ranges of Peninsular India south of the Vindhya Mountains, up to about 8,000 feet. Also Ceylon. Five races are recognized mainly on depth of colouration and size of bill.

HABITS: This Scimitar-Babbler is confined to densely wooded country, preferably when it is broken and hilly. It is most partial to secondary evergreen or moist deciduous jungle with patches of bamboo, cane and thorn brakes and *Strobilanthes* undergrowth. The birds go about in pairs or small scattered flocks of four to ten individuals, which rummage on the ground among the mulch, flicking the leaves aside or digging into the moist earth with their scimitar bills in search of insects and grubs. They also clamber up and hop about the moss-covered branches of forest trees or amongst the bamboo clumps in quest of food. The members of a flock keep in touch with one another by means of mellow bubbling or gurgling calls. In tone quality these are rather similar to the 'Crossword Puzzle' calls of the Indian Cuckoo, but consist only of three notes: *oo-pu-pu* as against the cuckoo's four. In the case of pairs, the male acts as leader and is followed from one thicket to another by his spouse, who is prompt to acknowledge by a subdued high-pitched *kroo*) or *krokant* ? every one of his musical flute-like calls. These calls are usually the first indication of their presence in any locality, for they are shy birds, difficult to observe, and permit merely occasional glimpses of themselves as they skulk amongst the thickets. When suspicious or alarmed and making a get-away, a sharp *kir-r-r-r* is uttered. In quiet hill-stations, however, they often enter gardens, and may also be seen along the less frequented roads. Like all babblers, their flight is feeble and ill-sustained. Their food consists mostly of insects, but berries are also eaten, as well as flower nectar.

NESTING: The season ranges between December and May, varying somewhat in different areas. The nest is a loosely put together domed structure—a ball of grass, moss, rootlets and leaves. It is placed on the ground at the foot of some bush growing on the side of a dry ravine or nullah in forest, and is inconspicuous in its surroundings. Three to five eggs are laid, pure white, thin shelled and translucent. Both sexes share in the nest building. The position of the nest is often given away by the sitting bird suddenly darting out of it when almost trod upon.

THE RUSTY-CHEEKED
SCIMITAR-BABBLER

Pomatorhinus erythrogenys Vigors

PLATE 17

SIZE: About that of the Myna.

FIELD CHARACTERS: An olive-brown and rust coloured babbler with white throat, continued as a broad white band down the centre of the underparts. No white streak above eye but a dark moustachial streak. Rather heavy yellowish, curved, pointed bill. Sexes alike. Pairs or family parties in scrub-covered ravines, etc.

The Slaty-headed Scimitar-Babbler (*Pomatorhinus schisticeps*) is another Himalayan species with a more or less overlapping distributional range. It is slightly smaller in size, olive-brown above, maroon-chestnut and white below. It has a dark slaty head and conspicuous white eyebrow. Its calls are almost indistinguishable from those of the peninsular Indian bird.

DISTRIBUTION: Himalayas between about 3,000 and 10,000 feet elevation, from about Murree east to the extreme NE. frontier (also across into Yunnan and China) and down through the Assam and Burma hills into Tenasserim. Five races are recognized on slight differences of size, colouration and markings.

HABITS: The Rusty-cheeked Scimitar-Babbler haunts densely scrubbed ravines as well as hill forest with plenty of undergrowth. Not infrequently it may be found on the opener hillsides with tall grass and thickets, or stony land dotted with sparse berberis and other bushes. It usually keeps in pairs or family parties of four to six, which search among the fallen leaves and undergrowth for grubs and insects. These comprise the greater part of their diet, but various berries are also eaten. They are very shy birds and seldom leave cover. When suddenly come upon feeding some distance from cover, they utter little shrieks of alarm and dash to safety by a series of long hops. Their calls are amongst the more familiar bird voices to be heard in a morning's walk at most Himalayan hill-stations, but owing to their skulking habits it is usually some time before the visitor can track these down to their source. The male, who acts as leader and is followed from thicket to thicket by his devoted wife, constantly utters his distinctive call of two notes, *cue-pee* (accent on first syllable), and is promptly answered by a *kip* or *quip*. The call and its response follow each other so promptly and unfailingly that they sound as though from one and the same bird, thus *q-p . . . quip, q-p . . . quip* and so on.

When agitated, the birds utter a harsh, chattering quick-repeated *che-che-che-che*, etc., rather like that of the Jay, eight to fifteen times.

NESTING: The principal breeding months are from April to June. The nest is a cup of rootlets, etc., domed with a loose canopy of dry bamboo leaves. It is fitted into an earth pocket in the side of a scrub-covered ravine, or sheltered by some bush or rock on a grass-covered hillside. The whole structure looks very like a natural accumulation of rubbish. The eggs—normally three—are white with a pinkish tinge when fresh, and roundish oval in shape.

THE SPOTTED BABBLER

Pellorneum ruficeps Swainson

PLATE 16
SIZE: About that of the Bulbul.
FIELD CHARACTERS: A small olive-brown babbler with a reddish-brown cap. Underparts whitish with the breast heavily streaked or

PLATE 15
1 THE GILGIT STREAKED LAUGHING-THRUSH (*see* page 31)
2 THE STRIATED LAUGHING-THRUSH (*see* page 32)
About 1/3 Nat. Size

PLATE 16
1 THE RUFOUS BABBLER (*see* page 33)
2 THE SPOTTED BABBLER (*see* page 36)
About 1/3 Nat. Size

PLATE 17
1 THE PENINSULAR INDIAN SCIMITAR-BABBLER (*see* page 34)
2 THE RUSTY-CHEEKED SCIMITAR-BABBLER (*see* page 35)
About 1/3 Nat. Size

PLATE 18
THE BLACK-HEADED SIBIA (*see* page 39)
About 1/2 Nat. Size

spotted with dark brown. Sexes alike. Pairs or family parties, skulking in undergrowth and on the ground.

DISTRIBUTION: From the Punjab Himalayas eastward through Garhwal and Nepal to Assam, Burma and beyond into Malay Peninsula, Annam and Cochin-China. Absent in the Indo-Gangetic plain, but occurring in the mountains and broken plateau country throughout peninsular India south of about Khandesh. Not in Ceylon. Five or six races are recognized, differing from one another in details of colouration and markings.

An allied species, the Brown-capped Babbler (*P. fuscocapillum*) is peculiar to Ceylon. It is olive-brown all over with obsolete streaking on sides of neck and breast. The upper part of its head is chocolate-brown.

HABITS: Over its extensive range, the Spotted Babbler is found from almost sea level to about 6,000 feet elevation. It keeps to dense thickets and undergrowth in evergreen as well as deciduous jungle, and is particularly fond of overgrown ravines and nullahs, and well wooded hillsides. Pairs or family parties of four or five are usually met with rummaging quietly on the ground amongst the mulch and humus, flicking aside the dry leaves in search of insects. The members keep in touch with one another by a subdued musical *weet*, repeated at intervals of a second or so. They are usually very shy and difficult to observe, but sometimes surprisingly bold, even haunting roadside hedges in or near villages and feeding complacently within a few feet of passers-by. The call most commonly heard is a pretty, rather plaintive one of three or four rich, mellow whistling notes which may be rendered as *pret-ty sweet* or *he'll beat you*. It is repeated with great persistence and monotony at intervals of five seconds or so, for over fifteen minutes at a stretch from up within the thickest bushes or bamboo clumps, chiefly in the mornings and evenings. The birds answer one another. On an observer's approach the calls suddenly cease; the bird noiselessly drops into the undergrowth and disappears. Sometimes, but not always, a subdued harsh *chr-r*, *chr-r* or *kraa*, *kraa* announces that it is slinking off, and the monotonous plaint soon recommences some distance away. But the Spotted Babbler is a remarkable songster. It sings principally in the breeding season, of course, but short sporadic bursts may be heard at all times. The song is a percussive loud, clear whistling of several notes, rambling up and down the scale, with many variations, sometimes lasting fully three minutes or more with practically no break. It is uttered from some branch where the singer is usually well concealed by the foliage.

Its food consists principally of insects.

NESTING: The season varies considerably in the different portions of its range, but the months from about February to July more or less cover the entire period. The nest is a large ball of leaves with the entrance hole at the side. It is placed among dead leaves, on the ground on steep banks, etc., in forest. The normal clutch is of two or three eggs, white or faint dull cream with numerous small specks, spots and blotches of brown.

THE QUAKER BABBLER

Alcippe poiocephala Jerdon

SIZE: Between the Sparrow and the Bulbul.

FIELD CHARACTERS: A sober olive-brown babbler with a grey cap. Rather tit-like in shape. Sexes alike. Parties of 7–10 in undergrowth and trees in forest.

DISTRIBUTION: Eastern and Western Ghats and all the hills and hilly country (between about 1,000 and 6,000 feet elevation) of peninsular India south of a line from about the Surat Dangs in the west to Lower Bengal on the east. Assam and Burma. Six races are recognized on the basis of minor differences in colouration and markings.

An allied species, the Nepal Babbler (*A. nepalensis*) is found in the Eastern Himalayas and hills of Assam and Burma up to about 4,000 feet elevation. It can be readily identified by the conspicuous ring of white feathers round the eye.

HRBITS: This dainty little babbler is primarily a bird of evergreen biotope, but it extends all through the intermediate zone and well into the deciduous. Flocks of six to ten individuals are normally met with amongst undergrowth as well as up in the canopy foliage of trees and at all heights in between. They are invariably to be found among the mixed hunting parties of small insectivorous birds that rove the forest. The birds hop from sprig to sprig, often clinging upside down, sideways or back to ground to peer into the angles of the leaf-stalks and various nooks and crannies for lurking insects. They freely descend into the forest undergrowth of seedlings, cane-brakes and the like in search of food, but only rarely to the ground. The clear, whistling, quavering song of four notes, of the tone quality of the Magpie Robin's vocal effort, is constantly uttered as the birds move about. This is usually the first indication of their presence in any locality. The scattered members of a flock keep in touch with one another by a harsh, rather subdued *chur-r, chur-r.*

Their diet consists chiefly of insects, but the birds are also very fond of flower nectar. In season they may invariably be seen probing into the blossoms of Coral (*Erythrina*) and Silk Cotton (*Bombax*) trees.

NESTING: The Quaker Babbler breeds more or less throughout the year, but May and June are perhaps the best months for eggs in peninsular India. The nest is a rather flimsy cup of rootlets, lichens, leaves and grass, built 4 to 8 feet up in the crotch of a sapling or slung hammockwise between two horizontal twigs of upright seedlings in dense moist jungle. There is usually no effort at concealment. The normal clutch is of two eggs, rarely three. They are pale salmon in ground colour with blotches and smudges of deep purple-brown or purple-black, and fainter markings of pale or inky-grey. Many eggs have short broad lines and hieroglyphics of the same colours. In shape they are moderately broad ovals, fine textured and slightly glossed.

THE BLACK-HEADED SIBIA

Leioptila capistrata Vigors

PLATE 18

SIZE: About that of the Myna, with a longer tail.

FIELD CHARACTERS: A handsome rufous or rust coloured bird with a black crest, and with some blue wash in the wing feathers. Rather bulbul-like appearance. Flight reminiscent of the Minivet's. Sexes alike. Noisy pairs or parties in trees in Himalayan forest. Purely arboreal.

DISTRIBUTION: The Himalayas from Hazara in the NW. to about Dafla Hills in Assam, between about 5,000 and 8,000 or 9,000 feet elevation. A darker eastern race (*capistrata*) and a paler western (*pallida*) are recognized.

HABITS: The Black-headed Sibia is a common bird about most Himalayan hill-stations, perhaps particularly so about Darjeeling. It haunts the hillsides and ravines covered with dense moist forest, especially the oak and rhododendron zone. The birds are usually in pairs in summer, but they collect into noisy flocks during the winter months. They are strictly arboreal and never descend to the ground. They hunt for insects actively among the tree tops, hopping along the branches, clinging to the sprigs upside down and in all manner of tit-like positions and peering into the leaves. Occasionally, one may be seen clinging sideways to the moss-covered trunk to investigate a crevice in the bark for lurking prey.

A soft rattling chuckle is uttered as the birds move about in search of food. They are usually shy. Their diet consists of insects, seeds and berries, but they are also very fond of flower nectar. Parties are constantly seen probing into rhododendron flowers, and by transferring the pollen adhering to their cheek and forehead feathers the birds doubtless do useful service in cross-pollinating them. One of its loud, shrill, ringing calls, to be heard throughout the year, has been likened to *tiri-rere-rere-ree*. Another is described as *titteree-titteree-tweeyo*, the final *tweeyo* being uttered in a subdued tone after a short pause. I have myself recorded it as a clear, rather mournful high-pitched whistling call *chi-whichee-yew-yew-yew*, curiously reminiscent in the distance of the Iora and also of the Quaker Babbler. Besides these it has a very high-pitched alarm note, rather like that of the blackbird, but more subdued and quickly repeated. The crest is erected when the alarm note is being uttered.

NESTING: The season is April to July. The nest is a neat, compact, deep massive cup of moss, grass and roots firmly interwoven and lined with roots of maidenhair fern, etc. It is placed in a bush or small tree from 8 to 20 feet up; sometimes high up in a dense fir tree. It is well concealed and difficult to locate, but the birds often give away the site by keeping up a shrill cry in its vicinity. The normal clutch is of two or three eggs, very pretty pale bluish-grey in ground colour, spotted blotched and streaked with various shades of reddish-brown and faint markings of greyish-purple. Both parents feed the young.

THE RED-BILLED LEIOTHRIX
OR 'PEKIN ROBIN'

Leiothrix lutea Scopoli

PLATE 19

SIZE: Between the Sparrow and the Bulbul.

FIELD CHARACTERS: A sprightly, well-groomed, little olive-green bird somewhat like an enlarged Tit, with bright yellow breast, a patch of yellow round the eye, yellow and red margins to flight feathers, and conspicuous coral-red bill. Tail slightly forked as in the Rosefinch. The female is somewhat duller coloured with no red but only yellow on the wing. Parties, frequenting dense overgrown ravines in open Himalayan forest.

DISTRIBUTION: The Himalayas between 3,000 and 8,000 feet from about Dharamsala in the west, all through to East Assam. Khasi Hills, Chin Hills and Northern Arakan. The Indian race (*callipyga*) occupies the whole of this range. Other races represent it in its distribution eastward into China.

HABITS: The Red-billed Leiothrix, commonly called 'Pekin Robin', though a purely Himalayan species, is a popular cage bird and well known as such throughout the country. Its exquisite appearance, lively manners and sweet song coupled with adaptability to a captive life, make it a charming adjunct to any aviary. Except in the breeding season, when pairs is the rule, the birds go about in small parties of half a dozen or so. They keep to the undergrowth in fir and pine, as well as oak and rhododendron forest. At lower elevations they are particularly attached to the dry outscoured ravines thickly overgrown with evergreen scrub of wild raspberry and other species so characteristic of the outer Himalayan foothills. They are restless and lively little birds, ever on the move among the thickets and secondary growth in search of insects, which form the major portion of their diet. The call notes ordinarily heard are a pleasant conversational *tee-tee-tee*, etc. The song uttered by the male in the breeding season, from the exposed top of a bush, is a loud and cheerful melody, rich in tone and variations. While singing, the throat feathers are fluffed out and a quivering of the wings accompanies the performance.

NESTING: The season is a prolonged one, but May and June appear to be the principal months for eggs. The nest is a largish, rather well made and substantial cup of dead leaves, moss, lichen, and pliant twigs, lined with roots, moss and finer material. It is placed at heights between 2 and 8 feet among tangled bushes in the horizontal fork of a twig, or in the crotch of a sapling, growing in a ravine in dense forest. The normal clutch is of three eggs, sometimes four, and rarely five. They are a beautiful pure white to pale blue, boldly blotched with dark brown or umber brown, and exhibit many variations. The texture is hard and fine with a bright gloss.

Both sexes share in nest-building and incubation. Their fussiness and excited jumping about near the observer usually gives away the position of the nest.

THE RED-WINGED SHRIKE-BABBLER

Pteruthius erythropterus Vigors

PLATE 20

SIZE: About that of the Myna.

FIELD CHARACTERS: A handsome, but rather stocky short-tailed, shrike-like bird, with crown of head and tail jet black. Back grey. Underparts white. Wings bright chestnut. The long, broad white streak above the eye is a conspicuous feature. In flight the white inner edges to the primaries flash into prominence, giving the bird a very white general appearance. In the female the crown is bluish grey. She has much olive greenish and yellowish in her upper plumage and is pale buff below. Pairs or parties in trees—in Himalayan hill forests.

DISTRIBUTION: Western and Eastern Himalayas to East Assam, Manipur and Chin Hills, between 3,500 and 9,000 feet.

HABITS: This Shrike-Babbler is not uncommon in mixed oak, chestnut and rhododendron forests and also in the zone of firs and deodars higher up. It moves up and down to some extent with the seasons, occupying higher elevations in summer than it does in winter. The birds are met with in pairs or small parties and commonly amongst the usual bands of insectivorous species that roam about in the forest. They are not shy as a rule, but rather difficult to observe as they have an uncanny knack of always putting leaves between themselves and the observer. They are not particularly active and hop about the branches of trees in leisurely fashion. They are purely arboreal, keeping mostly to the leafy portions of trees, and while occasionally descending into low bushes in search of food, they never actually set foot on ground. The call, which is quite intriguing when heard for the first time, is a loud *kik . . . kew-kew . . . kew-kew . . . kew-kew* repeated three or four times. It has the same tone-quality as the call of the Tailor-bird, but is louder and bigger. I have likened it to the wail of a disconsolate chicken, about a month old, that has got separated from its mother! The initial *kik* is rather subdued, and audible only at close quarters. Their food consists of insects, but various seeds and berries are also eaten.

NESTING: The season is uncertain, but eggs have been taken in April, May and June. The nest is a moderately deep cup, loosely made, of green moss with a lot of wool and cobwebs incorporated in the structure, which also serve to bind it in position. The lining is of fine roots. It is usually suspended like a cradle between horizontal twigs always high up near the top of the tallest trees of fir, oak, etc. The nest is not only difficult to find, but usually also impossible to get at. The eggs—two or three—are white with a faint tinge of lilac or pink, with numerous tiny flecks of reddish-brown or purplish-brown, forming broad rings at the larger end. They resemble the eggs of both the Red-vented and the Himalayan Black Bulbuls.

THE ORANGE-BELLIED CHLOROPSIS

Chloropsis hardwickii Jardine and Selby

PLATE 21

SIZE: About that of the Bulbul.

FIELD CHARACTERS: An elegant restless grass-green bird with bright deep orange underparts. Chin, throat and upper breast velvety black with purple sheen. Slender slightly curved black bill. In the female the blue moustachial streak is less bright and the underparts a paler orange. Pairs or parties in leafy trees. Purely arboreal.

The Gold-fronted Chloropsis (*C. aurifrons*) has a more or less overlapping Himalayan distribution, but is also commonly found in most of the peninsular hills and in Burma and Ceylon, between 1,000 and 6,000 feet. It has a bright golden forehead, purple and black chin and throat, and green underparts like the back.

DISTRIBUTION: Himalayas from Simla and Mussooree to Eastern Assam, and south through Manipur and Burma to Tenasserim. Beyond into Malay Peninsula. From foothills up to about 6,000 feet elevation.

HABITS: The Orange-bellied Chloropsis is essentially a forest bird and keeps to the foliage canopy of trees in well-wooded tracts. Its colouration harmonizes so perfectly with the leaves that it is much oftener heard than seen. Normally, the only glimpse one gets of the bird is as it flies across from one tree top to another. It is mostly seen in pairs, but small parties commonly collect to feed on the nectar of flowers like Coral (*Erythrina*) and Silk Cotton (*Bombax*). Clusters of the *Loranthus* tree-parasite when in bloom form an irresistible attraction, and the birds doubtless play an important part in cross-pollinating the flowers. They also hunt industriously among the foliage for insects, clinging to twigs in all manner of acrobatic positions.

This Chloropsis is a remarkable songster, and mimic. Its song is a beautiful performance of uncommon richness and melody, with a wide range of notes and variations. The imitations of the calls of numerous birds met with in its habitat are so perfect and convincing that even an experienced ornithologist may be repeatedly taken in. These accomplishments, coupled with the fact that it bears captivity easily, make it a popular cage bird, and it finds eager purchasers in all bird markets. It is of an extremely pugnacious disposition, however, and unsuitable for mixed aviaries with small birds. It eats insects as well as fruit and, in captivity, thrives on a diet of bananas and bread and milk.

NESTING: The season is chiefly May to July. The nest, like that of the Gold-fronted species, is a cradle of roots and fibres and small twigs, etc., with a lining of finer roots. It is suspended between leaf stalks or end twigs towards the extreme top of tall trees, 20–40 feet from the ground, usually well concealed in foliage. The eggs are somewhat darker editions of those of the Gold-fronted Chlorposis, pale cream or buffy cream in ground colour, stippled, freckled or lightly blotched all over with pale reddish. They are long ovals a little pointed at one end, and of a smooth and fine texture.

THE SILVER-EARED MESIA

Mesia argentauris Hodgson

PLATE 19

SIZE: Slightly smaller than the Bulbul.

FIELD CHARACTERS: A bright coloured babbler-like bird chiefly olive-yellow, fulvous-yellow and slaty-green, with black head set off by the glistening silver-white earcoverts. A crimson patch above and below root of tail. Wings edged yellow and crimson. The female differs chiefly in having the upper and lower tailcoverts orange-buff instead of crimson. Pairs or parties, in trees and scrub in evergreen secondary jungle.

DISTRIBUTION: The Himalayas between about 500 and 5,000 (and sometimes up to 7,000 feet) from Garhwal to NE. frontier, and down through Manipur, Lushai, Chin, Kachin, and other hills to Central and South Burma; Shan States and Siam, and beyond, eastwards. Only the one race *argentauris* occurs within our limits.

HABITS: Like the 'Pekin Robin', the Mesia is a bird of Himalayan broad-leafed evergreen forest of oak, chestnut and rhododendron, sometimes mixed with pines where it frequents the out.<kirts and opener portions.

PLATE 19
1 THE SILVER-EARED MESIA (*see* page 44)
2 THE 'PEKIN ROBIN' OR LEIOTHRIX (*see* page 40)
About 1/2 Nat. Size

PLATE 20
THE RED-WINGED SHRIKE-BABBLER (*see* page 42)
Male (above).   Female
About 1/2 Nat. Size

VIEW PLATE THIS WAY

PLATE 21
THE ORANGE-BELLIED CHLOROPSIS (*see* page 43)
About 1/2 Nat. Size

PLATE 22
1 THE YELLOW-BROWED BULBUL (*see* page 48)
2 THE SOUTHERN INDIAN BLACK BULBUL (*see* page 45)
About 1/3 Nat. Size

Scrub jungle growing along outscoured ravines in broken foothills country and on the site of abandoned forest clearings for cultivation forms a favourite haunt. Mesias go about in pairs or small parties, but in the winter months they join up into large flocks of some twenty or more individuals. They are restless little birds and hunt energetically among the foliage of shrubs, as well as up in the canopy of tall trees, for insects, clinging on to investigate the leaves and flitting from sprig to sprig. Occasional short fly-catching sallies into the air are also made. The flocks work tree after tree in feverish succession and move on to the next in disorderly follow-my-leader style as if in hurry to catch a train. A chirruping cry is constantly uttered as the birds move about, punctuated now and again with clear, loud whistling notes. Their diet consists chiefly of insects. They are favourite cage birds and thrive well in captivity. In their sprightliness and many of their actions and behaviour they are strongly reminiscent of their cousin the 'Pekin Robin'.

NESTING : The season is from April to August, but apparently most eggs are laid in May and June. Their nests and nesting habits closely resemble those of the 'Pekin Robin'. The nest is a largish well-made and substantial cup of dry bamboo and other leaves, grass and moss, lined with fine roots. It is placed in a horizontal or vertical fork of twigs in a bush, usually between 2 and 10 feet from the ground. In Sikkim and about Darjeeling, tea bushes in the plantations are largely patronized. There is seldom any effort at concealment, and the position of the nest is further given away by the agitated fussiness of the owners when it is approached. The eggs, normally four, but sometimes three, and rarely five, are a beautiful pure white to pale blue, boldly blotched with dark brown or umber brown. They are difficult to differentiate from the eggs of Leiothrix and also exhibit the same range of variations. Both sexes take part in building the nest and incubating the eggs.

THE BLACK BULBUL

Microscelis psaroides Vigors

PLATE 22

SIZE : About that of the Myna; slightly slenderer.

FIELD CHARACTERS : A dark slate-coloured bird with an untidy black crest, a slightly but distinctly forked tail and red bill and legs. Sexes alike. Noisy flocks in leafy tree tops in evergreen hill forest. Arboreal.

13

DISTRIBUTION: The Himalayas between about 2,000 and 10,000 feet from Hazara in the west to Assam. In winter it descends to lower elevations, and may be met with down to about 500 feet in the Siwaliks and Himalayan foothills. Burma, Eastern and Western Ghats (south of about the latitude of Matheran), Nilgiris, Palnis, and other hills of SW. India and Ceylon, from the foothills up to about 8,000 feet. In the areas of particularly heavy rainfall it migrates locally to drier areas at the height of the SW. Monsoon—about July–August. Five races are recognized in the above range—the Himalayan *psaroides*, the Assam *nigrescens*, the Burmese *concolor*, the South Indian *ganeesa*, and the large-billed Ceylonese race *humii*. They differ from one another slightly in size and colouration.

HABITS: The Black Bulbul early intrudes itself on the notice of the visitor to the hills by its vulgar loudness and garrulity. About Srinagar and most of the other Himalayan hill-stations, it is particularly common and noisy in spring and summer, and in its South Indian range its bearing and abundance are no different. In the Himalayas it affects the evergreen forests of broad-leaved species such as oak and rhododendron; in the South, the rain forests of the Ghats and the *sholas* of the Nilgiris and adjacent hills form its favourite habitat. The birds move about among the tops of the lofty trees in flocks of six to ten, but at certain seasons enormous gatherings numbering up to a hundred may be seen, and the forest fairly resounds with their creaky calls. Even in the breeding season the flocks do not entirely break up. When chasing one another among the tree tops, as is their wont, a sharp, long drawn *weenh*-like scream 'as of a young porker' is constantly uttered. They also have a pretty and most attractive whistle *whew-whé, whew-whé*—sometimes *whee-whé*—which has been well likened to the musical creaking of a rusty gate hinge. Usually preceding this whistle are a couple of drongo-like notes like *squeaky-squeak*. Their food consists of *ber, jamun, lantana* and a large variety of fruits and berries. They are exceedingly fond of the nectar of flowers such as rhododendron, *Eucalyptus, Grevillea* and *Erythrina*. Clamorous flocks collect to feed on these trees in season, incidentally doing useful service in promoting cross-pollination. The birds also take insects visiting the flowers and may commonly be seen launching short aerial sallies in their pursuit.

NESTING: In the Himalayas, as well as in the S. Indian hills, April, May and June appear to be the principal breeding months. The nest is a neat but flimsy-bottomed cup of dead leaves, grasses and fine woody stalks well plastered on the outside with spiders webs, with a lining of fine tendrils and bast and other fibres. It is placed in the fork of a horizontal branch of some tall tree in open forest or dense *shola*, between 25 and 30, and even up to 60 feet, from the ground. The eggs exhibit a wide range in colouration and markings. Perhaps the commonest type is white, or almost white, in ground colour, finely and sparsely speckled with red-brown or purple-brown.

THE WHITE-CHEEKED BULBUL

Molpastes leucogenys Gray

PLATE 23
SIZE: That of the better-known Red-vented Bulbul of the plains (8 inches).

FIELD CHARACTERS: A sprightly earth-brown bulbul with a jaunty forwardly curving pointed crest, glistening white earcoverts ('cheeks') and bright sulphur-yellow under the tail. Sexes alike. Pairs or small parties in gardens and open scrub country.

DISTRIBUTION: The truly hill-inhabiting race of this bulbul is the typical *leucogenys* with long crest as illustrated. It occupies the Himalayas between about 2,000 and 9,000 feet elevation from Afghanistan in the west, right across to Assam north of the Brahmaputra. The north-western part of the peninsula from Baluchistan (and including Sind, Gujerat and Kathiawar) south to about Bombay, and east to Jhansi, is occupied by the almost crestless race *leucotis*. The third intermediate-crested race *humii*, connecting these two forms, is found in the NWF. Province.

The Bulbul of the peninsular and South Indian hills is the Red-whiskered species, *Otocompsa jocosa*. It is brown above, white below, with a broken dark collar on breast. An upstanding pointed black crest, crimson 'whiskers' and crimson patch under root of tail, are other diagnostic features. It is also found in the Assam hills.

The Red-vented Bulbul (*Molpastes cafer*), smoke brown, with partially crested black head, scale-like markings on breast and back, and a conspicuous crimson patch under the tail, is common in the Himalayas as well as in most peninsular and S. Indian hills up to about 5,000 and 3,000 feet elevation respectively.

HABITS: The White-cheeked Bulbul is found in open scrub jungle and on hillsides dotted with wild raspberry, *Berberis* and other bushes. It is tame and confiding and a great favourite everywhere, making itself completely at home in orchards and gardens adjoining inhabited bungalows. Visitors to Kashmir are charmed by the abundance and friendliness of the Bulbuls in Srinagar. They are some of the commonest birds in the gardens and environs of that town, and also fearlessly enter the house-boats for scraps. The birds usually go about in pairs, but gatherings of up to fifty or more will collect where the prospects of feeding are good, such as a thicket in ripe berry or a swarm of winged ants emerging from the ground. They have a number of cheerful rollicking notes which express the joy of living, but nothing that can be termed a 'song'. Their food consists of fruits and berries of various kinds, as well as insects, grubs and spiders. Thus, while they may do some damage in the orchard and kitchen garden, they more than make up for it by the enormous quantities of injurious insects they destroy, especially while they have nest-young to feed.

NESTING: The season is principally from April to June. The nest is the usual bulbul structure—a shallow, flimsy cup of fine stems of herbaceous plants and grass blades, lined with finer grass. It is placed in a crotch, or horizontal fork of twigs, in a bush or low tree growing in scrub jungle or overgrown clearings. The eggs—normally three in a clutch—are typical of the genus *Molpastes*—pinkish-white, profusely blotched with purplish brown or claret.

THE YELLOW-BROWED BULBUL

Iole icterica Strickland

PLATE 22

SIZE: That of the Red-vented Bulbul.

FIELD CHARACTERS: A bright-plumaged Bulbul, olive-yellow above, bright yellow below. Sexes alike. Noisy parties or flocks in trees in ever-green jungle.

DISTRIBUTION: The Western Ghats south of about Khandala and hills within the evergreen forest biotope of SW. India, and Ceylon. From about the level of the plains and foothills up to 4,000 or 5,000 feet elevation, sometimes higher.

HABITS: This conspicuous bulbul is one of the commonest birds of the heavy rainfall zone of south-western India to which it is confined. It is found in evergreen as well as wet deciduous forest. It moves about in noisy parties of five to seven, which sometimes swell into large loose flocks of fifty or more birds where food is plentiful. The parties do not completely break up even when nesting is in progress. Its loud, clear and mellow double whistle, frequently uttered, is seldom out of earshot at Nilgiri and Palni hill-stations where the birds are particularly abundant. But it is essentially a shy forest bird and never becomes as trustful of man as, for example, the Red-whiskered Bulbul does. And it seldom enters gardens in the same confiding way. The dense *sholas* or ravines covered with tall evergreen forest, and separated from one another by open grassy hillslopes so characteristic of the south-western hills, are the typical habitat of this species. The birds feed among the foliage canopy of the lofty trees as well as lower down in the bushes. Their diet consists mostly of berries and fruits of numerous species, and like their cousins, they act as important agents in seed dispersal. A number of these bulbuls feeding in a tree top often form the nucleus of the mixed hunting parties of insectivorous birds. Their fluttering and restless activity in the foliage while plucking the berries invariably helps to dislodge a number of lurking insects which are promptly seized upon by their 'Co-prosperity' partners. They themselves are not averse to taking a juicy moth, and may frequently be observed launching short aerial sallies in pursuit.

NESTING: The season is principally from February to May. The nest is of the typical bulbul-pattern—a moderately deep round cup made of grass bents and lined with finer grasses. It is suspended like a hammock between horizontal twigs in a sapling growing as a rule in thick cover, 6 to 10 feet from the ground. The normal clutch is of two or three eggs, pale creamy pink to warm salmon-pink in ground colour covered all over with innumerable specks, freckles and blotches of various shades of red. The markings are slightly more numerous at the big end.

THE HIMALAYAN TREE-CREEPER

Certhia himalayana Vigors

PLATE 24

SIZE: Smaller than the Sparrow.

FIELD CHARACTERS: A tiny mottled brown bird with a longish stiff pointed tail, distinctly cross-rayed at close quarters, and slender curved bill. Sexes alike. Singly or pairs, creeping up tree trunks like a woodpecker.

DISTRIBUTION: The Western Himalayas between 4,000 and 12,000 feet from Baluchistan and the Afghan frontier through Kashmir, to Garhwal and Kumaon. Possibly also further east to Sikkim and Bhutan.

In this area two races are recognized on differences in shades of colouration. In winter it leaves the highest elevations and may then be met with in the foothills as well as plains of NW. India. Here it frequents sparsely wooded country and groves of trees about villages and cultivation, and is particularly fond of shisham trees.

The Sikkim Tree-Creeper (*C. discolor*), more richly coloured, with the lower parts earthy brown instead of pale greyish, is found in the Eastern Himalayas from Nepal to east Assam and down into the Shan States and Chin Hills of Burma.

The beautiful Wall-Creeper (*Tichodroma muraria*), a grey square-tailed bird like the Nuthatch with a slender black bill and bright crimson in its wings, occurs in the Himalayas between 12,000 and 16,000 feet elevation in summer. It descends lower in winter and may then be met with in the foothills, and even the plains at their base. This bird lives on cliffs and rock scarps moving up their vertical faces in the same way as the Tree-Creeper does on tree trunks. It has a peculiar slow-flapping, or fluttering, butterfly-like flight: flap . . . pause (with wings closed) . . . flap . . . pause, and so on.

HABITS: The Tree-Creeper inhabits both broad-leaved and coniferous forests. It usually moves about in pairs, but sometimes family parties are met with, either by themselves or in the customary roving bands of insectivorous birds such as tits, nuthatches and warblers. The bird clings to the rough bark of a tree like a nuthatch and runs up the trunk in short spurts either directly or in irregular spirals. It stops now and again to peer into or probe with its slender bill some promising looking crevice in the bark for hidden insects. Often after hopping up for a few feet the bird suddenly drops lower in 'reverse gear' to investigate some crevice it has missed and works up again. Having thus worked its way up to near the top of the tree it flies off to another nearby, alighting near the base of its trunk and working up in the same way. Thus the birds follow one another from tree to tree all day long. Their large feet and claws and stiff tail feathers help them in clinging to and climbing up the tree trunks. Its squeaky notes, uttered from time to time, sound something like *chi-chi* . . . *chiu-chiu-chiu*. In volume and quality they are reminiscent of the *tsee-tsee* of the Red-winged Bush-Lark (*Mirafra*) of the plains.

NESTING: May and June are the months when breeding is at its height. The nest is a shapeless thick mass, rather like the House-Sparrow's, of small feathers mingled with a few pieces of dry grass, straw, etc. It may be placed fairly low down in a tree stump—at about 4 feet or so—or in crevices and bulges of broken or loose bark of a deodar, rhododendron or hill oak tree up to 40 or 50 feet above ground. The normal clutch consists of four eggs, sometimes five. They are mostly white or pale pinkish-white in ground colour, heavily spotted and speckled with reddish-brown chiefly at the broad end where they form irregular caps or zones. Both sexes share in building the nest and feeding the young, but apparently the female alone broods. Incubation takes thirteen to fourteen days.

THE WHITE-BREASTED OR KASHMIR DIPPER

Cinclus cinclus Linnaeus

PLATE 25

SIZE: About that of the Myna.

FIELD CHARACTERS: A dumpy, stub-tailed thrush-like bird, slaty and chocolate-brown with glistening white throat and breast. Sexes alike. Singly, or separated pairs at Himalayan torrents.

The Brown Dipper (*C. pallasi*), wholly chocolate-brown, is also commonly seen on Himalayan streams. Both have more or less the same distributional range and habits, and are often met with side by side.

DISTRIBUTION: The Kashmir race (*Kashmiriensis*) is found in the NWF. Province, Kashmir, and all along the Himalayas east to Assam north of the Brahmaputra river. Chiefly between about 6,000 and 15,000 feet elevation, but occasionally up to 17,000 feet.

HABITS: The Dipper is an inhabitant of clear, swift running, icy Himalayan torrents. Its harsh, shrill cry *dzchit dzchit*, makes suitable music to the deafening roar of the waters as they leave their cradle of eternal snow among the mighty peaks and glaciers, and dash their thunderous way down to the parent river, tumbling in cascades, leaping over rocks, hurrying under snow-bridges, and breaking up into showers of foam and spray against the gigantic boulders. Such are the wild surroundings the Dipper loves. It is a hardy creature, indifferent to the severity of wintry conditions and found at high altitudes even in the coldest season, although most descend to lower levels then. It spends its time perched upright on the slippery boulders in mid stream, cocking its stub tail and bobbing the forepart of its body. It is fascinating to watch a Dipper plunge into the ice-cold water from time to time in search of food. It remains submerged for quite half a minute or more at a time, walking freely along the bottom. It has been shown that the bird does not grip the stones at the bottom, but keeps submerged without effort merely by tilting its body at an angle at which the vertical force of the current is sufficient to keep it pressed down. It also uses its wings in a sort of submarine flight. When it reappears above the surface, it jumps on to a stone and shakes the water off its plumage, bobbing its plump body up and down, bending and stretching its legs and turning its head from side to side—bowing and curtseying—in a manner reminiscent of the Brown Rock-Chat. In flight the short rounded wings are rapidly vibrated with almost imperceptible pauses every little while. When perched on a stone with the swirling torrent around it, or skimming along a foot or two above the water, it is often difficult to pick out the bird from its background, so well do its white underparts break up its contours to blend with the ripples and foam. It swims freely on pools, looking like a miniature moorhen, diving and disappearing below the surface now and again for quite ten seconds or so at a time. Its food consists of aquatic insects and their larvæ, water spiders, and apparently also tadpoles and tiny fish.

In the breeding season the male sings a merry, loud wren-like song. NESTING: The season is from April to late July, earlier at lower levels, later higher up. The nest is a large, untidy, round or oval ball of grass, leaves, weed stalks, etc., lined with dry leaves and grass. It is very inconspicuous and looks like a natural collection of rubbish. It is always placed on banks or beds of streams, on a ledge or crevice of rock, a stranded log or a pile of caught-up debris. The eggs—three or four—are pure white, smooth but without gloss.

THE SHORTWING

Brachypteryx major Jerdon

SIZE: Somewhat larger than the Sparrow.
FIELD CHARACTERS: A rounded, winged, short and square-tailed cousin of the familiar Robin, dark blue above with a white rump. Slaty-blue breast; pale chestnut and whitish belly. Sexes alike. Singly, in evergreen undergrowth in South Indian *sholas*. Terrestrial.

A closely allied species, Hodgson's Shortwing (*Hodgsonius phoenicuroides*), represents it in the Himalayas from Kashmir to NE. Assam, between 6,000 and 12,000 feet elevation. It is about the size of the Bulbul, slaty-blue with a predominatingly chestnut tail. The tail is normally spread out and carried low—not cocked—with the wings drooping at the sides. It is flicked up momentarily from time to time. The female is chiefly

G.M.Henry

VIEW PLATE THIS WAY

PLATE 23
THE WHITE-CHEEKED BULBUL (*see* page 47)
About 1/2 Nat. Size

G. M. Henry.

PLATE 24
THE HIMALAYAN TREE-CREEPER (*see* page 49)
About 5/8 Nat. Size

PLATE 25
THE WHITE-BREASTED OR KASHMIR DIPPER (*see* page 51)
About 1/2 Nat. Size

olive-brown and rufous-chestnut. This Shortwing frequents open scrub-covered hillsides and has a rather mournful whistling call: *pee-pée-pit* (accent on second syllable).

DISTRIBUTION: Nilgiris, Brahmagiris, Palnis, and other hill ranges of SW. India, including those of Mysore, Travancore and Cochin. Chiefly between 3,000 and 7,000 feet.

The race *albiventris*, found in the Palnis and Travancore and Mysore ranges, has the chestnut on sides of belly replaced by slaty-blue.

HABITS: The Shortwing is confined to the hills in the heavy rainfall zone of south-western India. It is a shy and retiring bird haunting thick undergrowth in the *sholas*, or evergreen ravine forest, that are such a feature of those hills. It is only in the evening twilight that it usually leaves the seclusion of cover, and then, if one moves quietly along a forest path it may be come upon round a bend hopping out into the middle or sitting on a bank or on the roadside. When alarmed the bird flies up into a tree, but descends almost immediately. The only call heard in the non-breeding season is a loud chattering, and occasionally a faint high-pitched whistle, but the birds are, on the whole, very silent. During the nesting season, however, the male pours forth a lively and beautiful song, long sustained and varied, as he moves from twig to twig among the shadows. It is rather similar in style and tone-quality to that of the Southern Blackbird, but not so loud and also covering a smaller range of variations. Its food consists entirely of insects.

NESTING: The season is March to June, but May appears to be the most popular month. The nest is a soft mass of green moss with a cup-like depression in the centre lined with dark moss roots. It is usually placed in holes in trees under four or five feet from the ground within well-wooded *sholas*; sometimes in holes in earth banks. There is no effort at concealment and the nests are not, as a rule, difficult to find. The normal clutch is almost invariably of two eggs, very pale olive-brown in ground colour but so completely covered with minute freckling of reddish-brown that they look quite brown. They are fine and smooth textured, with a light gloss.

THE INDIAN BLUE CHAT

Luscinia brunnea Hodgson

PLATE 26

SIZE: About that of the Sparrow.

FIELD CHARACTERS: A forest-haunting chat, slaty-blue above, bright chestnut below with a conspicuous white streak over the eye. Female olive-brown above, whitish below. Singly, in evergreen undergrowth; Himalayas summer—SW. Indian hills winter.

DISTRIBUTION: *Summer*: Himalayas between 5,000 and 10,000 feet from Kashmir and Garhwal to Bhutan. *Winter*: Chiefly hills of the heavy rainfall zone in SW. India and Ceylon, between about 2,500 feet and 5,000 feet elevation.

HABITS: The Blue Chat arrives on its breeding grounds in the Himalayas early in May. Thence onward until about September it is quite common everywhere. Like its cousin the Shortwing, the greater part of its life is passed on the ground or among low bushes. It frequents dense undergrowth in the opener parts of fir and mixed forest growing on the hillsides and is a confirmed skulker. It seldom shows itself except when the male constantly sings from some perch not far from the nest. But its presence is usually given away by the loud clear notes which emanate from within the undergrowth as the bird hops about in search of food, now on the ground, now a few inches up in some thicket. From time to time it jerks up and expands its tail, usually accompanied by a feeble *chr-r-r*. At this season also, the male has a short sweet song consisting of three or four monotonous notes—rendered by Whistler as *jerri, jerri, jerri,* or *phwee—phwee—phwee—* in an ascending scale, followed by a rapidly-repeated trill *tree-tre-tre-tretre*—the last reminiscent of a Robin's song. This is one of the commonest bird sounds in the hill jungles during the breeding season. In its winter quarters in the SW. Indian hills—from September to May—the favourite habitat of this chat is dank ravines in cardamom plantations and evergreen *sholas* with dense brakes of rattan and screw-pine. The bird is also freely met with under coffee bushes in plantations. At this season it is mostly silent, the only note heard being a feeble monosyllabic squeak, repeated about once a second and usually punctuated at intervals by *chr-r-r* or *chick-chick* like the Brown Flycatcher as the bird hops about under thickets. Like the last named also, it jerks its tail up and flicks it open when uttering these sounds. Its food consists of insects.

NESTING: The season in the Himalayas is from May to July, earlier at

54

lower elevations and later at higher ones. The nest is a pad of dry leaves, moss and roots lined with hair and a few feathers. It is placed in a hollow on the ground in the side of an earth cutting often beside some jungle path, or well concealed among the roots of a bush, ferns or brackens in deep jungle. The normal clutch consists of four eggs—occasionally three, and rarely five—beautiful unspotted deep blue of the shade known as 'Hedge-Sparrow blue'. This chat does not breed in S. India as has been sometimes presumed from its late departure northwards.

THE PIED BUSH-CHAT

Saxicola caprata Linnaeus

SIZE: About that of the Sparrow.

FIELD CHARACTERS: A jet black chat with white patches on rump, abdomen and wings, the last more conspicuous in flight. The female is earth-brown with a pale rust-coloured rump. Pairs, on bush-tops, etc., on open grassy hillsides.

The Collared Bush-Chat (S. torquata) breeds throughout the Himalayas between 2,000 and 8,000 feet elevation from west to east in summer, usually occupying higher zones than the Pied species. It has a black head, orange-brown breast, prominent white collar and white patches on shoulders and above base of tail. The female resembles the female Pied Bush-Chat, but is streaked darker on the upper parts. In winter it spreads out over the plains and most peninsular hills.

DISTRIBUTION: The Himalayas up to about 8,000 feet from west to east, and all the plains, plateaux and hills of peninsular and South India and the central hills of Ceylon. Four races are recognized on slight differences in size of wing and bill, and extent of white on underparts of male.

HABITS: The Pied Bush-Chat inhabits open country, grassland, bush and scrub covered hillsides and plains, and is often found in the neighbourhood of villages and cultivation. In the Mysore, Travancore and Cochin hills it frequents grass-covered areas at the edge of *sholas*. It is a particularly familiar and abundant species in the Nilgiris and Palnis. The bird is seen singly, but invariably has its mate somewhere close at hand. It takes up a position on some stake, grass-tuft or stone, twitching open its tail now and again, and makes frequent little darts to the ground to pick up a grasshopper or bug. Sometimes it will spring up into the air or make short sallies after winged insects. The note commonly uttered is a harsh *chek, chek*, ending in a subdued *trweet*. In the breeding season the male has a pretty whistling song beginning with a double *chick-chick* and resembling in cadence and tone-quality that of the Indian Robin or the Crested Bunting. It is uttered either from a perch or during the short arc-like display flight with 'delayed action' wing beats above his back, as in a pigeon 'clapping'. Occasionally, the singing bird takes short ludicrous leaps into the air. The song is also uttered in defiance to a rival. During this challenging gesture the back is slightly arched, the neck stiffly craned forward, and the wings drooped at the sides flaunting the white shoulder patches. The tail is depressed and fanned out, while the white rump is fluffed out menacingly.

NESTING : The season varies somewhat with locality and altitude, ranging between February and May. The nest is a pad of grass lined with hair or wool. It is placed in hollows in earth cuttings, a depression in the ground under some bush, or in crevices or holes in piled-up stone boundary walls, etc. The eggs—three to five in number—are usually very pale bluish-green, speckled and blotched with reddish-brown. Incubation takes twelve to thirteen days. Only the female broods, but the male helps in building the nest and feeding the young.

THE DARK GREY BUSH-CHAT

Rhodophila ferrea Gray

PLATE 27

SIZE : About that of the Sparrow.

FIELD CHARACTERS : An unmistakable cousin of the Bush-Chat. General effect of the male grey, white and black; of the female rufous brown. Pairs on open hillsides with scattered bushes, trees and rock outcrops.

DISTRIBUTION : The Western or typical race *ferrea* occupies the Himalayas between about 4,000 and 9,000 feet elevation from the Afghan border, and through Kashmir east to Assam, north and south of the Brahmaputra. The Eastern race, *haringtoni*, in which the male is paler grey above and whiter below, is found in the Chin and Kachin Hills of Burma, Yunnan, etc. In winter the birds descend into the foothills and plains country along the base of the Himalayas.

HABITS : Open grass-covered hillsides with terraced cultivation here and there, and scattered bushes and trees and outcrops of rock form the typical habitat of the Dark Grey Bush-Chat. It freely enters hill gardens and the vicinity of bungalows. Single birds, or separated pairs, are usually met with perched on a boulder or tree top, whence they keep a look-out for crawling insects. From time to time the bird darts to the ground to pick up the quarry, battering it on the spot and bolting it down before returning. Its food consists entirely of insects. In its actions and behaviour it closely resembles the Pied Bush-Chat, except perhaps that it perches much more on tree tops and less on bushes and stones than that bird does. Telegraph and electric overhead wires afford ideal perches at hill-stations. They appear to have fixed territories both in the breeding season and out of it, and intrusion by others of their kind is actively resisted. The male has a pleasant, though rather feeble, whistling song, *sisiri-swirr*, uttered from a tree top in the proximity of its nest. Its display flight is very similar to that of the Pied Bush-Chat, in which the contrasting colours of its plumage are thrown into the fullest prominence. NESTING: The season is principally from April to mid-June. The nest is usually a neat and compact cup of grass, fine twigs and moss, lined with finer grass stems, horse-hair, soft fur, etc. It is placed in hollows in banks, under large roots and boulders, or amongst the loose stones of a boundary wall or revetment. The eggs—four or five—are light greyish or greenish-blue in ground colour, speckled faintly but profusely with pale reddish, denser, and forming a ring round the broad end. In appearance they are exactly like those of the Collared Bush-Chat, only a little larger. Incubation takes about thirteen days. It is uncertain whether the male takes any share in the brooding.

THE SPOTTED FORKTAIL

Enicurus maculatus Vigors

PLATE 28

SIZE: Between the Bulbul and the Myna.

FIELD CHARACTERS: A graceful spotted black-and-white bird, rather like a wagtail, with a long and deeply forked tail. The white 'Cross of St Andrew' across the back is a distinguishing feature of this species. Sexes alike. Singly or pairs on rocky, wooded Himalayan mountain streams.

The Little Forktail (*Microcichla scouleri*), slightly bigger than the

Sparrow, also black-and-white but with a short, square—almost stub-tail, is another common species found at Himalayan torrents, with an overlapping geographical range.

DISTRIBUTION: Throughout the Himalayas between about 2,000 to 12,000 feet more or less, from the extreme NW. frontier to the extreme NE. frontier. Also down into Shan States, Siam and Yunnan. The Eastern race *guttatus* differs from the Western *maculatus* chiefly in having the breast unspotted black.

HABITS: This delightful bird is a dweller on rocky Himalayan streams. Single birds or pairs may be seen tripping gingerly over the slippery or moss-covered rocks lapped by the swirling torrent, running along the water's edge or hopping from stone to stone in search of food. The long forked tail is raised well off the ground and carried horizontally. The general aspect and bearing of the bird is very wagtail-like, and its tail is also moved up and down vertically. But it is swayed gently rather than wagged, the movement being slow and full of elegance. The bird pivots slowly on its perch, now facing one way, now another, to the accompaniment of this slow swaying of its tail. The call note, uttered as it flies up or down the ravine when disturbed, is a sharp *kree* like the Whistling-Thrush's. It also utters both at rest and on the wing a sharp, creaky *cheek-chik-chik-chik-chik*, which I find to be almost identical with one of the calls of the Blue Magpie, though perhaps less loud. The tone-quality of this sound is akin to a finger rubbed along a plate-glass show-window. These lively calls heard above the rush of the torrent in the deep solitude of a forested ravine, make some of the most fascinating music that a bird lover can hear in this romantic setting. Its food consists principally of aquatic insects and their larvæ.

NESTING: The season is between April and July. The nest is a cup of moss, moss-roots, horse-hair, etc., lined with skeleton leaves and fine rootlets. It is always placed near some rocky stream in a niche or hollow in a steep bank, usually overhung by ferns and roots, and completely hidden from view. The moss, when collected, is carried to the water's edge, where the bird deliberately dips and soaks it to render it thoroughly pliant before plastering it on to the structure. The eggs—normally three or four—are pale buffy stone colour or pale grey-green, or creamy. The whole surface is usually freckled and spotted with light reddish-brown, sometimes more profusely at the broad end. Both sexes share in building the nest, incubation and feeding the young.

THE WHITE-CAPPED REDSTART

Chaimarrornis leucocephalus Vigors

PLATE 29

SIZE: Slightly bigger than the Sparrow.

FIELD CHARACTERS: A sprightly robin-like bird, black above, bright chestnut below, with a glistening snow-white cap, and a bright chestnut tail ending in a black band. Sexes alike. Singly, on stones and boulders in Himalayan torrents.

DISTRIBUTION:The Himalayas from extreme north-west to extreme north-east. Also N. Burmese hills, Shan States, Yunnan, etc. In summer between 6,000 and 16,000 feet elevation; in winter at lower levels, and on all North Indian rivers, where they leave the foothills. Also along irrigation canals at the edge of the plains, sometimes even where flowing through a town or village.

HABITS: The White-capped Redstart is inseparable from the rocky streams and torrents of the Himalayas at high altitudes during the summer months. Here it is extremely common, and it is not long before the trekker will strike up an acquaintance with it. As his path winds up the bank of a clear glacier-fed stream—its waters leaping over stones, dashing against the boulders or cascading over the little steps—his attention is constantly drawn by a loud, shrill and plaintive *teeee* heard above the tumult of the waters to this dainty little redstart. It is perched on a rock amid stream, wagging its tail violently up and down, and bobbing the forepart of its body. Every little distance along the course of the stream he will meet this bird either singly or in pairs. They seem to portion off definite territories within which they flit from stone to stone, or fly from one bank to another in their day-long hunt for food. Almost invariably there will be a pair or so of Plumbeous Redstarts nearby. Each time the bird alights on a stone the tail, which is normally carried cocked up like a robin's, is slowly but deliberately wagged up and down until it almost touches the perch. It is then fully expanded, displaying the deep orange-chestnut to fullest effect, with the black terminal band that finishes it off so admirably. Sometimes the bird runs swiftly over the stones with a mincing gait head lowered and tail slightly cocked—recalling the movements of the Bluethroat—then mounts a stone, standing erect and wagging its tail violently.

Its food consists entirely of aquatic insects, which are picked off the water as they float past, or when cast up high and dry by a ripple. It also makes short aerial sallies after winged insects in the manner of a Fly-catcher.

59

NESTING: This Redstart breeds normally between 8,000 and 14,000 feet elevation in June and July. The nest is a bulky cup of moss, mixed with leaves, etc., and lined with wool, hair and roots. It is placed in a hole or crevice of rock, in a hollow in a bank, or among the roots of a tree. Whatever the situation, it is never far from turbulent streams running either through forest or down a rocky, sparsely-scrubbed mountainside. The eggs—three or four—are pale sea-green profusely spotted all over with dark reddish-brown or rust colour, more densely round the broad end. Both parents feed the young.

THE PLUMBEOUS REDSTART

Rhyacornis fuliginosus Vigors

PLATE 29

SIZE: About that of the Sparrow.

FIELD CHARACTERS: Male, dark bluish-slate with a bright chestnut tail. Female greyish-brown with a white and brown tail. When expanded it shows a brown triangle broadly bordered with white. Singly or pairs, on Himalayan torrents.

The Blue-fronted Redstart (*Phoenicurus frontalis*) and the Common or Black Redstart (*P. ochruros*) both occur and breed in summer throughout the Himalayas west to east at elevations between 10,000 and 15,000 feet. In winter the former is common down at most Himalayan hillstations, while the latter spreads out practically all over the plains of India. The male of the former is dull dark blue with brilliant blue forehead and supercilium. Its lower plumage is chestnut and there is a black band at the end of its chestnut tail. The male Common Redstart is black or greyish-black with chestnut below the breast and a chestnut tail. In all redstarts the tail is an expressive organ and is constantly shivered or flirted.

DISTRIBUTION: The Himalayas from extreme west to extreme east. Tibet, Assam and Burmese hills, Yunnan, etc., between 4,000 and 14,000 feet. In winter down to lower elevations, same as the White-capped Redstart.

HABITS: The Plumbeous Redstart is found in identical habitats and mostly side by side with the White-capped species. The habits of the two are closely similar. The male and female are so different in appearance that they could easily be mistaken for entirely different birds. It is met

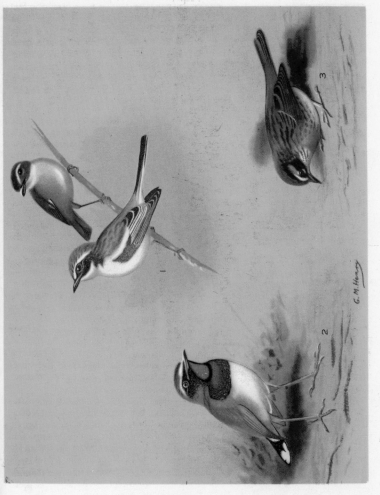

G. M. Henry

VIEW PLATE THIS WAY

PLATE 27
1 THE DARK GREY BUSH-CHAT (*see* page 56)
2 THE HIMALAYAN RUBYTHROAT   3 THE RUFOUS-BREASTED HEDGE-SPARROW
   (*see* page 61)   (*see* page 72)
About 3/8 Nat. Size

PLATE 28
THE WEST HIMALAYAN SPOTTED FORKTAIL (*see* page 57)
About 1/2 Nat. Size

PLATE 29
1 THE WHITE-CAPPED REDSTART (*see* page 59)
2 THE PLUMBEOUS REDSTART. Female (left). Male (*see* page 60)
About 1/3 Nat. Size.

PLATE 30
1 THE SHAMA (*see* page 64)
2 THE BLUE-HEADED ROCK-THRUSH (*see* page 70)
Female (above).   Male
About 1/3 Nat. Size

singly sitting on a rock or driftwood amid stream, opening and closing its tail laterally every now and again, or fanning it out and depressing it vertically until it almost touches the perch. It seems to be even more territorially inclined than the White-capped species and actively resents the intrusion of its feeding area, or 'zone of influence', by another of its kind, regardless of sex. In summer, however, pairs get on more harmoniously together. From its perch on a stone it makes short fluttering sallies into the air after winged insects above the foam and spray, and occasionally even snatches them up from the surface as they are borne past by the swirling ripples. Sometimes the bird leaps up, catches an insect and flutters down gracefully in an arc on to another stone nearby. All its antics are delightful to watch. The male has a pleasant but feeble whistling song, *chik . . . cheechik—cheechik*. In volume, tone-quality and cadence this is an 'identical twin' of the song of the White-throated Fantail-Flycatcher (*Rhipidura albicollis*). It is such a true copy in fact that even an experienced ornithologist may frequently be taken in.

NESTING: April to July are the breeding months over its range as a whole. May and June are the most favoured in the Western Himalayas. The nest is a compact cup of moss mixed with a few roots and leaves, and lined with fibres, horse-hair, wool, etc. It is placed in hollows in earth banks, crevices in boulders, and under roots of trees alongside streams. The normal clutch is of four eggs, pale greenish, speckled and blotched fairly heavily with reddish-brown.

THE HIMALAYAN RUBYTHROAT

Calliope pectoralis Gould

PLATES 27 AND 69

SIZE: About that of the Sparrow.

FIELD CHARACTERS: A robin-like bird ashy-slate above with a white forehead. Chin and throat bright crimson bordered with black. Abdomen white. Some white on base and tip of tail feathers, conspicuous in flight. Female olive-brown above, with chin and throat dull white. Singly on rocky or juniper-covered Himalayan hillsides.

The Common Rubythroat (*C. calliope*), which breeds in NE. Asia, is a common winter visitor to the eastern side of India, south to the Godavari river. It may be differentiated by its upper plumage being olive-brown, by absence of any white in tail, and by a white moustachial streak.

15   61

The Bluethroat (*Cyanosylvia svecica*) is another bird of remarkably similar general effect and habits, found about marshes, wet cultivation, etc., all over India during winter. It is divided into several geographical races, at least one of which breeds within Indian limits, in Kashmir and Ladakh, between 9,000 and 12,000 feet. The male in summer is brown above, whitish below with a conspicuous chestnut patch near root of tail, and bright blue chin and throat.

DISTRIBUTION: The Western Himalayas from Afghanistan and Baluchistan through Kashmir, etc., to Nepal. In summer between 9,000 and 14,000 feet; in winter down into the foothills and plains along their base.

HABITS: The Himalayan Rubythroat is an inhabitant of steep rocky and grassy slopes at high elevations, in the zone above the level of tree growth and just below the snows. It also frequents rocky hillsides with Juniper, *Berberis* and *Lonicera* scrub, and small overgrown nullahs. It runs and hops about on the ground, dodging among the bushes and boulders, wings partly drooping, tail cocked, and switched over the back now and again. When approached it takes a short flight near the ground —a few wing beats punctuated by a short pause—and dives behind some bush. The white patches at the base and tip of its tail now present an easy identification mark. Or it scuttles secretively from bush to bush with lowered head very like a Bluethroat. In all its movements and behaviour it is extremely reminiscent of the familiar Bluethroat of the plains in winter, and in some ways also of the Indian Robin. It has a somewhat metallic single call note rather like a Sparrow's. In the breeding season the cock utters a lively pleasant song from a bush top in the proximity of its nest. The song is very similar to that of the Pied Bush-Chat, and the stance taken by the singer is also the same: wings and tail drooping. It is of three or four seconds' duration, and repeated with short breaks— to the point of monotony—sometimes for over an hour at a stretch.

Its food consists entirely of insects.

NESTING: The nesting habits of this bird are also remarkably like those of the Bluethroat. The season is from May to July, but June is the time when breeding is at its height. The nest is either domed, with a large opening on one side near the top, or cup-shaped. It is made more or less entirely of grass and lined with finer grass, and usually well concealed under a tuft of grass or small bush on an open rocky, sparsely scrubbed hillside. The eggs—three or four—are dark bluish-green, or 'Hedge-Sparrow blue', with pale reddish speckling and freckles, denser at the broad end. Rubythroats' nests are largely parasitized by the Asiatic Cuckoo (*Cuculus canorus telephonus*).

THE RED-FLANKED BUSH-ROBIN

Ianthia cyanura Pallas

PLATE 26

SIZE: About that of the Sparrow.

FIELD CHARACTERS: A small robin-like bird purplish-blue above, ashy white below, with an orange-chestnut patch on each side of the body. A broad bright blue supercilium. The female is rufous olive-brown above, with orange-chestnut patches on the flanks and whitish down centre of abdomen. Upper tailcoverts and tail blue. Singly, or separated pairs, in high Himalayan forest.

DISTRIBUTION: The Himalayas from extreme NW. to extreme NE. between 7,000 and 14,000 feet in summer; down to about 5,000 feet in winter. Also Chin and Kachin Hills, Shan States, Yunnan, etc. Two races occur within our area: the paler Kashmir or West Himalayan *pallidiora*, and the darker East Himalayan *rufilata*.

HABITS: The Red-flanked Bush-Robin is a common but shy and retiring bird, affecting steep slopes in birch and rhododendron forest at high altitudes, wherever there is plenty of undergrowth. It is partial to stream beds, especially those bordered with dense bushes in which it can take refuge on the least alarm. The bird hops about restlessly on the ground and in low bushes in its quest for insect food. Every now and again it flicks open its wings and tail in the characteristic Bush-Chat manner. Its general behaviour is very similar to the English Robin's. The ordinary call note is a plaintive *pheeou*. It has no song as such, but in the breeding season the male utters a rather pleasant three-noted call. The first and third notes of this are the same, the middle one being a tone lower. The calls of concern, as for instance when its nest is approached, are very like those of the Pied Bush-Chat: a sharp *kek – kek*, rather like a tree-frog, sometimes followed by a whistle, *trweet*.

NESTING: The principal breeding months are May and June. The nest is a rather rough cup of grass, moss, roots, dead leaves, etc., usually lined with wool or hair. It is well concealed under the projecting roots of some large tree or in herbage on a steep grass- and bush-covered hillside in thin birch or silver fir forest. The eggs—three to five, but most often four—are pure chalky white or slightly pinkish, usually faintly freckled at the larger end with pale pink, forming an ill-defined ring. Sometimes they are unmarked. Both sexes feed the young.

THE SHAMA

Kittacincla malabarica Scopoli

PLATE 30
SIZE: That of the Bulbul, but with a relatively much longer tail.

FIELD CHARACTERS: An unmistakable cousin of the familiar Magpie-Robin of the plains. In the male the head, back and throat are glossy black, the underparts rich chestnut. A white patch on the rump and white outer feathers of the long graduated black-and-white tail are diagnostic features even in a flashing glimpse of the flying bird. In the female the black is replaced by slaty-brown, the underparts are paler and duller, and the tail shorter. Solitary, in deep forest.

DISTRIBUTION: Patchily throughout the well-wooded plateau country and hills of peninsular India, Burma, Andamans and Ceylon. Also the Himalayas east of the Kumaon Terai from the foothills up to about 3,000 feet, and occasionally up to 5,000 feet elevation. Not in the arid tracts of NW. India.

HABITS: The Shama is essentially a bird of evergreen and moist-deciduous forest-clad foothills and *ghats*. It haunts the seclusion of dense undergrowth of seedlings and saplings, and is particularly fond of mixed bamboo jungle and well-wooded ravines. On account of its shy and retiring disposition, and also the remoteness of its natural habitats, it is perhaps more likely to be met with as a cage bird by readers than in its wild state. In the hill-stations of Matheran and Mahableshwar (Western Ghats) however, it may commonly be seen in the forest surrounding the bungalows and along the roadsides, and here it does not seem to mind observation and people passing to and fro. Its general habits closely resemble the Dhyal's. Although largely arboreal, most of its food is obtained on the ground, the bird constantly descending to pick up an insect, hopping about, flicking open its wings and tail to stampede lurking prey and flying up into a branch. Sometimes it will also make a short sally into the air after a winged insect. Although entirely insectivorous in its wild state, the Shama thrives well in captivity on a diet of *suttoo* (gram paste), varied occasionally with insects or a little minced meat. It is one of the finest song birds we have in India and is as highly prized for its own vocal accomplishments as for its aptitude in mimicking to perfection the calls of other birds. The song of the male Shama heard in the depth of the forest at dusk has a peculiar charm. Its phrases are rather like those of Tickell's Blue Flycatcher, but it is louder, more musical and possesses an infinitely richer tone-quality. It has a curious mixture of the Oriole and the White-throated Ground-Thrush rolled into it.

NESTING: The principal months are April to July, varying somewhat in the different portions of its range. The nest is built in some natural hollow in a dead tree stump or amongst the rubbish collected in the rootstocks of a bamboo clump. It is a shallow, untidy cup of rootlets, grass and bamboo leaves, usually 4 to 6 feet, and occasionally up to 12 feet from the ground. The eggs—normally four, rarely five—are very like small dull coloured eggs of the Magpie-Robin, pale blue-green, densely blotched with brown or reddish-brown. Both sexes share in nest-building, incubation and feeding the young.

THE SOUTHERN BLACKBIRD

Turdus simillimus Jerdon

PLATE 31

SIZE: About that of the Myna.

FIELD CHARACTERS: A sober grey-brown bird with a black cap and yellow eyelids, legs and bill. The female is more ashy above and paler generally, with the cap brown. On trees or ground, in *ghat* and peninsular hill forests. (This description applies particularly to the Black-capped race *Mahrattensis* of the Bombay *ghats*).

Several allied thrushes or 'blackbirds' are common in the Himalayas. They all have a delightfully loud, rich song during the summer months, uttered chiefly in the mornings and evenings. During winter some of them wander a great deal down into the Himalayan foothills and the plains and hills of peninsular India.

Tickell's Thrush (*Turdus unicolor*) is uniform ashy-grey above, slaty-grey and whitish below, with chestnut underwing coverts. Female olive-brown. Chin and throat white, streaked on sides with black. Exceedingly common in gardens and orchards in and around Srinagar. Singing everywhere morning and evening, March to May.

The Grey-winged Blackbird (*Turdus boulboul*) found at medium elevations, about 6,000 to 8,000 feet, common about Mussooree, Ranikhet, and other W. Himalayan stations, is probably the finest songster of all our thrushes. It is glossy black with a conspicuous pale grey patch on the wings. The female is ashy-brown with pale rufous patch on wings instead of grey.

65

The White-collared Blackbird (*Turdus albocinctus*) is met with between about 9,000 and 12,000 feet in Himalayan oak, fir and birch forests. It is black with a broad white collar; the female is brown with a dull ashy collar instead of white.

The Grey-headed Thrush (*Turdus rubrocanus*) occurring from Kashmir to Bhutan is chestnut coloured with head, neck, upper breast and centre of abdomen creamy-grey.

DISTRIBUTION: Mt. Abu; hills of peninsular India roughly south of the Vindhya Mountains in Central India, and Ceylon. Five races are recognized on minor differences in size and colouration.

HABITS: This Blackbird is a resident of well-wooded hills, but it wanders freely down into the plains in winter. It frequents deep *sholas* as well as groves of trees near villages, and gardens and compounds in hill-stations. It is exceedingly common at Mahableshwar and Panchgani; also at Ootacamund and other Nilgiri and Palni resorts, and elsewhere, especially between 3,000 and 6,000 feet elevation. Single birds, pairs or small parties, are usually met with either on the ground or in trees. But it is mainly terrestrial in its feeding habits and more commonly seen hopping about, turning over and flicking aside dry leaves in search of insects and ripe wind-fallen fruits and berries. During the hot weather the forests resound with their chorus of full-throated song from every direction as each bird tries to outdo its neighbour. The rivalry does not end with music alone, for the males become extremely quarrelsome at this season. The song is of the typical blackbird pattern, loud and rich, and with a fine range of notes. It is heard mostly in the early mornings and evenings, often until well after sunset. This thrush is also an accomplished mimic and its own melody is invariably interlarded with the calls of a large variety of other birds, all perfectly reproduced. In the cold weather the birds are shy and mostly silent. The only note then heard is a sharp, high-pitched *kree-ee* uttered from time to time, and varied occasionally by a throaty, quick-repeated *chuk-chuk-chuk*. The flight is swift and direct without pauses or gliding.

Its diet consists of insects, grubs, fruits and berries. But it is also very fond of flower nectar and an unfailing habitué of Silk Cotton and Coral trees in bloom.

NESTING: The season ranges between May and August. The nest—typical of this group of thrushes—is a deep cup of moss, rootlets and grass, into which a good deal of wet mud is incorporated, and lined with soft ferns and root hairs. It is placed in a bush or small tree, rarely over 10 feet from the ground. The normal clutch is of three to five eggs—pale greenish-white, blotched with ruddy-brown, rather densely at the broad end.

66

THE GROUND-THRUSH

Geokichla citrina Latham

PLATE 31

SIZE : About that of the Myna.

FIELD CHARACTERS : A rather short-tailed orange-chestnut thrush with bluish-grey wings and tail. The female is a paler chestnut with the bluish-grey replaced by brownish-olive. A white patch on the wing-quills conspicuous in flight. Usually singly on ground in overgrown nullahs or undergrowth in forest.

DISTRIBUTION : Divided into several races with a vast general distribution. The two which mainly concern us are the orange-headed race *citrina* described above, and the White-throated *cyanotus* (illustrated). The former breeds in summer in the Himalayas up to 5,000 feet from Murree through Simla, Garhwal, etc., to Assam; Lower Bengal, Burma, and beyond eastwards. In winter it descends into the foothills and plains, and spreads sparsely over the greater part of N. India and Ceylon. The White-throated Ground-Thrush is a resident of practically all peninsular India south of a line roughly from W. Khandesh through Pachmarhi to Surguja State up to 4,000 feet elevation. It moves about a great deal with seasons, especially monsoon, but as yet its movements are not properly understood.

HABITS : The Ground-Thrush is an inhabitant of well-wooded broken country among the foothills and up to moderate elevations, and is found in both deciduous as well as evergreen types of jungle. It is fond of overgrown nullahs and ravines. In the southern hills cardamon *sholas* and coffee plantations constitute its favourite haunts. It hops about on the ground under the canopy of the bushes, rummaging amongst the mulch, turning over and flicking aside the dry leaves for insects lurking underneath, or digging into the moist earth for them. When disturbed it flies silently up into a low branch, where it sits motionless, descending again to resume its quest immediately its suspicion is allayed. Its food consists largely of insects and grubs, but ripe windfallen fruits and berries are also eaten. During the winter months it is silent except for the sharp typical thrush-like *kree-ee* which is occasionally uttered. As the hot weather advances and its breeding season draws nigh, the male pours forth a clear rollicking song of several rich whistling notes into which are rolled imitations of the calls and songs of numerous other birds such as the Spotted Babbler, Tailor-bird and Magpie-Robin. The song is heard mostly in the early mornings and evenings, the singing bird taking up its position on some bare branch up in a tree. While singing, the tail is held low or depressed and the wings partly drooping at the sides.

This ground-thrush is much prized as a cage bird and soon becomes reconciled to captivity.

NESTING: The principal months for the northern race are May and June, for the southern June and July, with a month or so on either side of these. The nest is a shallow cup with a neat egg cavity, made of moss mixed with roots, leaves, grass stems, etc., lined with finer grasses and roots. Sometimes a little mud is employed as by other thrushes, sometimes not. In the southern race there is usually no moss used, and the structure always seems to have a clay foundation. The nest is placed in some well-foliaged bush or small tree in forest, generally between 4 and 15 feet from the ground. In South India coffee bushes are largely patronized. The eggs—three to five, usually four—are pale bluish or creamy white, blotched and freckled with pale reddish all over, sometimes more thickly at the broad end. Both sexes share in building the nest, incubation and feeding the young.

THE MOUNTAIN-THRUSH

Oreocincla dauma Latham

PLATE 32

SIZE: About that of the Myna.

FIELD CHARACTERS: An ochraceous-brown, rather short-tailed thrush with little black crescent-shaped marks on the back. Underparts whitish, barred with crescentic black spots. In flight a pale coloured wing-bar conspicuous. Sexes alike. Singly, on ground in forested hillsides, and in *sholas*.

The Plain-backed Mountain-Thrush (*O. mollissima*) is somewhat similar but slightly longer-tailed and with a plain, unmarked olive-brown back and upper plumage generally. The underparts are marked as in *dauma*. It is found in the Himalayas, west to east, at high elevations.

DISTRIBUTION: The race *dauma* occupies the Himalayas from Hazara, in the west, to Assam in the east. In summer above about 8,000 feet; in winter down into the foothills. Also mountains of Central and NE. Burma. The race *nilgiriensis*, with much darker upper parts, is confined to the hill ranges of S. India from the Nilgiris to Central Travancore, above 2,000 feet elevation. A third race *imbricata*, darker above and with

VIEW PLATE THIS WAY

PLATE 31
1 THE SOUTHERN BLACKBIRD (*see* page 65)
2 THE WHITE-THROATED GROUND-THRUSH (*see* page 67)
About 1/3 Nat. Size

PLATE 32
1 THE MOUNTAIN-THRUSH (*see* page 68)
2 THE HIMALAYAN WHISTLING-THRUSH (*see* page 71)
About 1/3 Nat. Size

PLATE 33

1 THE KASHMIR SOOTY FLYCATCHER (*see* page 74)

2 THE RED-BREASTED FLYCATCHER
Male. Female (above) (*see* page 75)

3 THE RUFOUS-TAILED FLYCATCHER
(*see* page 80)

4 THE WHITE-BROWED BLUE FLYCATCHER
Male. Female (*see* page 76)

5 THE WHITE-THROATED FANTAIL-FLYCATCHER
(*see* page 88)

About 1/2 Nat. Size

PLATE 34

About 3/16 Nat. Size

lower parts ochraceous-buff instead of whitish, is endemic in the forested hills of Ceylon, above 3,000 feet.

HABITS: In the Himalayas the Mountain-Thrush inhabits densely forested hillsides in summer, being particularly fond of such as have broken ground with outcrops of moss-covered rocks and a sprinkling of *Rubus, Berberis*, and similar bushes. In the Nilgiris and other South Indian hills, the dense evergreen *sholas* or forested ravines form its typical habitat. The bird is usually seen singly and is shy and difficult to observe. But if one remains perfectly quiet one may watch it hopping along noiselessly searching for insects and grubs or windfallen berries among the humus, turning over the dry leaves or flicking them aside in the quest. The posterior part of its body is wagged violently up and down as the bird moves. Every now and again the tail is flicked open fanwise to its fullest extent, often accompanied by the sudden opening and closing of the wings as well. This is a habit common to many insectivorous birds of diverse families; it serves effectively in 'stampeding' lurking insects from the unevenness of the ground, which are then promptly seized. When disturbed, the bird flies silently up into a tree, sitting motionless and descending almost immediately to resume its hunt. Its flight, which is swift and direct, is curiously reminiscent of the Hawk-Cuckoo or Brain-fever Bird's, as also is its habit of gliding upwards into a branch for perching. The Mountain-Thrush is an exceedingly silent bird, but in the breeding season it is said to have a rich, varied and far-reaching song. Although this is what one would expect from its family connections, curiously enough, the song never seems to have been properly described.

NESTING: The season, both in the north and in the south, is between March and June. The nest is a substantially built cup—wide, but not deep—of moss, twigs, roots, fern stalks or pine needles, lined with fine roots. It is placed in the fork of a tree in dense deodar forest or *shola*, between 6 and 20 feet from the ground. The normal clutch in the northern race is three or four eggs; in the south, two eggs is normal, three rare. They exhibit many variations in colour and markings, but usually are pale yellowish or greenish-grey to dull clay-brown, finely freckled or feebly blotched with pale reddish.

THE BLUE-HEADED ROCK-THRUSH

Monticola cinclorhyncha Vigors

PLATE 30

SIZE: About that of the Bulbul.

FIELD CHARACTERS: *Male*: Head blue; rest of upper plumage blue and black; rump chestnut. Chin and throat blue; rest of lower plumage chestnut. A white patch on wings conspicuous, both at rest and in flight. *Female*: Brown above, whitish below squamated with dark brown, producing a scaly effect. Singly, or separated pairs, on lightly forested hillsides.

The Chestnut-bellied Rock-Thrush (*M. rufiventris*), of similar habits, is also found in the Himalayas from Kashmir to Assam, in summer between 4,000 and 8,000 feet. The male is brilliant blue above, chestnut-maroon below, with no white wing patch. The female is like that of *cinclorhyncha*, but has the entire back and rump barred instead of only the rump.

The Blue Rock-Thrush (*M. solitaria*) is a uniformly leaden blue bird commonly seen perched bolt upright on rocks about cliffs and on boulder-strewn hillsides. It breeds in the Himalayas in summer, up to about 13,000 feet, and spreads out practically all over India and Assam plains and hills in winter.

DISTRIBUTION: In summer breeding throughout the Himalayas west to east, between 4,000 and 9,000 feet elevation. Also Chin and Kachin Hills. In winter visiting practically all India—plains and hills—and West and Central Burma.

HABITS: During summer the Blue-headed Rock-Thrush affects openly forested Himalayan hillsides of Chir pine and oak. In its winter quarters it is partial to broken ground and stony hillsides covered with light deciduous forest and bamboo jungle, often in the neighbourhood of villages and cultivation. It is also found in moister localities where lightly wooded, but seldom ventures into the dense evergreen type. In the South Indian hills, cardamom and coffee plantations under the thinned-out natural *sholas* form favourite haunts. Its feeding habits are a compromise between those of the Ground-Thrush and the Bush-Chat. From its perch on a branch, where it sits bolt upright, it descends to the ground to pick up an insect, either returning with the quarry or disposing of it on the spot. At other times it rummages amongst the mulch for its food like a Ground-Thrush, and has the same habit of flying silently up into the overhanging vegetation when disturbed. Its food consists of insects, principally, but small animals such as frogs and lizards are also eaten with relish. During the breeding season the male has a loud, clear song, heard chiefly in the mornings and evenings. It consists of three notes repeated with varying emphasis, but rather monotonously. In winter the bird is silent.

NESTING: The season is between April and July, and often two successive broods are raised. The nest is an untidy shallow pad or cup of moss, grass, roots and similar material. It is placed in a hollow in a bank on a steep hillside, on a ledge of rock overhung by herbage, or amongst the roots of a tree clinging to a cliff. The eggs—three to five—are creamy white to deep buff, densely covered with tiny reddish freckles, sometimes forming a ring at the broad end. Both sexes share in building the nest, incubation and tending the young.

THE WHISTLING-THRUSH

Myiophoneus caeruleus Scopoli

PLATE 32

SIZE: Between the Myna and the Pigeon.

FIELD CHARACTERS: A blue-black bird with brighter blue wings and tail. In good light appears spotted all over with glistening blue. Strong black legs; stout yellow bill. Sexes alike. Singly, on rocks in Himalayan torrents.

A closely related species, the Malabar Whistling-Thrush or 'Whistling Schoolboy' (*M. horsfieldii*), with brilliant cobalt blue forehead and shoulder patches, and a black instead of yellow bill, is found perhaps at Mt. Abu and practically along the entire length of the Western Ghats. Also at Pachmarhi, in the Central Provinces. On the eastern side it has been recorded from Sambalpur (Orissa) and the Shevaroy Hills.

DISTRIBUTION: The Himalayas from extreme west—Afghanistan and Baluchistan—to extreme east Assam; Chin and Kachin Hills, and Arakan. In summer from the foothills, commonly up to 6,000 feet, and locally to 10,000 feet or more. In winter down to lower elevations.

Eastern Burma, Pegu, Tenasserim, Shan States, Yunnan, etc., are occupied by the Burmese race *eugenei* which lacks the white tips to the wingcoverts present in the Himalayan *temminckii*.

HABITS: The Whistling-Thrush is a common inhabitant of all Himalayan hill-streams and torrents. It is particularly fond of such as run

71

through deep rocky gorges with abrupt moss-covered banks overgrown with ferns and other vegetation, and with large boulders lying helter-skelter in wild confusion. Here its sharp high-pitched *kree-ee*, uttered as the bird flies from one part of the stream to another, and its remarkably fine loud song may commonly be heard above the tumult of the waters. The rich whistling song, so much oftener heard in its native haunts than the songster is seen, is a delightful performance with a considerable range of notes and variations, but it is far inferior to that of the Malabar species.

The diet of the Whistling-Thrush consists of aquatic insects, snails and crabs, but it will also eat windfallen ripe berries, and it is not uncommon to disturb a bird picking at the droppings of pack-mules and horses along secluded bridle paths. It hops from stone to stone in the midst of a rushing stream, snatches the quarry as it floats past and batters it on the stone. Or it digs into the wet mud banks for food with its strong bill. Every now and again the bird does a 'bend-stretch' on its legs and raises and lowers its tail, sometimes very slowly and deliberately. It is fully expanded on the downward movement when it almost touches the ground.

NESTING: The season is April to August, and frequently two successive broods are raised. The nest is a massive strongly built cup of moss and lichens with a copious admixture of mud, lined with moss- or fern-roots. Almost invariably it is placed on a ledge of rock near or over-hanging a mountain stream, or similar situation. But sometimes it is built on a ledge inside a natural cave or within a bungalow or outhouse—even an occupied one and well removed from water. Individual pairs appear to stake out large territories and there is never more than a single pair for considerable stretches of a stream. The eggs—three to five—are very similar to those of the Mountain-Thrush, pale clay in colour, sometimes pinkish or with a buff tinge, sparsely and faintly covered all over with pale reddish freckles, spots and blotches more numerously at the broad end. Both sexes share in building the nest, incubation and care of the young.

THE RUFOUS-BREASTED HEDGE-SPARROW

Prunella strophiata Blyth

PLATE 27
SIZE: About that of the Sparrow.
FIELD CHARACTERS: A grey-brown sparrow-like bird, streaked above

with black. The white chin and throat, the rufous-coloured breast, and the broad rufous supercilium bordered above with black forming conspicuous broad lateral bands on either side of the crown, are useful identification marks. Sexes alike. Singly, or small flocks, on ground on open scrubby high Himalayan hillsides.

Several other species of Hedge-Sparrows, or Accentors, occur in the Himalayas at more or less high altitudes. They are all birds of about the size and general effect of the Sparrow, soberly clad and patterned in grey and brown, with slender finely-pointed bills (not thick and conical like the Sparrow's), and square or slightly forked tails. In their habits they resemble fairly closely the species described.

DISTRIBUTION: The Himalayas from Afghanistan and Baluchistan, through Gilgit and Kashmir, eastwards to North Assam and Tibet. In summer between 9,000 and 12,000 feet (locally up to 16,000 feet); in winter between 6,000 and 4,000 feet, or somewhat lower. Two races are recognized: the East Himalayan *strophiata* differs from the West Himalayan *jerdoni* (described) in being rufous-brown above, and having a deep ferruginous breast.

HABITS: The Rufous-breasted Hedge-Sparrow frequents bleak open hillsides with moraines, etc., at high elevations, usually above the zone of forest growth. It is not uncommon in the low scrub of Juniper, *Lonicera*, *Berberis*, *Viburnum*, and other species that grow at these altitudes. It is also met with somewhat lower down in open localities outside thick silver fir and birch forests, and amongst the terraced hill cultivation. The birds go about singly or in small flocks, which join up into larger ones during winter. They are usually seen in stony country or in low scrub hopping along with belly close to the ground in a way that reminds one of the Black-bellied Finch-Lark. Although normally shy, and great skulkers, they may sometimes be seen feeding about the piled stone boundary walls of mountain villages and in the neighbourhood of the houses picking seeds out of animal droppings. When flushed, they settle abruptly again after a short flight at the base of some cover. The flight is strong and direct with rapid wing strokes. Their food consists of seeds, spiders, insects and their larvæ.

The note normally uttered has been described as a rather high-pitched *tr-r-r*, like the noise produced by striking two stones together. In the breeding season the male has a short, rather pretty song like a wren's, but less loud and not so penetrating. It is interspersed with occasional harsher notes.

NESTING: The season is from early June to mid-July. The nest is a cup of sticks, moss and lichens, lined with fine dry grass, a little hair, wool and feathers. It is usually placed in low bushes, or in the foliage of a lower branch of a silver fir, normally much under 10 feet from the ground. The eggs—three to five—are a beautiful blue of the shade that is so well known as 'Hedge-Sparrow blue'. Both sexes incubate.

THE SOOTY FLYCATCHER

Hemichelidon sibirica Gmelin

PLATE 33

SIZE: Smaller than the Sparrow.

FIELD CHARACTERS: A sooty brown little bird with a white ring round the eye and white abdomen. The tips of the closed wings reach almost to end of tail. Sexes alike. Seen singly, perched bolt upright in typical flycatcher fashion on tree tops in Himalayan forest, or hawking insects.

An allied species, the Ferruginous Flycatcher (*H. ferruginea*) is found in the Eastern Himalayas from Garhwal, and in the higher North Burmese Hills, 4,000–6,000 feet elevation in summer, and all Burma, Malay Peninsula, etc., in winter. It is very common about Darjeeling.

DISTRIBUTION: The Himalayas from extreme west to extreme east. In summer between 6,000 and 11,000 feet or higher; in winter down into the foothills and practically to plains level. The two races that concern us are the Nepal, or East Himalayan *fuliginosa*, and the Kashmir or West Himalayan *gulmergi*, differentiated on shades of colouration.

HABITS: This flycatcher frequents silver fir, birch and spruce forest in summer, and is an exceedingly common species in Kashmir from about 8,000 feet elevation up to the limit of tree growth at 11,000 feet or so. It is partial to open glades in the midst of forest, where it may be seen hawking insects from the tip of a tall fir tree, or nearer the ground from some brushwood, the dead branches of an uprooted tree, or a boulder. While not a gregarious species, it is usual to find four or five individuals in the same glade making nimble aerial sallies in pursuit of prey. Like all flycatchers, these birds are possessed of remarkably keen eyesight. I have frequently observed one making looping sorties after tiny winged insects from its perch on a tree top fully twenty-five yards away, snapping up the quarry in mid-air and returning to its base in a graceful gliding sweep. Its diet is wholly insectivorous.

It is a very silent bird normally, but in the breeding season the male utters a feeble little twittering song.

74

NESTING: The season is chiefly from April to August. The nest is a large, compact cup of moss and lichen, bound with spiders' webs and lined with hair. It is placed on a horizontal branch of some large spruce, or similar tree, in open forest, generally 30 to 40 feet from the ground. Several pairs often nest within a circumscribed area and the territorial instinct does not appear to be stongly developed in this species. The normal clutch is of three or four eggs, pale olive-grey or olive-stone in colour, sparsely freckled all over with very pale reddish. The freckling is denser at the broad end, where it sometimes forms a well-defined ring or cap.

THE RED-BREASTED FLYCATCHER

Muscicapa (*Siphia*) *parva* Bechstein

PLATE 33

SIZE: Smaller than the Sparrow.

FIELD CHARACTERS: A plain, brown flycatcher with orange-chestnut throat and breast, whitish underparts and black-and-white tail. The tail is jerked up or carried Robin-wise, with wings drooping at the sides. It is a passable miniature of the English Robin, with a white patch added on in the tail. The female and young male lack the red breast. Seen singly, in trees, in open forest.

A closely related species, the Indian Red-breasted Flycatcher (*Siphia hyperythra*), is found in the Western Himalayas between 6,000 and 8,000 feet in summer, when it is common, and also breeds in Kashmir. It is distinguished from the above by having a broad black line bordering the chestnut (almost brick-red) throat and breast on either side. In winter it migrates south into the hills of Ceylon above 2,500 feet elevation, and curiously enough, is not found in peninsular India at all.

Another allied Himalayan species, the Orange-gorgeted Flycatcher (*Siphia strophiata*), common about Darjeeling, has more white in the basal half of its tail. Its throat and breast are sooty, and there is just an orange spot below the throat.

Two migrant races of the Red-breasted Flycatcher are common during the winter months—October to May—throughout peninsular India, both hills and plains: the European *S. p. parva* and the East Asiatic *S. p. albicilla*. They differ from each other in minor details of colouration. The following description of habits chiefly applies to them.

HABITS : The Red-breasted Flycatcher frequents lightly-wooded country and is partial to orchards and groves of leafy trees planted about villages and cultivation. It is usually met with singly perched on a low branch, jerking up its tail every now and again. From here it makes short agile sallies into the air after winged insects, sometimes hovering momentarily in front of a flower or sprig in its search. Occasionally, it will hop down to the ground, give a couple of jerks to its cocked-up tail accompanied by a distinctive low double *click-click*, pick up an insect, and flit back to its perch. It also hunts insects that collect at the flowers of Mango, Silk Cotton and other trees. During its sojourn in India no song is heard. It does not breed within our limits.

NESTING : On its breeding grounds in Kashmir, the Indian Red-breasted Flycatcher affects mixed forests of walnut, hazel, cherry and willow, especially where there is a dense undergrowth of *Perrottia*. The most important months for eggs are May and June. Its nest is a rough cup of moss, skeleton leaves, strips of bark etc., lined with softer material such as hair and feathers. It is placed in holes in the trunks and branches of trees, usually between 5 and 20 feet from the ground. The normal clutch is of four or five eggs, pale grey-green in colour with tiny specks of pale pinkish-brown, sparse over the entire surface but dense and forming a ring or cap at the broad end.

THE WHITE-BROWED BLUE FLYCATCHER

Muscicapula superciliaris Jerdon

PLATE 33

SIZE : Smaller than the Sparrow.

FIELD CHARACTERS : A dainty little flycatcher blue above, white below, with a prominent broad white supercilium. There is a broken blue-black band across the breast and a white patch at base of the tail feathers. The female is greyish-brown above, whitish below with a glistening white throat and upper breast. Singly, or separated pairs, in mixed Himalayan forest.

The Slaty-blue Flycatcher (*M. tricolor*) with an almost overlapping Himalayan distribution, is slaty-blue above, greyish-white below tinged with fulvous on flanks and breast, and without the interrupted blue-black collar. It also has a white patch at the base of the tail feathers, but no

PLATE 35
THE RUFOUS-BELLIED NILTAVA (*see* page 84)
Female (above).   Male
About 3/8 Nat. Size

PLATE 36
THE BLACK-HEADED SHRIKE (*see* page 89)
About 1/2 Nat. Size

PLATE 37
THE ORANGE MINIVET (*see* page 91)
Female (above).   Male
About 1/2 Nat. Size

PLATE 38
1 THE LARGE CROWNED WILLOW-WARBLER (*see* page 96)
2 TICKELL'S WILLOW-WARBLER 3 THE GREY-HEADED FLYCATCHER-WARBLER
(*see* page 95) (*see* page 97)
4 THE BROWN HILL-WARBLER 5 THE RED-HEADED FANTAIL-WARBLER
(*see* page 99) (*see* page 93)
About 1/3 Nat. Size

white supercilium. It is common in Kashmir between 6,000 and 9,000 feet.

DISTRIBUTION: The Himalayas from the Afghan frontier on the west, to NE. Assam. Also Manipur, Lushai, Chin and Kachin Hills. In summer between 5,000 and 10,000 feet in W. Himalayas; 4,000 to 5,000 feet in E. Himalayas. It is extremely numerous about Simla, Mussooree, Murree, etc. In winter at lower elevations and down into North and Peninsular India, sparingly as far south as Mysore. A West Himalayan race (*superciliaris*) and an East Himalayan (*astigma*) are recognized. The latter differs from the former in the male having no, or almost no, white supercilium.

HABITS: The White-browed Blue Flycatcher affects mixed forests of conifers and broad-leaved species such as blue pine, silver fir, hill-oak and rhododendron. It captures winged insects by making short aerial sallies after them in the typical flycatcher manner, either from a perch high up in a tree or amongst low undergrowth. The subdued song, or effort at song, indulged in by the male in summer is a sweet but feeble *chiri-ri-ri*. The bird constantly jerks its tail, fluffing out the head feathers now and then and uttering *chr-r-r* or *tr-r-r*. It is often met with amongst the roving bands of insectivorous species in the Himalayan forests. The birds are not shy and will freely take possession of nesting boxes in hill-station compounds, even where fixed to the walls of occupied outhouses, going about their domestic tasks unmindful of the comings and goings of the inmates.

NESTING: The season is from April to July, and frequently two succes-sive broods are raised. The nest is a well-made little cup of dry moss lined with fibre and roots or hair. It is placed in a rift or small hole in a tree trunk in well-forested country, between 5 and 25 feet from the ground. The eggs—three or four—are usually pale olive-greenish to dull stone-buff with minute freckles of reddish-brown, sparse over the surface and coalescing to form a cap at the broad end. But some eggs are without markings, and variations are considerable. Both sexes share in building the nest and feeding the young; presumably also in incubation.

THE WHITE-BELLIED BLUE FLYCATCHER

Muscicapula pallipes Jerdon

PLATE 34

SIZE: About that of the Sparrow.

FIELD CHARACTERS: Male dark indigo-blue with white abdomen; female brown with rusty-red throat and breast, and white abdomen. She looks rather like an enlarged Red-breasted Flycatcher, or like the English Robin. Singly, or separated pairs, in moist Western Ghats forest.

The Blue-throated Flycatcher (*Muscicapula rubeculoides*) is found in summer throughout the Himalayas from Kashmir to Assam, chiefly between 2,500 and 6,000 feet, and also in the Burmese hills. In winter it spreads over many parts of the peninsula, including the range of the White-bellied species. The male is dark blue above, with a blue throat, rusty-red breast and white underparts. The female is, in general, rather similar to that of *pallipes*.

Tickell's Red-breasted Blue Flycatcher (*M. tickelliae*) is found practically throughout the hills and plains of Peninsular India (excepting Sind), Assam, Burma and Ceylon, but is rare in the sub-Himalayan tracts. It is a species with which *rubeculoides* can easily be confused. The male may be differentiated by its pale rusty, not blue, throat; the female is like the male, only duller and paler.

DISTRIBUTION: The typical race *pallipes* is resident in the Western Ghats from Belgaum to South Travancore, including the Nilgiri and Palni Hills, between about 1,000 and 4,000 feet elevation. The brighter coloured race *hainana* occurs in peninsular Burma and beyond our limits, in Siam, Cochin-China, Hainan, etc.

HABITS: The White-bellied Blue Flycatcher inhabits the heavy rainfall tracts of evergreen and moist deciduous forest-clad hills in south-western India, and here it is fairly common. It is a shy and unobtrusive little bird, mostly seen singly in the dense undergrowth of tall lanky seedlings and *Strobilanthes* plants in the *sholas*. It is partial to cardamom plantations and loves the neighbourhood of the evergreen nullahs that run through them. It hawks insects in the air in the typical flycatcher manner and is frequently to be met amongst the mixed hunting parties of insectivorous birds that move about in the forest. When perched on a branch bolt upright, the bird has a peculiar habit of screwing open its tail from side to side in a way that reminds one of the Thick-billed Flowerpecker (*Piprisoma*). It is an exceedingly quiet species on the whole, but the male has a sweet, rich and varied song which it sings in the early mornings and late evenings, sometimes till well after dusk.

NESTING: The season is between February and September, but principally during the SW. monsoon months. The nest is a rough, untidy structure of moss on the outside with a neat cup-shaped lining of lichen, fine grass and roots. It is placed inside a large hollow in a dead tree stump or a hole in a bank fairly low down in damp forest. The normal clutch consists of four eggs. They resemble small eggs of the Dhyal or Shama, varying in colour from dull sea-green to warm yellowish stone, richly and profusely blotched all over with dark brown or chocolate brown. The blotches are more numerous at the broad end, where they sometimes form zones or caps. There is very little on record concerning the breeding biology of this species.

THE VERDITER FLYCATCHER

Eumyias thalassina Swainson

PLATE 34
SIZE: About that of the Sparrow.
FIELD CHARACTERS: A conspicuous bright blue-green flycatcher (of the shade of the 'green rust' of copper), with a black patch in front of the eyes. The female is duller. Singly, on openly forested hillsides, in well-wooded gardens and on electric wires, etc., at Himalayan hill-stations.

The Nilgiri Verditer Flycatcher (*E. albicaudata*) is very similar but rather more indigo-blue, and with a white patch at base of tail. It is resident and common in evergreen *sholas* above 2,000 feet elevation and up to the highest in the Nilgiris, Palnis and other hills of SW. India. It also frequents gardens, roadside trees and the neighbourhood of hill-station bungalows. Its habits closely resemble those of the Himalayan species described below. Males have a pleasant trilly song of five to ten seconds duration, uttered from some exposed twig on the top of a tree. It is somewhat feebler than, but similar in quality to the song of the Pied Bush-Chat. It breeds from March to June, sometimes building its nest on beams, etc., in verandahs of occupied bungalows.

DISTRIBUTION: The Himalayas from west to east between 4,000 and 10,000 feet in summer. Also hills of Assam, Burma, Shan States and beyond. The only race found within our limits (excepting extreme South

Burma) is the typical *thalassina*. In winter its spreads out more or less over the entire peninsula except Sind, and is then also found in the range of the Nilgiri species, often side by side with it. In the hills of Ceylon, above 2,000 feet, it is represented by an allied species—the Dusky Blue Flycatcher (*E. ceylonensis*). This is bluish ashy-grey with a bright blue supercilium, white undertail coverts, and no white at base of tail feathers.

HABITS: The Verditer is without doubt the commonest and most familiar flycatcher of at least the West Himalayan hill-stations. It is seen everywhere, especially in the open forest of oak that clothes the hillsides, perched bolt upright on some exposed twig near the top of a tree, or on an overhead electric wire, beside a shady path. Every now and again the bird twitches its tail up and down and utters the typical flycatcher *click, click*. From here it launches agile sallies after winged insects. It is also commonly met with as a member of the mixed hunting parties of insectivorous birds. It is a bold and confiding little creature and freely enters gardens and orchards in the proximity of bungalows. From some exposed perch the male constantly sings his pleasant jingling song, very similar to that of the White-eye (*Zosterops*), only a trifle louder.

NESTING: The season is principally from mid-April to mid-June. The nest is a thick-sided cup of green moss mixed with roots and fibres and lined with fine moss-roots. It is placed in pockets in earth banks, or in hollows in rotten tree stumps, fairly low down. The side of a ravine or a steep hillside-cutting for a path are favourite sites. The nest is usually concealed from view by overhanging herbage, but frequently betrayed by the sitting bird darting out in front of the passer-by. I have seen a nest placed twelve inches inside a disused horizontal drain pipe through the wall of an occupied bungalow! The eggs—four or five, sometimes only three—are mostly pale creamy-pink, sparsely freckled over the surface with reddish, more densely and forming a ring round the bigger end. Both sexes share in building the nest, incubating and feeding the young. Incubation takes twelve to thirteen days.

THE RUFOUS-TAILED FLYCATCHER

Alseonax ruficaudus Swainson

PLATE 33

SIZE: Smaller than the Sparrow.

FIELD CHARACTERS: A small flycatcher, dull olive-brown above, pale ashy-brown or whitish below. The chestnut tail is its most distinctive features. Sexes alike. Solitary, flitting among foliage of tall trees in Himalayan forests.

Layard's Flycatcher (*Alseonax muttui*) is a bird of more or less similar appearance, resident above 4,000 feet elevation in the Eastern Himalayas. In winter it migrates to the hills of South India and Ceylon, and has also been met with in the Deccan. It is ruddy-brown above, dirty whitish below. A conspicuous white ring round the eyes, and a glistening white chin and throat bordered by a faint dusky 'necklace' are its chief recognition marks. It affects low thickets rather than the leafy crowns of trees.

Both these species must be differentiated from the Brown Flycatcher (*A. latirostris*), which has a wide breeding distribution in the Himalayas as well as in the W. Ghats and other peninsular hills, and extends through Eastern Asia to Japan. It lacks the white throat and 'necklace' of *muttui*, the chestnut tail of *ruficaudus*, and has the throat, breast and flanks streaked and mottled with ashy-brown.

DISTRIBUTION: NW. Himalayas from Baluchistan, Afghanistan, Gilgit and Kashmir to the Simla Hills and Garhwal. In summer between 7,000 and 11,000 feet elevation; in winter over a large portion of NW., Western and Peninsular India south to Travancore.

HABITS: In the Himalayas, the Rufous-tailed Flycatcher affects spruce and deodar as well as open oak and rhododendron forest. In its winter quarters in South India it is met with in the heavy rainfall areas among lofty evergreen trees mostly standing on the edge of paths and clearings. It is usually seen singly keeping to the canopy foliage, and in this regard it differs rather markedly from most other flycatchers who seem to prefer low thickets. Its method of hunting, too, is somewhat different. It does not usually perch in exposed situations or sally after winged insects in the open, but flits and flutters within the canopy and boughs for them, restlessly wandering about the crowns of tall trees, from one to another, in its search. In the breeding season the male has rather a loud, short 'song' of three or four notes.

NESTING: The season is principally from the middle of May to the end of June. The nest is a neat cup made of soft moss and lichens, lined with hair and sometimes a few feathers. It is placed in a fork in the branch of a spruce, or at its junction with the main stem, 10 to 15 feet from the ground. Another favourite site is on the stumps of pollarded trees where the branches sprout. The eggs—three or four—are very like those of the Blue-throated Flycatcher (*M. rubeculoides*). They are pale olive or yellowish stone in colour, very closely and finely stippled over the entire surface with reddish olive-brown.

THE BLACK-AND-ORANGE FLYCATCHER

Ochromela nigrorufa Jerdon

PLATE 34
SIZE: Slightly smaller than the Sparrow.
FIELD CHARACTERS: A strikingly coloured flycatcher, well-named and mistakable for no other. In the female the orange is paler, and the black parts replaced by greenish-brown and dark brown. Singly, or separated pairs, in evergreen undergrowth in South Indian hills.
DISTRIBUTION: Restricted to the hill ranges of South India from Cape Comorin to the Wynaad at about 2,500 feet elevation and upwards. It is very common in the Nilgiri, Palni and Travancore hills, but rather local and patchy.
HABITS: This handsome flycatcher is essentially a bird of the dense evergreen forest-clad hills and *sholas* of South India, being commonest at elevations between about 3,000 and 5,000 feet. Here it flits about the dense undergrowth of upright lanky seedlings and *Strobilanthes* plants capturing winged insects by little aerial sorties. Cardamom *sholas* and dank ravines with brakes of screw-pine and rattan cane also form favourite haunts. Sometimes it descends to the ground momentarily to pick up an insect in the manner of the Bush-Chat, presently flitting back to its perch a foot or two up among the stems. It is usually met with singly, but often has its mate somewhere near at hand. It has no song worth the name, but the male constantly utters a somewhat metallic high-pitched *chiki-riki-chiki* or *chee-r-ri-ri-ri* every few seconds. It is not shy and does not resent observation even at close quarters, provided one remains quiet.
NESTING: The normal season is from March to May, but it sometimes continues until July. The nest is a loose, untidy ball of coarse grass or leaves of the eeta bamboo (*Ochlandra travancorica*), sometimes lined with fine grasses, sometimes unlined. It is placed low down in a clump of weeds, ferns, bramble or bracken from a few inches to about 4 feet off the ground—but usually between 2 and 3 feet. It is frequently built on the straight, thin evergreen seedlings that are so common in the *sholas*. The eggs—almost invariably two—are rather like those of the Verditer Flycatcher, pale greyish-white or buffy-white, freckled with pale pinkish-red, sometimes forming a cap at the broad end.

THE GREY-HEADED FLYCATCHER

Culicicapa ceylonensis Swainson

PLATE 34

SIZE: Smaller than the Sparrow.

FIELD CHARACTERS: A tiny greenish-yellow flycatcher with ashy-grey head and neck. Sexes alike. Singly, among leafy trees in well-wooded country.

DISTRIBUTION: Throughout the Himalayas from west to east. All India, excluding Sind and the dry portions of the NW. Ceylon; Assam and Burma. It has a wide range further to the east in Siam, Cochin-China, Java, Borneo, etc., and is divided into several geographical races. We are concerned only with two: *pallidior* breeds in the Himalayas between 3,000 and 8,000 feet elevation, and spreads out in winter over a large part of northern and peninsular India. The slightly richer coloured *ceylonensis* breeds in the hills of Ceylon as well as in the Nilgiris and other South Indian hills. This race also moves down into the plains after breeding, so that in winter there is a certain amount of overlapping and confusion in the peninsula.

HABITS: The Grey-headed Flycatcher haunts oak and deodar forest in the Himalayas, and particularly the neighbourhood of well-wooded ravines. In the South Indian hills it affects evergreen *sholas*, up to the highest, as well as forest of the type intermediate between the evergreen and the deciduous, and is partial to mixed bamboo jungle in foothills and broken country. It is an active, restless little bird for ever making lively swoops after winged insects from a base on some exposed twig, turning and twisting in the air with great dexterity and returning to its perch. A couple may invariably be seen amongst the mixed hunting parties of insectivorous birds that rove the forest. The flycatchers act as outriders to these foraging bands, snapping up tiny flies as they attempt to escape from the concerted hunt on the tree trunks and in the foliage. A pretty little interrogative whistling song of five notes, *chik! . . . whichee whichee!* is constantly uttered between the graceful sorties, and is surprisingly loud for the size of the bird. In the breeding season the male begins singing with morning twilight in the vicinity of its nest. The usual song is followed within three seconds by another—the answer to it, as it were—*whi-chi-chi*. Question and answer are repeated at quick and regular intervals, often for twenty minutes at a stretch in the early mornings. The bird also has a sharp, rather prolonged twittering note which always advertises its presence in a wood.

NESTING: The season over its range as a whole is April to June. The nest is a tiny half cup of moss, sometimes bedecked on the outside with lichens. It is attached like a bracket against a moss-covered tree trunk, usually from 5 to 20 feet up. Cobweb is used in felting the materials and securing it to the site. Its nest merges into its surroundings completely and is admirably concealed. The eggs—three or four—are greyish or creamy-white, blotched sparsely with pale yellowish-grey. The markings are dense at the broad end where they form a ring.

THE RUFOUS-BELLIED NILTAVA

Niltava sundara Hodgson

PLATE 35

SIZE: Slightly larger than the Sparrow.

FIELD CHARACTERS: A brilliant plumaged flycatcher, dark blue above, bright chestnut below, with glistening black forehead, sides of head and throat. Female fulvous olive-brown with chestnut tail, and a patch of lustrous blue on either side of neck as in male. Singly, in undergrowth in Himalayan forests.

The Small Niltava (*N. macgrigoriae*), found throughout the Himalayas from Mussooree to Assam, and also in Burma, is smaller than the Sparrow. The male is bright purplish-blue above, ashy below, with purple sides of head, throat and breast. The female is rather like that of *sundara* but smaller, and also has a patch of brilliant blue on either side of the neck.

DISTRIBUTION: The Himalayas from Murree to extreme East Assam; Manipur and Lushai hills; Chin and Kachin Hills and down through hills of Central Burma to Tenasserim. Also beyond, eastward. In summer between 5,000 and 8,000 feet elevation in W. Himalayas; 3,000 to 5,000 feet or higher in E. Himalayas. In winter at lower elevations and down into the foothills. Two races are recognized: the East Himalayan *sundara* and the West Himalayan *fastuosa*, differing from each other in minor details of colouration.

HABITS: This magnificent flycatcher normally frequents moist broad-leaved Himalayan forests but is sometimes also found in pine woods provided there are rocky ravines with water running through them over-grown with herbage and plenty of vegetation on their banks. It hunts flies amongst the low undergrowth, making short sallies and capturing

PLATE 39
1 THE GOLDEN ORIOLE. Male (abcve). Female (*see* page 101)
2 THE FAIRY BLUEBIRD. Female (above). Male (*see* page 100)
About 1/4 Nat. Size

PLATE 40

About 1/4 Nat. Size

PLATE 41
1 THE COMMON SWALLOW (*see* page 115)
2 THE NILGIRI HOUSE-SWALLOW (*see* page 116)
About 1/2 Nat. Size

PLATE 42
1 THE WHITE WAGTAIL (*see* page 118)   2 THE EASTERN GREY WAGTAIL (*see* page 119)
3 THE INDIAN BLUE-HEADED WAGTAIL   4 THE INDIAN YELLOW-HEADED WAGTAIL
(*see* page 119)   (*see* page 119)
All in summer (breeding) plumage
About 1/3 Nat. Size

them on the wing in the typical flycatcher manner, but often also descends to the ground to pick up one in the style of the Bush-Chat. Its habits are somewhat reminiscent of those of the Black-and-Orange Fly-catcher of the Nilgiris and South Indian hills. In secluded glens and jungle it may frequently be seen amongst the mixed roving hunting parties of small insectivorous birds like tits, tree-warblers and the smaller babblers, but it keeps to the brushwood and seldom mounts into the higher trees. It is said to have a beautiful song like other Niltavas, but no details appear to have been recorded. In addition to insects it is said to eat a certain amount of berries, but this is also unconfirmed.

NESTING : The principal months for eggs are May, June and July. The nest is a neat and compact structure of fresh green moss lined with fine moss-roots. It is placed in a hollow among the roots of a tree, a hole in a moss-covered bank or some such situation, and is difficult to find. A normal clutch consists of four eggs, creamy-white or pinkish-white to warm buff. Most eggs are distinctly freckled with light reddish or brownish, sometimes so minutely and evenly that the surface looks unicoloured. Both sexes share in building the nest and brooding. Incuba-tion takes twelve to thirteen days.

THE PARADISE FLYCATCHER

Tchitrea paradisi Linnaeus

PLATE 34

SIZE : That of the Bulbul, excluding the tail ribbons which are between 10 and 15 inches long.

FIELD CHARACTERS: General effect of a Bulbul. Adult male, silvery white with two long ribbon-like feathers or streamers in tail, and crested metallic-black head. Female and young male, chestnut above, greyish-white below, with black head and crest. The young male has chestnut streamers in tail; the female is without. Singly, or pairs, in wooded country.

DISTRIBUTION : Baluchistan, Afghanistan and the Himalayas from Kashmir right across to and including Assam. In summer between 3,000 and 8,000 feet elevation; in winter down into the foothills and plains. Also Burma, Ceylon, and more or less throughout India in the plains as well as all peninsular hills. Over this area three races are recognized. In the Ceylon race, *ceylonensis*, the adult male apparently always remains chestnut instead of turning white. In the other two, adult white birds are practically impossible to differentiate, but chestnut males and females can be told by minor differences in colouration. It is largely migratory in winter, and the movements of the races are as yet imperfectly understood. Large numbers for example arrive from the south to breed in the Himalayan foothills about Dehra Dun in early April and by the beginning of September most birds have left again.

HABITS: This exquisite creature—variously known as Rocket-Bird, Widow-Bird or Ribbon-Bird—is a frequenter of light forest and bamboo jungle both hill and plain, and loves shady groves and gardens, often in the neighbourhood of human habitations. Its ethereal presence lends an indescribable charm to the magnificent chenars and poplars of Srinagar and the various Kashmir valleys, a charm that can be fully appreciated only by those who have watched it in that superb setting. The lithe, fairy-like movements of the male, as with streamers trailing in the breeze he makes his agile aerial sallies and contortions in pursuit of winged insects, or flits in graceful undulating flight from one part of a grove to another—surf-riding on air as it were—present an enchanting sight. Single birds or pairs are usually met, either by themselves or among the roving bands of mixed insectivorous species. The notes commonly heard are a harsh and grating *chē* or *chē-chwē*, but during the breeding season these are supplemented by a number of pleasant musical ones, seemingly uttered by both sexes. It has no song proper. Its diet consists of moths and flies, and a large variety of other insects. These are captured on the wing in the typical flycatcher manner.

NESTING: The season ranges between February and July. The nest is a compactly woven cup of fine grasses and fibres, plastered on the outside with cobwebs and spiders' egg cases. It is built in the crotch or elbow of a twig, usually 6 to 12 feet from the ground. Mulberry groves are largely selected in Kashmir. Mango orchards are general favourites. The eggs—three to five—are pale creamy-pink, speckled and blotched with reddish brown.

Both sexes take part in building the nest, incubation and care of the young, though the hen does the lion's share of the work. Incubation takes fifteen to sixteen days.

THE BLACK-NAPED BLUE FLYCATCHER

Hypothymis azurea Boddaert

PLATE 34

SIZE: Slightly larger than the Sparrow.

FIELD CHARACTERS: A longish and partially fan-tailed blue flycatcher with whitish abdomen. Its identity marks are a black patch on the nape and a black crescentic bar across the foreneck. The female is browner generally and lacks these marks. Solitary, or separated pairs, in trees in forest (non-Himalayan), restlessly flycatching.

DISTRIBUTION: Wide. From India, through the adjoining eastern countries, to the Philippine Islands. Several races are recognized, of which two chiefly concern us: the endemic Ceylonese *ceylonensis*, with nape-patch and throat-crescent indistinct, and the Indian *styani*. This latter occupies Burma, Assam and all India south of the Himalayas and east of a line roughly from Dhulia (Khandesh) to Lucknow (U.P.). It is confined largely to the peninsular hill-ranges up to about 4,000 feet, but is also found in the plateau country of the Deccan and South India.

HABITS: This flycatcher is an inhabitant of well-wooded country, preferably hilly tracts and where cut up by ravines, etc., with vegetation ranging from more or less pure deciduous to the humid evergreen type. It loves shady trees on the banks of streams and mixed bamboo jungle as well as opener teak plantations. Solitary birds, separated pairs, or sometimes family parties of four or five, are met with commonly amongst the mixed hunting parties that move about in the forest. It is an active, restless little bird constantly flitting amongst the foliage of large trees, hovering in front of a sprig or launching the usual flycatcher sallies after winged insects. Sometimes it will swoop down almost to the ground to capture a fly, and it also frequently descends to pick up a crawling insect. With wings drooping at the sides and tail partly fanned out and cocked, the bird pirouettes about, pivoting on its perch from side to side to the accompaniment of a lively, high-pitched though rather harsh *sweech-wich*. Sometimes it will swoop down and cling sideways to the trunk of a tree to take an insect from a crevice in the bark. It does not appear to have any song.

NESTING: The season ranges from March to August, but most eggs are laid in June and July. The nest is a deep compact cup of the same type but more massive than that of the Fantail-Flycatcher, made of fine grass stems (or moss where locally available) well-woven together and coated on the outside with cobwebs, spiders' egg cases and lichens. It is placed in a slender fork of a small sapling or high bush, usually between 5 and 10 feet from the ground. The eggs—normally three, occasionally four—are perfect miniatures of those of the Paradise Flycatcher. Both sexes assist in building the nest and brooding the eggs. Incubation takes about twelve days.

THE WHITE-THROATED FANTAIL-FLYCATCHER

Rhipidura albicollis Vieillot

PLATES 33 AND 66

SIZE : About that of the Sparrow.

FIELD CHARACTERS : A restless dark sooty-brown flycatcher with a white band across the throat, a short white supercilium and white-tipped tail. The most characteristic feature of all fantail-flycatchers is their tail cocked up and spread fanwise with the wings drooping at either side. Sexes alike. Singly, or separated pairs, dancing among the branches, in brushwood and secondary jungle, shrubby gardens, etc.

The White-spotted Fantail (*R. pectoralis*) is common at Mt. Abu and in the Nilgiris and other hills (and plains) of peninsular India. It differs from *albicollis* chiefly in having the lower breast heavily white-spotted and the abdomen whitish.

The White-browed Fantail (*L. aureola*) is another allied species common practically throughout India, Burma and Ceylon—hills and plains alike —and up to about 4,000 feet in the Outer Himalayas. It is easily recognized by its broad white forehead, and its white breast and underparts.

For the warbler-like Yellow-bellied Fantail-Flycatcher (*Chelidorhynx hypoxanthum*) see under Grey-headed Flycatcher-Warbler, page 98.

DISTRIBUTION : The Himalayas from Murree in the west to Eastern Assam; Burma, Shan States, and eastward beyond our borders. Up to 7,000 feet elevation, but normally under 4,000 feet. It wanders somewhat in winter, but its movements have not been studied. The specimens said to have been taken in the Central Provinces and Chota Nagpur were presumably these wanderers.

HABITS : This flycatcher is chiefly a bird of low elevations in the Himalayas, and is particularly fond of the foothills. It affects brushwood and low secondary growth on the sides of the outscoured ravines that are such a feature of these tracts. But it is also found in rambling jungly gardens in towns, and in suitable country on the outskirts of villages— mango orchards or thin Sal jungle with woody under-shrubs. The birds are usually seen in pairs, flitting tirelessly under the canopy of the thickets, from a low branch to a stone, from a stone to a sagging creeper-stem, and so on, tail fanned out and waltzing and pirouetting ceaselessly. Now and again it makes a graceful looping-the-loop sally after a fly which is snapped up in mid-air with a little castanet-like click of the mandibles. The note usually uttered is a somewhat harsh *chuck* or *chuck-r*, like that of the other fantails. Besides this it has a feeble rather jerky whistling song, *chik . . . cheechik – cheechik*, much inferior to those of its White-browed or White-spotted cousins. This, as I have remarked before, is an 'identical twin' of the song of the Plumbeous Redstart.

NESTING : The season extends from March to July, but May and June appear to be the months when most eggs are laid. The nest is exactly like that of the White-spotted Fantail, a beautiful little cup, or wine-glass, made of fine grasses and fibres, draped and plastered on the outside with cobwebs. There is an untidy bunch of grass, strips of bark etc., invariably left dangling underneath. It is built in the horizontal fork or elbow of a twig, seldom more than 8 feet from the ground. The eggs—three or four —are pale sandy white, with tiny brown spots forming a ring round the broad end.

THE BLACK-HEADED SHRIKE

Lanius nigriceps Franklin

PLATE 36

SIZE : Between the Bulbul and the Myna, with a relatively longer tail.
FIELD CHARACTERS : General aspect when at rest, rather like that of a miniature hawk. Typical stout, hook-tipped shrike bill. Crown of head, cheeks and neck black; rest of upper plumage chestnut. Underparts mostly white. A small white patch on dark wings, particularly noticeable in flight. Sexes alike. Singly, perched upright on exposed bush tops in openly-wooded country.

The more common Rufous-backed Shrike (*Lanius schach*), in four geographical races, has a very wide distribution in India. Head grey with a conspicuous black band across forehead and backward through the eyes. Lower back and rump bright rufous. Underparts white, washed with rufous. In flight, a broad white wing patch or 'mirror' is prominent. It is found in Baluchistan NWF. Province, Kashmir, and throughout the Himalayas (up to 12,000 feet in summer) to extreme NE. Assam, and beyond. It is also resident and breeds over large portions of peninsular India and NW. Ceylon. In winter it spreads out practically all over.

DISTRIBUTION: The Himalayas (between about 4,000 and 6,000 feet) from Garhwal east to Assam, and beyond. Chin and Kachin Hills. In winter it moves down into the foothills and adjoining plains, and is then common in the Vizagapatam Ghats, Orissa and Chota Nagpur.

HABITS: The Black-headed Shrike is an inhabitant of openly-wooded country. It loves orchards and the neighbourhood of cultivation, and avoids both heavy forest and arid tracts. Except when paired off for breeding, it is met with as a solitary bird. From a perch on some exposed twig or tree stump, whence it keeps a sharp look-out for crawling things, it drops to the ground from time to time to seize and carry off a victim. This is held underfoot and torn limb from limb with the sharp hooked bill before being bolted down. Shrikes maintain regular larders where surplus food is stored impaled upon thorns to be eaten at leisure. This habit is responsible for their popular name of Butcher Birds. Their food consists of crickets, grasshoppers, lizards, small birds and mice.

The usual call notes of the Black-headed Shrike, in common with its other cousins, are loud, harsh and scolding, but it is an exceptionally fine songster, and during the breeding season the male delivers a song of considerable sweetness, range and duration. It is also a good mimic of the calls of other birds.

NESTING: The season ranges between April and July, and during this time two broods are frequently raised. The nest is a large and deep compact cup of feathery grasses. It is placed in the fork of a branch in some small tree or bush standing on the edge of forest, and usually under 15 feet from the ground. The eggs—four to six—vary considerably in colouration. The ground colour ranges between pink, cream, yellowish, buff, greyish, and pale green. They are blotched and spotted with grey-brown, reddish-brown or purplish-brown, usually more densely at the broad end.

THE SHORT-BILLED MINIVET

Pericrocotus brevirostris Vigors

PLATE 37
SIZE: About that of the Bulbul.
FIELD CHARACTERS: A brilliantly-coloured glossy black and deep

scarlet bird with a broad scarlet band running through the black wing, and black-and-scarlet steeply graduated tail. Female grey above, yellow below. It has a yellow rump and black-and-yellow tail. Flocks in leafy tree tops in forest. Purely arboreal.

An allied and rather confusingly similar species, the Scarlet Minivet (*P. speciosus*), has a more or less overlapping distribution in the Himalayas, and is also found over a great part of Northern India. It may be differentiated from *brevirostris* by large, oval scarlet spots in the black wing, in addition to the broad scarlet band common to both species. The wing of the female presents the same pattern in yellow and black.

A third species of about the same size, the Orange Minivet (*P. flammeus*), is a common resident in the forests of the Nilgiris and associated hills, and the Western Ghats up to about 6,000 feet from the Surat Dangs to extreme South India. It also occurs in Ceylon. In this species the underparts of the male are orange-red instead of scarlet, and the yellow in the female much paler.

DISTRIBUTION: The Himalayas from Gilgit and Murree to Assam, and down through Burma into Tenasserim. In summer locally between about 3,000 and 10,000 feet; in winter it spreads out more or less throughout North India down to about the Central Provinces. The two races that chiefly concern us are the paler Indian *brevirostris*, and the darker Assam and North Burmese *affinis*.

HABITS: The Short-billed Minivet is a bird of well-wooded tracts and both in its summer as well as winter quarters it is met with in open forest, or country well supplied with large leafy trees. It moves about in small parties which, after the breeding season, sometimes attain considerable proportions, so that in winter twenty or twenty-five birds together is not an uncommon sight. They are strictly arboreal and keep to the foliage canopy of large trees, working industriously amongst the leaves, flitting from sprig to sprig or hovering airily in front of a flower to capture an insect or spider. Flying insects are hunted in the air in the manner of a flycatcher. Their food consists entirely of insects. A mixed flock of these gorgeous birds, with the brilliant scarlets and yellows of the sexes flashing in the sun as they flit among the verdant tree tops or fly across in a loose flock up or down a hillside, presents a spectacle of singular loveliness and charm. The call frequently uttered is a clear musical whistling double note, *wee-twee?* or *wi-weet?* with a distinctly interrogative intonation.

NESTING: The season is principally from April to June. The nest, typical of the minivets, is a compact delicate cup of fine twigs, roots, grass, pine needles, etc., neatly interlaced and densely coated with cobwebs. It is attached in the fork or on the upper surface of a horizontal branch 15 to 25 feet or more from the ground. The eggs—three or four—are pinkish or greenish white, spotted and blotched all over with light brown to blackish-brown and with faint secondary markings of lavender or inky grey.

THE GREY DRONGO

Dicrurus longicaudatus Jerdon

SIZE : About that of the Bulbul with a relatively longer tail. Same as of the more familiar Black Drongo.

FIELD CHARACTERS : A slim, glossy slaty-black bird, with duller underparts and a long deeply-forked tail. Sexes alike. Singly, on trees in hill forest.

The Black Drongo (*D. macrocercus*), known as *kalkanchi* or *kotwal*, so common on telegraph wires and about cultivation and grazing cattle in the plains throughout India, is also found in the Outer Himalayas and the peninsular hills. It is deep glossy black all over.

The Bronzed Drongo (*Chaptia aenea*) is a smaller edition of the Black Drongo, highly glossed with metallic bronze. It is found in forested country in the Outer Himalayas, Western and Eastern Ghats, Bengal and Burma.

The White-bellied Drongo (*D. caerulescens*) occurs throughout Ceylon and India south of a line from Kutch to Garhwal, in lightly forested hills and plains. It also ascends the Himalayas to 6,000 feet in a restricted tract. It is glossy indigo, with a white belly.

The Racket-tailed Drongo (*Dissemurus paradiseus*) is about the size of the Myna, glistening black with a conspicuous backward-curving tuft or crest from forehead, and two long, thin, spatula-tipped streamers in the tail. It is found in the Himalayas from Mussooree to Assam, and patchily throughout the forested peninsular hills and plains. Also Ceylon and Burma.

The Hair-crested Drongo (*Chibia hottentotta*) is about the size of the Myna, glossy black with a scraggy tuft of a few long hair-like feathers at the hind part of the crown. Its tail is almost square, twisted and upturned at its outer ends. It is a forest bird, with more or less the same distribution as the Bronzed Drongo's.

PLATE 43

1 THE WHITE-EYE (*see page* 127)

2 THE FIRE-BREASTED FLOWERPECKER
Female (above), Male (*see page* 132)

3 THE INDIAN STREAKED SPIDER-HUNTER
(*see page* 131)

4 MRS GOULD'S SUNBIRD
Male (above). Female (*see page* 128)

5 THE INDIAN YELLOW-BACKED SUNBIRD
Female (above). Male (*see page* 128)

6 THE SMALL SUNBIRD
Female (above). Male (*see page* 129)

About 1/4 Nat. Size

PLATE 44
1 THE BROWN-FRONTED PIED WOODPECKER   2 THE WEST HIMALAYAN PIED WOODPECKER
(see page 136)   (see page 136)
3 THE SCALY-BELLIED GREEN WOODPECKER   4 THE SPOTTED PICULET
(see page 135)   (see page 139)

About 1/4 Nat. Size

PLATE 45
THE MALABAR GREAT BLACK WOODPECKER (*see* page 137)
About 1/4 Nat. Size

PLATE 46
1 THE GREAT HIMALAYAN BARBET (*see* page 140)
2 THE SMALL GREEN BARBET (*see* page 141)   3 THE BLUE-THROATED BARBET (*see* page 140)
About 1/4 Nat. Size

DISTRIBUTION: The Himalayas from Hazara in the west to Assam, up to about 8,000 feet elevation. Practically all India, Burma and Ceylon, in the forested portions, both hill and plain. Resident in some areas, winter visitor in others. A number of races are recognized on measurements and differences in shades of colouration.

HABITS: The Grey Drongo is essentially a forest bird affecting hilly country for preference, and is found in all types from the deciduous to the evergreen. Here it replaces the Black Drongo of the open, cultivated plains. The bird is usually seen singly perched in a dry tree, or some such commanding position, whence it can keep a sharp look-out on insect movements. But gatherings of up to twenty-five or more may collect to hunt a swarm of winged termites. From time to time it pounces on some unwary grasshopper on the ground and carries it off to its perch, where it is battered and swallowed. It also makes aerial swoops and sallies after moths and winged insects. It is somewhat crepuscular, and may commonly be seen hunting till well after evening dusk. Its diet is chiefly insectivorous, but it is very fond of the nectar of flowers, and in season is in unfailing attendance on Silk Cotton, Coral, *Grevillea*, and other blossoms. This drongo has a number of harsh calls very like those of its black cousin, and it is a good mimic of other birds besides. It is every bit as bold and pugnacious as the celebrated 'Kotwal'.

NESTING: The season is principally April to June. The nest is a lightly-built deep saucer of grass and weed stems, bound with cobweb. It is cradled in a horizontal fork of a branch 10 to 20 feet or more from the ground. The eggs—three or four—are rather like those of the Black Drongo, whitish in ground colour with brownish-red spots, and show a range of variations.

THE RED-HEADED FANTAIL-WARBLER

Cisticola exilis erythrocephala Blyth

PLATE 38
SIZE: Much smaller than the Sparrow.
FIELD CHARACTERS: A tiny brownish bird with a bright chestnut crown. The female (and male in winter plumage) have the head rufous, streaked with brown, and paler underparts. The short, rounded tail is constantly jerked open like a fan. Singly, or loose parties, on open, grassy hillsides (SW. India).

An allied species, the Streaked Fantail-Warbler (*Cisticola juncidis*) is dark-streaked fulvous-brown above, whitish below, with no distinctive reddish cap. It is our common *Cisticola*, found throughout the Indian Empire, in the plains as well as up to 5,000 feet in the hills. It affects open grassland, reed-beds by jheels, and standing paddy crops.

DISTRIBUTION: Hills of Mysore and Travancore, Nilgiris, Palnis, Brahmagiris, and adjacent ranges. Apparently, also locally in the Western Ghats, and as far north as Saugor in the Central Provinces.

A second race *tytleri* with yellow head and underparts occurs from Bhutan to E. Assam, Bengal, Manipur, Lushai, Chin and Kachin Hills.

HABITS: Not many visitors to the usual South Indian hill-stations will agree that the Red-headed Fantail-Warbler is a common bird deserving a place in this book. It is true that unless specially sought, one is hardly likely to come across it; but the species is quite abundant in its accustomed haunts in the Nilgiris and Palnis, and in many of the Coorg and Mysore ranges. It frequents the tall coarse grass mixed with *Strobilanthes*, bracken and other scrub that clothes the open hillsides and plateaux alternating with forested ravines or *sholas*, which are such a characteristic feature of our southern hills. The bird is, however, curiously local and patchy; one may meet with a loose collection of twenty or more in a small area, and then not strike another such 'colony' over miles of identical country. They are unobtrusive little creatures, keeping low amongst the grass stems and seldom seen out of cover. But an individual mounting to the top of a blade now and again gives their presence away, and if one walks up a surprising number may often be flushed, one by one, in the same patch of ground. When disturbed the bird pops out of cover, flies a few yards hurriedly, then dives headlong into the grass. It works its way rapidly through the stems, and when pressed rises again from quite a different spot from where it disappeared. During the breeding season the male indulges in the same sort of erratic mounting, zig-zag and dipping flight as the Streaked Fantail-Warbler, but the call uttered is very different from the *chip . . . chip* of that bird. Lynes has well described it as a scratchy hissing note *scrrrrrrr*, followed after a short pause by a loud, almost explosive bell-like tinkle, *plook*, repeated *ad lib.*, and with a peculiar ventriloquial quality. Its food consists of tiny insects.

NESTING: It is a standing slur on the ornithologists of this country that, in spite of its local abundance, the nest of this warbler is still unrecorded. From juveniles collected in Mysore, it can be deduced that November–December are at least part of its breeding season there.

THE YELLOW-BELLIED OR TICKELL'S
WILLOW-WARBLER

Phylloscopus affinis Tickell

PLATE 38
SIZE: Smaller than the Sparrow.
FIELD CHARACTERS: A small warbler olive-brown above, bright yellow below, with a conspicuous yellow supercilium. No wing-bar. Sexes alike. Singly, or loose parties, on ground or in bushes.

Among the numerous species of tree-warblers found in our country, one that could be readily confused with Tickell's is *P. griseolus*, the Olivaceous Tree-Warbler. It is greyish-brown above, oil-yellow below, with a supercilium of the same colour and a brown streak through the eye. In breeds in the Himalayas and is a common winter visitor to a large part of western, central and peninsular India. It is met with singly in tall trees, on stony hillsides, ancient fort walls, cliffs, etc., running up and down the trunks and rock faces like a tree- or wall-creeper, and constantly flicking its wings and uttering *pick . . . pick*, etc.

DISTRIBUTION: Baluchistan and throughout the Himalayas from the Afghan frontier across to N. Assam and SE. Tibet. In summer between 7,000 and 15,000 feet elevation; in winter practically all over India (excepting Sind) and Burma. Not Ceylon.

HABITS: Tickell's Willow-Warbler is perhaps the commonest of the many warblers of this group that breed within our limits. In summer it keeps mostly to open alpine scrub and rock valleys with bushes of dwarf juniper, rhododendron and berberis, above the limit of tree growth. Osmaston remarks that no other bird approaching it in small-ness is found at these altitudes. In its winter quarters it frequents scrub-covered fallow cultivation, gardens and secondary jungle, both hill and plain. It feeds much more on the ground than other willow-warblers do, and is also more gregarious. Parties of up to twenty or more collect and feed on the ground, but loosely, and not in any organized flock. The individuals act independently, scattering to take refuge among the bushes when disturbed, every one for itself, and reassembling one by one on the ground. The wings are nervously flicked from time to time as the birds hop about, now this way, now that, and they constantly utter a feeble monosyllabic sparrow-like *tsip*. They also feed amongst the foliage of bushes and trees. Small insects form their food exclusively. The song uttered by the male from a bush top in the breeding season consists of a single note repeated four to six times in rapid succession, preceded by a single high-pitched one, thus: *pick . . . whiw-whiw-whiw-whiw*, etc.

NESTING: This warbler breeds in June and July at high elevations, generally over 10,000 feet, in open treeless country, characteristically placing its nest very low down in bushes. The nest is an untidy ball of coarse grass well lined with feathers. The eggs—four or five—are pure china white, sometimes faintly marked with scanty minute red specks at the large end. The male is said to take part in incubation, contrary to the general rule in willow-warblers.

THE LARGE CROWNED WILLOW-WARBLER

Phylloscopus occipitalis Blyth

PLATE 38

SIZE: Smaller than the Sparrow.

FIELD CHARACTERS: Greyish olive-green above, pale yellowish-white below. A pale band down middle of crown, two faint yellowish bars in the wing and the call note *tiss-yip* are good recognition marks. Sexes alike. Arboreal. Singly, or parties, in forest—commonly amongst the mixed hunting bands.

A bird with which it could be confused in its breeding grounds is the Kashmir Crowned Willow-Warbler (*P. reguloides kashmiriensis*). The latter, however, is brighter yellowish-olive above and more yellow below, with the double wing-bars more conspicuous. It winters in the Himalayan foothills and Indo-Gangetic plain, but is rare.

Three other common willow-warblers need mention. The Greenish, and Green (*P. trochiloides viridanus* and *nitidus*) are exceedingly plentiful over most of India in winter, hills and plains alike. They breed doubtfully in Kashmir and Baluchistan, but extensively in the Inner Himalayas and Russia. They are both dull olive-green above, dirty yellowish-white below, with a supercilium of the same colour and a faint wing-bar, and are practically indistinguishable from each other in the field. Call note: a cheerful *chiwee*.

The Chiff-chaff (*Phylloscopus collybita*) is olive-brown above; earthy-buff below, with a narrow pale buff supercilium. No wing-bar. A distinctive feature is its sulphur yellow underwing coverts and axillaries. On the closed wing these show out at close quarters as a small bright yellow patch on the edge of the shoulder. Breeds in NW. Himalayas; winters practically all over India. Usually met singly amongst reed-beds and babul trees, and scrub growing near water. Call note: a plaintive *tweet*. Song: a distinct *chiff-chaff, chiff-chaff*.

Numerous other species of willow-warblers also breed in the Himalayas and visit the plains and hills of the Indian Empire abundantly during winter. They are all tiny birds, mostly much smaller than the Sparrow, olive-green or olive-brown above, yellowish or dirty whitish below, without or with one or two pale bars on the wing. They flit about restlessly amongst the foliage of trees and bushes, nervously flicking their wings, hunting tiny insects on the sprigs, leaf-buds and flowers, and are never quiet for a moment. They cling upside down or sideways on the leaves in their quest, and also launch short agile sallies in the air after winged insects. Many of them are so alike and confusing that it is difficult to tell them apart in the field. The call notes of the different species, however, and their nesting characteristics when once learnt, are sufficiently distinctive as a rule to furnish reliable clues to their identification.

DISTRIBUTION: Breeding in Kashmir and Western Himalayas between 6,000 and 9,000 feet elevation in summer; all India (except Sind) in winter.

HABITS: In general, typical of the willow-warblers. Parties are met with in almost unfailing association with Tits, Grey-headed Flycatchers, White-eyes, and other small insectivorous birds. Song: a high-pitched, rather monotonous *chik . . . wee-chwee, wee-chwee, wee-chwee*, quickly repeated all day.

NESTING: One of the commonest breeding birds from Kashmir to Garhwal, nesting in gardens and the vicinity of villages and buildings—May to July. The nest is a rough globe of moss, grass, dead leaves, etc., lined with moss, wool or hair. It is placed in holes in tree stumps, between stones in a roadside embankment—sometimes even in a hole low down in the wall of a building. The normal clutch is of four eggs—pure white.

THE GREY-HEADED FLYCATCHER-WARBLER

Seicercus xanthoschistos Gray

PLATE 38
SIZE: Much smaller than the Sparrow.
FIELD CHARACTERS: A tiny warbler, yellowish-green above, bright yellow below. Crown and sides of head greyish-brown. A white super-

cilium and a pale line down centre of crown. Easily mistaken for some willow-warbler, especially the Large Crowned, but the white in its outer tail feathers will settle all doubt. Sexes alike. Singly, very common in trees and bushes about Himalayan hill-stations.

In the neighbourhood of Darjeeling its place in abundance is taken by the Black-browed Flycatcher-Warbler (*Seicercus burkii*), which has a parallel distribution in the Himalayas. It differs chiefly in having the sides of the head yellowish instead of grey-brown, and a prominent yellow ring round the eye. The yellow of its underparts is tinged with orange.

These must not be confused with the Yellow-bellied Flycatcher (*Chelidorhynx hypoxanthum*) of about the same size, also found throughout the Himalayas. This is dark olive-brown above, bright yellow below. There is a black line through its eye, and a broad bright yellow supercilium. The tail is broadly tipped with white. As in other fantail-flycatchers, this is fanned out and partially cocked while the bird prances among the branches uttering a feeble *tsi, tsi*, like some willow-warbler.

DISTRIBUTION: Baluchistan, Afghanistan and the Himalayas from extreme west to extreme east; hills of Assam and Chin Hills. In summer between 5,000 and 8,000 feet elevation (somewhat lower in Assam); in winter found also in the foothills and adjacent plains. Two races are recognized: the West Himalayan *albosuperciliaris* differs from the East Himalayan *xanthoschistos* in having grey-brown cheeks as against blackish-brown in the latter.

HABITS: The Grey-headed Flycatcher-Warbler is perhaps the commonest bird of its size to be met with at any of the West Himalayan hill-stations. No roving hunting party is complete without its quota of a couple or more of this species. It keeps to wooded hillsides, feeding up in the foliage of pine, oak and other tall trees, but also descending into the secondary growth and bushes. It is an active, lively little creature hopping about from sprig to sprig, peering into the leaves for insects, and sometimes also capturing them on the wing like a flycatcher. Its habits are a cross between those of a tree-warbler and a flycatcher, and thus its double-barrelled name seems singularly well-fitting. As it goes about its business, the bird constantly utters a distinctive, somewhat plaintive high-pitched call-note which the hill visitor will soon learn to recognize as one of the most familiar bird calls on the air. In summer its monotonous but pleasant little apology for a song may also be heard at all hours of the day. As it hops restlessly amongst the foliage it spreads its tail every little while and shivers its wings in a way that reminds one of the Grey-headed Flycatcher. The white feathers in its tail now displayed serve as an 'identification disc'.

Its food consists entirely of tiny insects.

NESTING: The principal months are May and June. The nest is a large globe of grass and moss on the outside, lined with wool, fur and sometimes a few feathers. It is placed on the ground in a hollow, under a bush or the roots of a tree, on a grassy bush-dotted hill-slope. The eggs— three or four— are typical of the genus, pure white glossy broad ovals. This little warbler is commonly parasitized by the cuckoo. The hefty young impostor, with the nest fitting around him like a loose-knit pullover to the point of bursting, and the silly little foster-parents continuing to feed him the while, are an amazing and ridiculous sight.

THE BROWN HILL-WARBLER

Suya criniger Hodgson

PLATE 38

SIZE: Slightly smaller and slimmer than the Bulbul.

FIELD CHARACTERS: A long-tailed brown bird, finely dark-streaked above, with a strong family likeness to the wren-warblers of the plains. Tail steeply graduated, tipped with white and black, and indistinctly cross-rayed. Sexes alike. Singly, in scrub on open hillsides and about terraced cultivation in the Himalayas.

DISTRIBUTION: Hills of Sind and Baluchistan, and Punjab Salt Range; the Himalayas from NW. frontier right across to Assam; down through North Cachar and Khasi Hills into the hills of Burma, and eastward beyond our boundaries. Commonly between 3,000 and 7,000 feet; locally at lower elevations. Five races are differentiated on details of colouration and markings.

HABITS: The Brown Hill-Warbler is common about most Himalayan hill-stations and should soon become familiar to visitors with an eye and ear for birds. It frequents the bare stony hillsides and steep dry ravines sparsely dotted with bushes, and the grass-and-scrub-covered neighbourhood of terraced cultivation on the slopes. It is frequently also seen within the actual precincts of the station. It is met with as a solitary bird or as one of a pair, skulking in the low brushwood, clambering among the stems and grass tussocks, or mounting to the top of a bush or small tree whence to utter its scraping, reeling song. Its general appearance and habits are strongly reminiscent of the wren-warblers of the plains, and there is in them something also distinctly of the Common Babbler. The bird is a poor flier, with a feeble and jerky flight. When disturbed, it seldom flies far before tumbling headlong into another bush. But a Hill-Warbler hurtling almost perpendicularly down a steep ravine is a different proposition. The tail is then doubled over the back, the wings pulled in and depressed at the sides and the head and bill form the arrow-head of the superbly executed dive, the velocity of which is astounding.

In the breeding season the male spends much time on some bush top, whence he continually pours out his heart in the wheezy, grating and rather monotonous *tsee-tswee-tsee-tswee*, etc., that is meant to be his love song. From time to time he jumps up and performs curious aerial evolutions consisting of a series of wave-crests and nose-dives which are accompanied by a low fluttering sound. This manœuvre is obviously another version of the rather similar giddy-goat antics of the wren-warbler in love. Its ordinary call notes are very like those of the Jungle Wren-Warbler—*p'ty, p'ty, p'ty*, etc., but louder. Its diet consists wholly of insects.

NESTING: The season is principally May and June, but continues till October. The nest is a neatly domed, egg-shaped structure of fine grasses, with a largish entrance near the top. It is built among tufts of grass or in a bush, within a foot or two of the ground. The eggs—three to five, but commonly four—are pure china white to very pale pink, with tiny blotches, freckles and specks of reddish or purplish-brown, dense at the broad end.

THE FAIRY BLUEBIRD

Irene puella Latham

PLATE 39
SIZE: Slightly bigger than the Myna.
FIELD CHARACTERS: A gorgeous deep black and glistening bluebird, shaped rather like an oriole. The female is much duller blue-brown or peacock-blue. Parties in tall trees in evergreen forest—East Himalayas and SW. India.
DISTRIBUTION: Himalayas from Sikkim eastward. Assam Hills; Burma and down into Malay Peninsula, Siam, etc. Also Ceylon, the Western

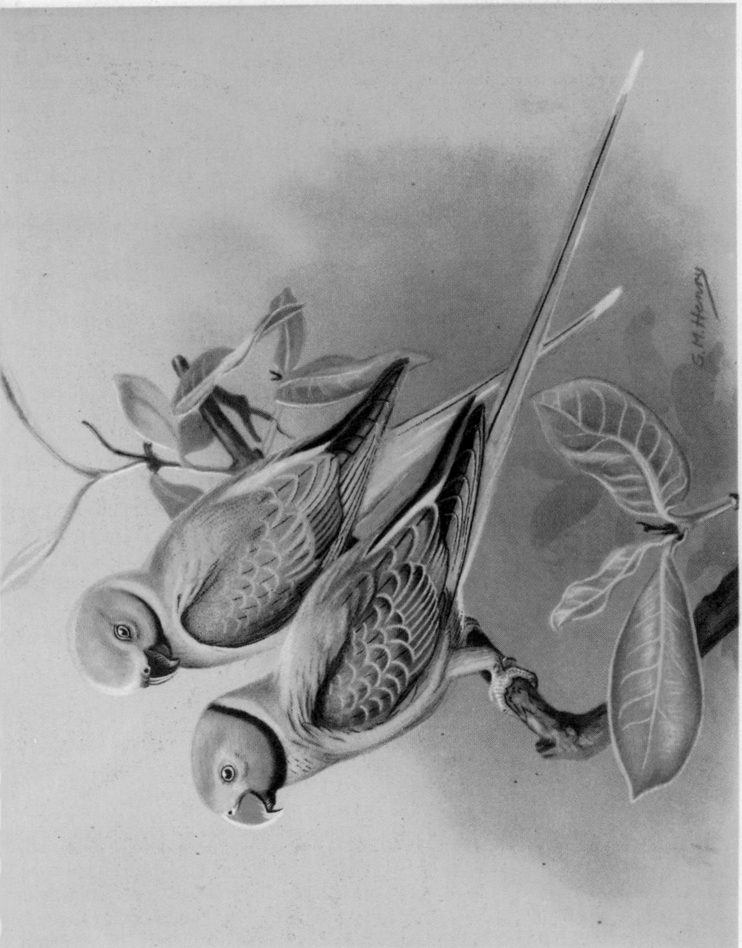

VIEW PLATE THIS WAY

PLATE 47
THE BLUE-WINGED PARAKEET. Female (above). Male (*see* page 146)
About 1/3 Nat. Size

PLATE 48
THE BLUE-BEARDED BEE-EATER (*see* page 147)
About 1/3 Nat. Size

PLATE 49
THE MALABAR TROGON. Female (above). Male (*see* page 150)
About 3/8 Nat. Size

PLATE 50
THE ALPINE SWIFT (*see* page 151)
About 1/3 Nat. Size

Ghats (from Travancore to Belgaum) and the Shevaroy and Chitteri Hills (and possibly others too) of the Eastern Ghats. Two races are recognized within Indian limits: the typical or South Indian *puella*, and the longer-winged Sikkim race *sikkimensis*.

HABITS: The Fairy Bluebird is essentially a bird of humid evergreen forest, and within this habitat, it is found both in the low country and foothills, and up to about 5,000 feet elevation. Parties of seven or eight individuals— sometimes larger flocks—are usually met with flying about among the lofty tree tops, and their sharp percussive call notes—*peepit* or '*be quick*', constantly uttered, are amongst the commonest bird voices in the localities they frequent. Numbers often collect on forest trees to feed on wild figs and fruits of various kinds in company with hornbills, green pigeons and other frugivorous birds. They also descend into the bushes to eat ripening berries, and down to the ground to drink and bathe. Their food consists almost entirely of fruits and berries, but they are very fond of flower nectar and are regular visitors to the blossoms of the *Erythrina*s and *Grevillea*s so largely grown for shade in the tea and coffee plantations of the South Indian hills. The birds transport the pollen adhering to their chin feathers from flower to flower, and thus do useful service in cross-pollinating them.

NESTING: The season in SW. India is not well-defined, but most eggs are found in March–April. In Assam, the principal month is May. The nest is a fragile-looking shallow saucer of roots, twigs, and a few bents mixed with green moss, and has a good deal of moss on the outside. It is usually placed 5 to 20 feet up in a tall, thinly-foliaded, straggling bush in the interior of deep, damp, sunless forest; sometimes in the leaves of a fern-palm. The clutch is almost invariably of two eggs—olive-grey or greenish-white in colour with irregular blotches of brown all over the surface, but denser and forming a ring at the broad end. This species is frequently parasitized by the Hawk-Cuckoo or Brain-fever Bird (*Hierococcyx varius*).

THE GOLDEN ORIOLE

Oriolus oriolus Linnaeus

PLATE 39
SIZE: About that of the Myna.
FIELD CHARACTERS: Bright golden yellow with black in the wings

and tail, and a conspicuous black streak through the eye. Female and young male usually duller and greener. Singly or pairs, among trees in wooded country.

The Black-headed Oriole (*Oriolus xanthornus*) is also found in the Himalayas up to about 4,000 feet elevation and in most of the peninsular hills. It is a brilliant golden-yellow bird about the size of the Myna, with jet black head, throat and upper breast, and with black in wings and tail. Its bill is livid pink.

Another very beautiful oriole, locally common in the Himalayas and Assam hills, is the Maroon Oriole (*Oriolus traillii*). It is deep black and shining maroon red. In overhead flight against the sky it arrests attention as a blackbird with a claret-crimson tail.

DISTRIBUTION: All India from Kashmir and about 6,000 feet in the Himalayas down to Cape Comorin, and from Baluchistan to Bengal. Resident in many localities; local migrant in others. For instance, to the Himalayas and a large part of Northern India it is only a summer (breeding) visitor arriving about March and leaving in September. We are concerned chiefly with the Indian race *kundoo*, which differs from the European in that the black eyestreak of the adult male extends behind the eye.

HABITS: The Golden Oriole, popularly known as the Mango Bird, is a dweller of open, but well-wooded country, and is particularly fond of orchards and groves of large leafy trees such as chenar, mango, shisham, and *toon*. In summer it is numerous about Srinagar and in the various side-valleys of Kashmir—the favoured haunts of the tourist and the hiker—and it must be a dull ear indeed that fails to catch the magic of its mellow, flute-like notes that are so constantly on the air. The bird is usually met with in pairs, which fly about from tree to tree, flashing through the dappled foliage like a streak of gold with a peculiar strong and dipping flight. It is entirely arboreal and never seen on the ground. While of a shy and retiring disposition the bird will commonly enter gardens and frequent roadside trees even in the midst of noisy and populous cities. The ordinary call notes are a harsh *chee-ah*, followed as a rule by liquid musical whistles that sound something like *pi-lo-lo*. Its food consists of fruits and berries, but insects are also eaten. The nectar of flowers such as of the Silk Cotton and Coral trees is regularly imbibed.

NESTING: The season over the greater part of its range is from April to July. The nest is a beautifully woven, deep cup of bast fibres. A good deal of cobwebs are used to bind the material together. It is suspended like a hammock in a horizontal fork of twigs near the end of an outhanging branch of some large leafy tree, 12 to 30 feet from the ground. The eggs—two or three—are white, spotted with black or reddish-brown. Both sexes share in building the nest, incubation, and tending the young.

THE JUNGLE MYNA

Æthiopsar fuscus Wagler

SIZE: That of the Myna.

FIELD CHARACTERS: Similar to the Common Myna in general appearance, but distinctly greyish-brown. No bare yellow skin round the eye, and a conspicuous tuft of erect black feathers at base of bill on forehead. Large white wing-patches conspicuous in flight, same as in Common Myna. Sexes alike. Pairs, and loose flocks in wooded country, about villages and forest cultivation.

The Common Myna (*Acridothers tristis*), all too familiar to most people, has now penetrated to practically all hill-stations throughout the country —in the Himalayas locally up to about 10,000 feet.

The Grackle or Hill Myna (*Gracula religiosa*), well known as a cage bird and talker, is found in the Outer Himalayas, Western Ghats and other peninsular hills. In size, it is between the Myna and the Pigeon, glossy jet black, with yellow bill and legs, and bright orange-yellow naked patches and wattles on the head.

Another common Myna of moderate elevations in the Himalayas (between 3,000 and 5,000 feet) is the Spotted-winged Stare (*Saroglossa spiloptera*). It is roughly the size of the Bulbul or Grey-headed Myna; brownish-grey above, rusty-white below. Head black-and-grey above, with chestnut chin and throat. In flight the dark head, rufous-brown rump and blackish wings, with a conspicuous white patch (as in the the Blue-headed Rock-Thrush) are diagnostic. Flocks of eight to ten in flowering and fruiting forest trees.

DISTRIBUTION: Practically all India and Burma, including the Himalayas up to about 7,000 feet elevation, as well as the peninsular hills. It is not found in Sind, Rajputana, or the drier portions of the NWF.P., nor in Ceylon. Two races are recognized: the Northern *fuscus* and the Southern *mahrattensis*. The latter is less grey, more brown. Its iris is whitish-grey ('wall-eyed'), as against yellow in the Northern race.

HABITS: The Jungle Myna is a bird of open well-wooded country, and usually found in the neighbourhood of forest clearings and cultivation, and forest plantations. It is not so dependent for its livelihood upon man, and therefore does not live in such intimate familiarity with him as its better-known cousin. Neither is it disposed to be so cheeky or so 'pushing'. At certain hill-stations, however, such as Ootacamund (Nilgiris) and Kodaikanal (Palnis), it has, strangely enough, more or less completely usurped the position of the Common Myna as a 'house' bird, and is freely seen about the bungalows and bazaars. A curious thing about the Jungle Myna is the patchiness of its distribution. Its absence from large tracts of country, apparently just as suitable as the ones it occupies, needs explanation. It wanders about to some extent with the seasons, but these movements are not sufficient to account for the local gaps. Small parties or larger flocks are often seen in association with Common and Brahminy Mynas in wet fallow fields and grassland, or attending on grazing cattle. It feeds on grasshoppers and insects as well as wild figs and berries, and often does considerable damage to orchard fruit. Flowers such as those of *Erythrina* and *Bombax* are regularly visited for the nectar. The tuft of feathers on the forehead serves as an efficient brush for collecting and transporting pollen and seems particularly well adapted for the purpose of cross-pollinating the flowers. In voice and other habits it does not differ appreciably from the Common Myna.

NESTING: The season is principally from April to June or July, and often two successive broods are raised. The nest is a collection of twigs, roots, paper and miscellaneous rubbish placed in holes in trees. Large nesting colonies occupy weep-holes in revetments alongside the hill roads in the Himalayas and elsewhere. The same sites are frequently occupied year after year. The eggs—four to six, sometimes only three—are a beautiful turquoise blue, smooth and rather glossy. They are indistinguishable from the eggs of the Common Myna.

THE BLACK-AND-YELLOW GROSBEAK

Perissospiza icteroides Vigors

SIZE: About that of the Myna.

FIELD CHARACTERS: An overgrown finch black and deep yellow, somewhat of the colour scheme of the Black-headed Oriole, with a very heavy conical bill. The female is dull ashy with fulvous underparts. Pairs or parties in Himalayan pine forests.

The very similar Allied Grosbeak (*P. affinis*), is found in the Himalayas from Hazara to Bhutan. The male is more orange-yellow in its upper parts and has the thighs yellow instead of black; the female is greenish-yellow underneath instead of ashy and fulvous.

Bullfinches of the genus *Pyrrhula* are also met with in the Himalayan pine forests. They are birds of the size of the sparrow, of orange-brown or ashy-brown plumage. A short, rather abrupt, swollen bill; a white rump particularly conspicuous in flight; glossy black wings and square or distinctly forked black tail are amongst their chief characteristics. They are rather solitary and unobtrusive, and have soft, clear, low call notes.

DISTRIBUTION: Western Himalayas from the Afghan frontier through to Kumaon (Murree, Mussooree, Naini Tal, etc.), between about 5,000 and 10,000 feet elevation in summer; slightly lower in winter.

HABITS: This large and handsome finch is essentially an inhabitant of coniferous woods, but it occurs in other types of Himalayan forests as well. It is met with in pairs or small flocks, keeping largely to the tall firs and deodars, biting into the pine cones and eating the seeds. It also descends into the shrubs and undergrowth to feed on various berries, and may commonly be seen hopping about on the ground picking seeds. A clear, high-pitched call, *pir-riu, pir-riu, pir-riu,* etc., is uttered at frequent intervals as the birds move amongst the branches. It is highly reminiscent of a railway guard's whistle—the sort that has a pea in it—but the blasts are rather short and subdued. In the breeding season, when the birds have paired off, the rich, clear and pleasing 'song' of the male, *pr-r . . . toweet-ā-toweet,* may commonly be heard.

NESTING: The season is principally May and June. The nest is a large and compact cup of fine twigs, lichen and plant-stems with occasionally a little moss, lined with dry grass and rootlets. It is placed on a branch usually at its junction with or close to the main stem of a spruce or deodar tree, between 18 and 60 feet from the ground, and is practically invisible from below. The normal clutch is of two or three eggs, pale french-grey in colour with deep purple-black spots and broad scrolls, and specks and lines of pale brown and lavender-grey. The markings are denser at the broad end. Both sexes share in building the nest.

THE ROSEFINCH

Carpodacus erythrinus Pallas

PLATE 40

SIZE: A trifle larger than the House-Sparrow.

FIELD CHARACTERS: A sparrow-like bird with beautiful crimson-pink head, breast, back and shoulders. Female brown with an olive tinge. In both sexes the heavy conical finch bill, the distinctly forked tail and a pale double bar in the wing are conspicuous features. Flocks in wooded country, hill and plain. In summer, Himalayas only.

Several other species of Rosefinch occur in the Himalayas, varying in intensity of redness, pattern of plumage, and also in size. The most remarkable of them all is certainly the Scarletfinch (*Haematospiza sipahi*) of the Eastern Himalayas, somewhat smaller than the Bulbul. The male is an almost unbelievably brilliant scarlet, with black in wings and tail. Female dusky brown with a bright yellow rump.

DISTRIBUTION: The Indian race *roseatus* is found in summer up to about 10,000 feet elevation and higher, from Kashmir through Kumaon and Garhwal to East Tibet, down through Yunnan to the Shan States and eastward beyond our borders. In winter it spreads out over all India and Burma. At this season the paler European race *erythrinus* also visits NW. and Central India.

HABITS: In summer the Rosefinch is found at high altitudes in the Himalayas, where it keeps to birch and silver fir forest and thickets of wild rose, bracken and tall weeds. Large flocks pass through Kashmir to their high breeding haunts in May and June, and during March and April similar flocks may be encountered on northward migration over the *ghats*, and many of the peninsular hills also. The song of the male, heard only on its breeding grounds is, according to Osmaston, a 'bright, cheery refrain of five to eight notes repeated at intervals from a tree or bush not far from the nest'. The ordinary call-note uttered at all seasons is a pleasant interrogative whistling *tooee?* or *chuee?* In its winter quarters—the hills and plains of peninsular India—this Rosefinch is found chiefly between October and April. It usually keeps in small flocks of ten to fifteen birds in wooded country and on the outskirts of cultivation, feeding amongst bushes, scrub and standing crops. In the southern hills, scrub at the edge of evergreen *sholas* and open secondary bush jungle bordering tea, coffee and cardamom plantations are favourite haunts. Its diet consists of flower buds, *Lantana* and other berries, Banyan figs, bamboo seeds, as well as jowari, linseed and other grains. The nectar

106

of *Butea*, *Woodfordia* and *Erythrina*, besides a large variety of wild flowers is habitually eaten. Like other bird visitors they transport quantities of pollen adhering to their forehead and chin, and are doubtless instrumental in cross-pollination.

NESTING: The season is from June to August. The nest is a cup of grass lined with fine roots and hair. It is built in wild rose and similar bushes between 2 and 6 feet from the ground. The eggs—three or four—are blue in colour, spotted and speckled with blackish and light red. Both sexes share in building the nest and tending the young.

THE HIMALAYAN GOLDFINCH

Carduelis caniceps Vigors

PLATE 40

SIZE: About that of the Sparrow.

FIELD CHARACTERS: A pointed and slender-billed finch of greyish-brown (sandy) plumage, with bright crimson face and a broad golden patch in the black wings. Tail black-and-white with a pure white patch above its base. The female has the crimson face somewhat paler, and the golden wing-patch smaller. In flight a pale yellowish band across wings, bordered in front and behind with brown, the black-and-white tail and white rump are diagnostic features. Parties, or flocks, in open Himalayan forest or orchards, etc.

DISTRIBUTION: The Himalayan race *caniceps*, with which we are chiefly concerned, is found from Gilgit and Kashmir to Kumaon, Simla States and Garhwal. In summer between 5,000 and 11,000 feet elevation; in winter lower, some even descending into the foothills and adjoining plains.

HABITS: The Himalayan Goldfinch is common in Kashmir and in suitable localities throughout its range. In summer it keeps in pairs or small parties, largely frequenting pinewoods. Later in the season and during winter the birds band themselves into larger flocks and are then commonly met with in opener country, in orchards and willow groves near villages, amongst weeds and thistles growing on bare hillsides or on sparsely scrubbed meadows and fallow land about cultivation. A party of goldfinches diligently exploring the thistle-heads for seeds, fluttering airily around them or clinging on like tits, is a delightful thing to watch. In this typical setting it makes a picture of the most exquisite composition, and it is small wonder that so many bird painters love to depict the goldfinch in one of its characteristic attitudes on a thistle-head. The birds utter soft twittering notes as they go about their business, and the twitters are also heard as a flock flies overhead, or flits from one weed patch to another. The flight is typically sparrow-like—slightly dipping—consisting of a few quick wing beats followed by a short break. The song, which commences to be heard as early as February or March and remains 'on the air' throughout the breeding months, is a pleasant twittering of considerable range and variations. It has rather the quality of a canary's performance. Several birds may often be heard singing together in a sort of chorus. Its food consists chiefly of seeds, but insects are also eaten. The seeds are taken mostly on the plants, but occasionally the birds descend to the ground, hopping along like a sparrow and picking them up.

NESTING: The season is from May to July. The nest is a beautiful, neat and compactly woven cup of lichens, fine grass and vegetable fibres, lined with soft willow down or hair. It is placed either in a large bush or in a willow or pine tree usually between 5 and 25 feet from the ground. A number of pairs sometimes nest in company in a small pine wood, and occasionally two or three nests may be found in the same tree. The normal clutch is of three to five eggs, pale skim-milk blue in colour, spotted and streaked with reddish or greyish-brown.

THE HIMALAYAN GREENFINCH

Hypacanthis spinoides Vigors

PLATE 40

SIZE: About that of the House-Sparrow; slightly smaller.

FIELD CHARACTERS: A particularly pointed and slender-billed finch—greenish-brown and black above, bright yellow below. A yellow eye-brow, yellow 'collar' on hindneck, yellow rump, and yellow markings in wings and tail are points to confirm its identity. The female is duller and paler. Gregarious, in high Himalayan forests.

DISTRIBUTION: The typical race *spinoides*, which concerns us principally, is found in Baluchistan and throughout the Himalayas from the Afghan border in the west, to Manipur (Assam) in the east. In summer between 6,000 and 11,000 feet; in winter lower, also down into the foothills and plains about their base. The Shan States, Yunnan and eastward, are inhabited by the duller coloured race *ambiguus*.

PLATE 51
THE INDIAN LONG-TAILED NIGHTJAR (*see* page 153)
About 3/8 Nat. Size

PLATE 52
THE FOREST EAGLE-OWL (*see* page 154)
About 1/6 Nat. Size

PLATE 53
1 THE WEST HIMALAYAN BARRED OWLET (*see* page 157)
2 THE WESTERN SPOTTED SCOPS OWL (*see* page 156)
About 1/3 Nat. Size

PLATE 54
THE SHAHIN FALCON (*see* page 162)
About 1/5 Nat. Size

HABITS: In summer the Greenfinch frequents openly forested hillsides in the Himalayas, especially those with deodar, fir and pine, from about the elevation at which most of our hill-stations are situated (6,000 to 8,000 feet) up to the limit of tree-growth. The birds may also be seen in the neighbourhood of hill cultivation, feeding amongst the weed patches, busily investigating the browning heads for seeds. Seeds of the wild hemp (*bhang*) are greatly relished, and ripening sunflower seeds form an irresistible attraction at all times. In quest of these, flocks will freely enter hill-station gardens and it is a familiar sight to see the birds hanging on to the flowers or flitting from one flower to another. The green-and-yellow colour scheme of their plumage blends admirably with the sunflowers.

It is a sociable bird even in the breeding season. In winter, at lower elevations, flocks of considerable size may sometimes be met with.

It has a number of soft twittering call notes, not unlike those of the Goldfinch. The male has a pretty little song usually uttered from the topmost branch of a tree. The flight, typical of the finches, is swift and undulating, and a flock on the wing with their yellow undersides and wing-patches glinting in the sun against a background of dark green deodars presents a charming spectacle.

NESTING: The principal breeding months are July and August. The nest is a neat and compact cup of grass stalks, roots and moss, lined with roots, fibres, horse-hair and some feathers. It is placed on the upper surface of a horizontal pine or deodar branch near its end, usually between 6 and 30 feet from the ground. The birds do not actually breed in colonies but gregariously, so that sometimes a dozen nests may be found within a radius of fifteen yards. The normal clutch consists of four eggs, but three or five are sometimes laid. They are a pretty greenish-white or pale blue in colour, lightly speckled all over with black or reddish, more densely round the broad end. The female alone incubates and is fed by the male while thus employed. Incubation takes thirteen days. Both sexes share in feeding the young.

THE CINNAMON TREE-SPARROW

Passer rutilans Temm. and Laug.

PLATE 40

SIZE: About that of the Sparrow (slightly smaller).

FIELD CHARACTERS: An unmistakable cousin of the vulgar House-

Sparrow, distinguished from it chiefly by its bright cinnamon-rufous upper plumage and yellowish underparts with black chin and throat. The female is duller above and with a conspicuous pale 'eyebrow'. Pairs or flocks, in or on outskirts of Himalayan villages and hill-stations.

The familiar House-Sparrow (*P. domesticus*) has followed man's footsteps and established itself comfortably amidst his habitations at most hill-stations, Himalayan as well as peninsular.

The Tree-Sparrow (*P. montanus*), common at Darjeeling, is found throughout the Himalayas, west to east (in summer up to about 8,000 feet), and south through Assam and Burma. It keeps to human habitations as well as to forest and open cultivated country. It differs from the House-Sparrow in having the crown of the head chestnut instead of grey, and a black patch on the earcoverts. Also in male and female being alike.

DISTRIBUTION: The Himalayas from extreme west to extreme east and down through Assam and Burma; also Yunnan. In summer most commonly between 3,000 and 6,000 feet and up to 9,000 feet; in winter in foothills and plains at their base. Two races chiefly concern us: the West Himalayan *debilis* and the East Himalayan *cinnamomeus*. The former is slightly paler, especially on the chestnut parts.

HABITS: The Cinnamon Sparrow is essentially a forest-dwelling species, less closely dependent for its livelihood upon man and his concerns than its all-too-familiar cousin. It normally occupies the vicinity of hill villages and wooded country on the outskirts of terraced cultivation. But how far this preference is voluntary, and to what extent influenced by the fact that the more comfortable living has, in most places, already been appropriated by its more audacious and quarrelsome relative, is a question. For wherever it has the chance the Cinnamon soon establishes itself as the common 'town sparrow' and seems to thrive well enough in these surroundings. This is precisely the case in Mussooree and several other Himalayan hill-stations also, where for some reason or other *domesticus* has not yet penetrated in force. Large flocks collect in winter to glean grain in the harvested fields and to roost among trees. In food, general behaviour and habits, there is little appreciable difference between the two, except of course that this species is far less impudent and obtrusive. Even where living in man's proximity, it does not usually enter houses, is less boisterous, and therefore seldom the unmixed nuisance that the House-Sparrow invariably makes of himself. Its call notes are of the same general pattern but considerably pleasanter—almost musical by comparison. The *swee . . . swee*, etc., commonly uttered, in fact, sounds very like some notes of the Indian Robin. A soft *chilp chilp* is also uttered, which is rather reminiscent of a nuthatch.

NESTING : The season is a prolonged one—April to August—and often two successive broods are raised. The nest is an untidy collection of grass, roots and miscellaneous rubbish, lined with hair and feathers. It is placed in holes and hollows in trees and dead stumps in open forest at heights of up to 30 feet from the ground, or under the eaves or in thatch roofing of houses. The eggs—four to six—are very like those of the House-Sparrow, whitish or pale greenish-white marked with various shades of brown. Both sexes take part in building the nest, incubating the eggs and feeding the young. Incubation takes twelve to thirteen days.

THE MEADOW BUNTING

Emberiza cia Linnaeus

PLATE 40

SIZE : Slightly larger than the Sparrow.

FIELD CHARACTERS : A trim, sparrow-like bird, black-streaked chestnut-brown above, chestnut below, with bluish-grey throat and breast. A prominent grey 'centre parting' to black crown, broad white eyebrow, black and white markings on face, and white in tail (conspicuous in flight), are its chief recognition marks. The female is similar but duller. Small flocks on ground in open grass and cultivated country.

The White-capped Bunting (*E. stewarti*) is another common West Himalayan species found in summer between 4,000 and 10,000 feet elevation and wintering in the N. Indian plains. The male lacks the centre parting on the crown, which is all pale grey. The breast is chestnut.

The Grey-headed Bunting (*E. fucata*) is of rather similar general effect. It is distinguished by a prominent chestnut band, like a gorget, running across the breast. The lower plumage is pale fulvous.

DISTRIBUTION : The Meadow Bunting has a vast Palæarctic range from North Africa, through Southern Europe right across to Eastern Siberia and North China, and is divided into numerous races. We are chiefly concerned with the Eastern race (*stracheyi*), which is found in the Himalayas from the Afghan border through Kashmir to Kumaon. In summer between 4,000 and 11,000 feet elevation; in winter over a large part of the North Indian plains.

HABITS : In summer the Meadow Bunting frequents bush-covered rock-strewn hillsides in the neighbourhood of cultivation, and open grassy glades within or on the outskirts of spruce and deodar forest. It is one of the commonest birds in Kashmir at this season and no camper in any of the side valleys can fail to notice it. It keeps in loose scattered flocks, which feed on the ground picking up seeds of various kinds, and fly up into trees like tree-pipits when disturbed. Here and there a bird may be observed perched upon a bush or exposed branch of a tree, on a boulder or piled stone boundary wall, uttering a mousey *swip, swip*, etc., every second or two. This note is rather reminiscent of the sunbird or flowerpecker. The song, not often heard, is said to be short but quite pretty, resembling that of the goldfinch.

NESTING: The principal breeding months are June and July. The nest is a cup of grasses sometimes lined with hair. It is usually placed on the ground in sloping grass and flower meadows under the shelter of a bush, a tuft of grass or a stone, well concealed from view. The normal clutch is of three eggs—sometimes four—greyish cream in ground colour, handsomely marked with intricate scrawls of fine dark purplish or brownish lines. Both sexes take part in building the nest, but incubation appears to be undertaken by the female only.

THE CRESTED BUNTING

Melophus lathami Gray

PLATE 40
SIZE: Slightly larger than the Sparrow.
FIELD CHARACTERS: Male glistening black with chestnut wings, of about the same colour scheme as the Crow-Pheasant, with a prominent pointed crest. The female, also crested, is dark brown with some cinnamon in her wings. Small flocks on bush-covered hillsides and about cultivation.

The Striolated Bunting (*E. striolata*) is somewhat smaller than the Sparrow, dull brown with some rufous in the wings and black and white markings on the head. Both in flight and at rest at a distance it recalls the female Crested Bunting, minus the crest. It is resident in a portion of the NW. Provinces, Punjab and Sind down to Kutch and east to the Central Provinces and Hyderabad State. It haunts dry, stony hills and arid broken country. Everywhere patchily and sporadically distributed, and also locally migratory.

DISTRIBUTION: Himalayas from Kashmir to E. Assam, at moderate elevations and up to about 6,000 feet in summer. Also Mt. Abu, and peninsular India—hills and plateau country—south to about Mahable-shwar. Portions of Burma, and eastward into China.

HABITS: The Crested Bunting is a dweller of open country. It is fond of old forest clearings overgrown with tall, coarse grass and *dhak* scrub (*Butea*), and broken hillsides covered with short, scraggy grass dotted with cactus and such-like bushes. Ancient overgrown hill forts with their tumble-down ramparts form attractive haunts. The birds are very partial to cross-country cart tracks and to the *paraos* or 'parks' where bullock carts halt for rest during the mid-day heat. If there are any Crested Buntings in a locality they are sure to make their appearance in such places. Parties of five to ten birds are usually met with on the ground gleaning grass seeds and grain, and uttering *pink, pink*, as they move about, rather like a Munia's, but louder. When disturbed they fly up into trees. In the breeding season the male sings excitedly from a tree top, wall or other exposed perch. The song, of several pleasant notes, is rather similar in tone-quality and cadence to the Indian Robin's or the Pied Bush-Chat's, but it invariably starts with a subdued double *which*, thus: *which* (undertone) . . . *which* (undertone) *which-whee-whee-which* (accent on second *whee*).

NESTING: In the Himalayas the season is April to June; in the penin-sular hills and *ghats* July and August are the principal months. The nest is a deep cup of grass lined with fine rootlets, placed in a pocket or hollow in an earth cutting or hillside, under the shelter of a stone or grass tuft. The eggs—three or four—are pale greenish-grey, freckled with purplish-brown, densely at the broad end. Both sexes share in building the nest.

THE CRAG-MARTIN

Riparia rupestris Scopoli

SIZE: About that of the Sparrow.

FIELD CHARACTERS: A plain, sooty-brown bird, whitish ashy below, with short square or slightly forked tail, and swallow-like wings and flight. The dark undertail coverts contrast with the whitish underparts in over-head flight. Sexes alike. Small, loose parties about rock scarps, hawking winged insects.

The Dusky Crag-Martin (*Riparia concolor*), somewhat smaller and uniformly darker, is found as a resident species more or less throughout peninsular India, excepting Sind. It is common in all the hills, seen hawking insects about cliffs, ancient forts and rock-cut caves.

A rather similar bird, the House-Martin (*Delichon urbica*), with forked swallow-tail and white feathered or stockinged legs, frequently seen in Kashmir, is locally resident in the Himalayas from the Afghan border to Sikkim, between 5,000 and 15,000 feet elevation. It is glossy blue-black above, with white rump and underparts. As a rule it haunts rather desolate uninhabited areas, and breeds in colonies on cliffs, attaching its cup-shaped mud nests to the rock-face under an overhang.

DISTRIBUTION: The Crag-Martin has a wide Palæarctic distribution from N. Africa and S. Europe right across to W. China. Within our limits it breeds in the Western Himalayas from the Afghan and Baluchi borders to Kumaon, between about 6,000 and 14,000 feet elevation. In winter it migrates southward and spreads out over peninsular India, being then found in practically all the hills down to Travancore.

HABITS: This Martin, as its name indicates, is inseparable from crags. It is found in the hills, both summer and winter, wherever cliffs and rock scarps occur. Small loose parties are usually seen flying about the precipices and hilltops, capturing tiny winged insects, and often in company with other swallows and swifts. Unlike the last, the birds may frequently be seen resting on some ledge of rock, sitting low down on their short legs, either inert or preening themselves. A soft, low, musical *chit-chit*, etc., is constantly uttered while at rest as well as on the wing.

In the air, martins and swallows may be distinguished from swifts by their broader wings and comparatively slower and less direct flight. In the swift the outstretched wings are noticeably narrower and curved like a bow. Only their tips are rapidly vibrated up and down to propel the bird through the air.

NESTING: The season lasts from May to August, most eggs being laid in June and July. The nest is a deepish oval saucer of mud, attached like a bracket to a rock face usually under the shelter of an overhang. It is lined with grass and feathers. The birds breed in colonies, selecting inaccessible rocky cliffs and the steep sides of narrow gorges or *tangis*, often directly over a stream. The eggs—normally four—are white, boldly speckled and spotted with pale chocolate-brown, with a few faint purplish-grey markings.

THE COMMON SWALLOW

Hirundo rustica Linnaeus

PLATE 41

SIZE: About that of the Sparrow.

FIELD CHARACTERS: Glossy steel-blue above, creamy- or pinkish-white below, with chestnut forehead and throat, the latter bordered by a blue-black breast band. Typical deeply forked 'swallow' tail. Sexes alike. Gregariously, in open country.

The beautiful Wire-tailed Swallow (*H. smithii*) occurs in the Himalayas up to about 5,000 feet elevation, and throughout the well-watered hills and plains of peninsular India. It may be differentiated from the Common Swallow by its bright chestnut cap, the uniformly glistening white underparts, and the two long, fine 'wires', or filaments, in its tail.

DISTRIBUTION: The Swallow has a wide Palæarctic breeding range in Europe, North Africa and Asia. Within our limits it is found in Baluchistan and the Himalayas from the Afghan border and Kashmir to Assam. In summer between about 5,000 and 7,000 feet elevation; in winter throughout India, Burma and Ceylon. Two races, differing in minor details, chiefly concern us, viz., the European-West Himalayan *rustica*, and the East Asiatic East-Himalayan *gutturalis*. A third race—the NE. Siberian *tytleri*—with chestnut underparts, visits E. Bengal, Assam and Burma in winter.

HABITS: In spring and summer the Common Swallow is one of the most familiar birds about Quetta, Srinagar and other holiday resorts in Kashmir, and plentiful at most other Himalayan hill-stations as well. Everywhere it is tame and confiding, keeping to the neighbourhood of human habitations and freely entering houses for nesting, even in the midst of noisy bazaars. The birds are seen gregariously, in small loose parties or flocks, perched on telegraph wires or beating back and forth over reedy *jheels* and open spaces, capturing insects in the air or scooping them up from the surface of the water. The flight, swift and graceful, seems amazingly effortless; the agile turning and twisting movements are greatly helped by the forked tail. When they have finished raising their families and the downward migration is about to commence, as well as before dispersing on arrival in their winter quarters, the birds collect in enormous swarms which often cover long stretches of telegraph wires and overflow on to adjacent tree tops, and even the ground. The same massing movement is again noticeable before the birds start on the return journey to their breeding grounds.

This swallow has a number of pleasant twittering notes uttered both on the wing and while at rest. In the breeding season the male has a pretty, though rather feeble, twittering song lasting sometimes up to fifteen seconds or more.

NESTING: The season is between April and July, and two successive broods are frequently raised. The nest is like that of the Crag-Martin, a saucer of mud reinforced with grass and straw. It is fixed in the corner of a verandah near the ceiling, under eaves or against rafters in buildings and bazaar shops. A favourite site in Srinagar is under the hulls of house-boats just above the waterline. The eggs—four to six—are white, dotted and speckled with reddish-brown or purplish-brown, more densely at the broad end. Both birds share in building the nest, incubation and feeding the young. Incubation is said to take fourteen to fifteen days.

THE NILGIRI HOUSE-SWALLOW

Hirundo javanica domicola Jerdon

PLATE 41

SIZE: About that of the Sparrow.

FIELD CHARACTERS: Green-glossed black above, with deeply forked swallow tail; pale ashy below. Chin, throat, upper breast and a broad band across forehead, chestnut. Sexes alike. Loose parties hawking insects about cliffs and near human habitations in S. Indian hills.

Another common swallow with a very general distribution in the peninsular hills up to about 3,500 feet elevation (and plains) is Sykes's Striated Swallow (*H. daurica erythropygia*). It is deep glossy blue-black above except for a chestnut half-collar on nape and chestnut rump. Underparts pale rufous with fine blackish streaks. It lives gregariously about old mosques and buildings, and makes a retort-shaped earthen nest attached to ceilings of domes, porches, caves, etc. Several races of this Striated or Red-rumped swallow are found in India, Burma and Ceylon, either as resident or winter visitor. One of these *hyperythra*, with chestnut underparts, is restricted to Ceylon. Another, *nepalensis*, which has a paler rump and finer streaks, breeds throughout the Himalayas between 3,000 and 10,000 feet and spreads over all India and Burma during winter in large numbers.

DISTRIBUTION: Hills of Southern India from the Nilgiris to Travancore and Ceylon, about 3,000 feet elevation and upwards.

PLATE 55
THE HIMALAYAN GOLDEN EAGLE (*see* page 164)
About 1/12 Nat. Size

PLATE 56
THE BLACK EAGLE (*see* page 166)
About 1/14 Nat. Size

PLATE 57
THE WEDGE-TAILED GREEN PIGEON (*see* page 168)
About 1/3 Nat. Size

PLATE 58
THE NILGIRI WOOD-PIGEON (*see* page 169)
About 1/3 Nat. Size

HABITS: In general habits and behaviour the Nilgiri Swallow does not differ appreciably from the Common or other species of swallows. Numbers are commonly met with hawking insects over grassy hill-slopes on the edge of tea and coffee plantations and in the proximity of estate bungalows and cooly lines. The birds frequently perch huddled together on the bare upper branches of lofty dead trees. They are tame and trusting, and freely enter verandahs and living rooms of inhabited bungalows for nesting. Neither electric lights nor the blare of radios, the screeching of gramophones, domestic squabbles nor the constant comings and goings of the inmates appear to disturb them.

Flying young, just out of the nest, are fed regularly by the parent in mid-air, both birds fluttering and halting in their flight momentarily while the food is transferred to the youngster's gape.

NESTING: The season is principally March to June, but in Ceylon they also nest in September and October. Two broods are usually raised in quick succession. The nest is the usual half-saucer of mud pellets lined with feathers. It is attached to the wall or rock face under culverts and in tunnels, but most commonly under the eaves or against beams and rafters in bungalows. They do not nest in colonies, but two or three nests may sometimes be found in the same shed or verandah. The same site is used year after year. The eggs—two to four—are smaller replicas of those of the Common Swallow. Both sexes share in building the nest, incubation and care of the young.

HODGSON'S PIED WAGTAIL

Motacilla alba alboides Hodgson

PLATE 42

SIZE: About that of the Sparrow, with longer tail.

FIELD CHARACTERS: A slim and elegant black, white and grey bird seen running about on damp ground near water, constantly wagging its tail up and down. Gregarious.

In summer: upper parts black with white forehead and forecrown, and black earcoverts and sides of neck; underparts white with black chin, throat and breast. In winter the black back becomes grey and the black of chin and throat disappears, leaving only a black spot or 'bib' on breast. The female retains the grey back at all seasons, and she may easily be mistaken for the Masked Wagtail (*M. a. personata*).

Numerous other races of this wagtail visit the Indian Empire in restricted areas or more or less generally during winter. Only the two with the widest winter distribution need concern us here. The Masked Wagtail (*M. a. personata*), grey-backed at all seasons and with black ear-coverts, is very like the female of Hodgson's in appearance. Within our limits it breeds only in a limited area in Kashmir and the NWF. Province between 6,000 and 12,000 feet elevation.

The White Wagtail (*M. a. dukhenensis*), which breeds outside our limits, is the commonest here in winter. It has a grey back in summer as well as winter, and may be differentiated from the Masked and Hodgson's Wagtails at all seasons by its *white* (not black) earcoverts.

The male of Hodgson's Wagtail in breeding plumage must not be confused with the rather similar looking Large Pied Wagtail (*M. maderaspatensis*) commonly found at rivers and streams more or less throughout India and Ceylon, and up to 4,000 feet elevation in the Himalayas. The main points of difference are that the latter is larger—almost the size of the Bulbul—and has the forehead black (with only a conspicuous white eyebrow), whereas in the latter the entire front part of the head is white.

DISTRIBUTION: From Gilgit through Kashmir and Sikkim to E. Tibet. In summer between 6,000 and 10,000 feet, and occasionally higher; in winter at lower elevations, in the foothills and plains about their base from Kashmir to Assam, and in Burma.

HABITS: Hodgson's Pied Wagtail is extremely common in Kashmir during summer, and a pair or two may always be seen every little way along clear shingly streams studded with boulders, provided they are fairly smooth running and not torrential. The birds are quite at home amongst the house-boats on the Jhelum and on the lakes about Srinagar and may commonly be seen perched on their roofs. The birds run about on the banks and on the floating vegetation, sometimes wading into the shallows, to pick up the tiny insects cast up by the current, and they wag their tails incessantly. Occasionally, an individual will make a short nimble aerial sally above the spray to capture a winged insect, and then return to its base on some rock amid-stream. They seem to apportion off feeding territories and are quick to defend them against intrusion by others of their kind. The flight, like that of other wagtails, is a series of undulating curves caused by alternate flapping and closing of the wings. It is accompanied by a sharp *chichip, chichip*, etc.

NESTING: The season lasts from mid-May to the end of July. The nest is a fairly bulky cup of grass, roots, leaves, etc., lined with wool or hair. It is placed in a hole or pocket under a boulder or amongst a collection of drift rubbish on some islet in the bed of a stream. The eggs—normally four or five—are white with numerous small freckles and spots of reddish-brown, usually denser at the broad end.

THE INDIAN YELLOW-HEADED WAGTAIL

Motacilla citreola calcarata Hodgson

PLATES 42 AND 68

SIZE : About that of the Sparrow, but with a long tail.

FIELD CHARACTERS : Male in summer jet black above, bright lemon yellow or canary yellow below. Head and neck also bright lemon yellow. Some whitish in wings and tail. Female similar but paler; her back is brownish-black, and in some cases the yellow parts are almost whitish. Pairs on swamps, and streams through water-logged grass and flower meadows.

This and the following wagtails which are common over most of the Indian Empire—hills and plains—during the winter months—September–October to March–April—often keeping in mixed association, are simple enough to identify on their breeding grounds when in full adult summer plumage. In winter dress and in intermediate stages of moult, however, especially in the case of immature birds, their correct determination even with a specimen in the hand is notoriously difficult. And in the field it is seldom possible to be certain beyond a point.

The long-tailed Eastern Grey Wagtail (*M. cinerea melanope*) in winter is grey above with a greenish-yellow rump. Pale yellowish below, brighter on abdomen and under tail. Whitish eyebrows. In summer chin, throat and breast black in male, mottled in female. Breeds at 6,000 to 12,000 feet in Himalayas, and beyond our limits. Usually seen paired in summer, singly in winter.

The Indian Blue-headed Wagtail (*M. flava beema*) in summer has the back olive-green with conspicuous light blue-grey head, broad white supercilium and bright yellow underparts. Chin and throat white. Breeds Ladakh and SE. Russia. In winter gregarious; on water-logged ground.

The Black-headed Wagtail (*M. feldegg melanogriseus*) in summer plumage has crown, sides of head and nape black; underparts yellow; white line dividing black earcoverts from yellow throat. Differs from all yellow wagtails in absence of supercilium. Breeds Turkestan and Persia. Gregarious in winter; on wet grassland by *jheels*, etc.

As some individuals are already sufficiently advanced into breeding dress by the time they depart on northern migration, a knowledge of the summer plumages of the various species is useful for field identification.

DISTRIBUTION: Summer: the Himalayas from the NW. Frontier to Garhwal between 5,000 and 15,000 feet elevation. Winter: N. India south to Kutch, east to extreme E. Assam. Also Burma.

HABITS: In summer the Yellow-headed Wagtail is exceedingly common in Kashmir about all the swamps and *jheels*. It is perhaps the most aquatic of all the wagtails and is never seen away from water either in its summer or its winter quarters. Apart from this characteristic, it does not differ from other wagtails in general habits or behaviour. As in the others, its food consists entirely of tiny insects and molluscs.

NESTING: The season lasts from May to July. The nest is a neat cup of grass and roots thickly lined with wool or hair. It is well tucked away in some hollow at the foot of a little bush or among the roots of soft lush grass, in a squelchy water-logged meadow or on a diminutive islet in a stream running through such country. The eggs—normally four or five—are greyish-stone or pale khaki, with fine stipplings of a darker shade. Both sexes share in building the nest, incubation and feeding the young.

THE INDIAN TREE-PIPIT

Anthus hodgsoni Richmond

SIZE: About that of the Sparrow.

FIELD CHARACTERS: A sobre-coloured, slim wagtail-like bird, dark-streaked olive-brown above; fulvous- or creamy-white below heavily streaked on throat and breast with black. A whitish supercilium. White in outside tail-feathers conspicuous in flight. Sexes alike. Small scattered parties running and feeding on ground under trees, flying up into branches when disturbed.

The closely-allied Tree-Pipit (*Anthus trivalis*), breeding mostly in Europe and N. Asia (but also at high altitudes in the W. Himalayas), winters in considerable numbers practically all over the Indian Empire. It has no greenish tinge in the upper plumage, but is almost as heavily streaked underneath and has the same habits.

Several other species of pipits are also found in the Himalayas and hills of peninsular India, either more or less resident or as summer or winter visitors. In their dull general colour pattern they all resemble the female House-Sparrow or the larks, but they are slimmer and wagtail-like in shape. Many are so alike to look at that it is difficult to tell them apart in the field.

The one with the widest range is the Indian Pipit (*Anthus rufulus*). It is found in the Nilgiris and all the peninsular hills (as well as plains) and the Himalayas, up to about 5,000 feet elevation. It is distinguished from the Indian Tree-Pipit firstly by having no green tinge in the upper plumage, and secondly by being much less and finely streaked on upper breast. It frequents open country and fallow land, and does not perch on trees.

DISTRIBUTION: Within our limits breeding in summer in the Himalayas (8,000 to 13,000 feet elevation) from the Baluchi and Afghan frontiers and Gilgit, through Kashmir to Sikkim and probably Assam. In winter practically throughout India, Pakistan, Burma and Ceylon. Three races are recognized on shades of colouration and details of marking.

HABITS: In summer the Indian Tree-Pipit affects open grass-covered Himalayan slopes in the immediate vicinity of woods, open grassy glades sparsely forested with pines and birch, and scattered bushes and Alpine meadows beyond the limit of tree growth. In its winter quarters it frequents well-wooded country, deciduous as well as evergreen. Parties of four or five birds, or loose flocks of fifteen to twenty, are usually seen moving about silently and feeding on the ground under trees on the edge of forest, or under mango topes and groves of large banyan and shady trees on the outskirts of a village. They are partial to coffee and cardamom plantations in the S. Indian hills, and are also commonly met with feeding on forest footpaths and along shady highways everywhere. When disturbed the birds fly up into the branches of trees, often quite high, but soon descend to resume feeding. As it sits motionless on its elevated perch, its tail swings gently up and down like some mechanical toy. A single, sharp *tseep* is uttered from time to time, especially as the bird is flying away. The tail is constantly wagged up and down like a wagtail's, though somewhat less vehemently. In the breeding season the male has a pretty song uttered on the wing. The flight is undulating, similar to the wagtail's. Its food consists of weevils and other small insects.

NESTING: The season is May to July. The nest is a shallow cup of grass, roots and leaves, lined with finer grasses. It is placed on the ground in a shallow depression under shelter of a boulder or tuft of coarse grass. The eggs—normally four—are pinkish- or yellowish-stone, or greyish in ground colour, profusely speckled all over with reddish-brown. They show a wide range of variations.

THE RUFOUS ROCK-PIPIT

Anthus similis Jerdon

SIZE: That of the Bulbul.

FIELD CHARACTERS: A particularly large pipit, ashy brown above with dark streaks. Fulvous or sandy below, faintly streaked (almost unmarked) on breast. No white in tail. Singly, or widely scattered pairs on sparsely scrubbed hillsides and broken country. The large size usually distinguishes it from all other pipits. One which is only slightly smaller is Richard's Pipit (*Anthus richardi*). It has no ashy in its upper plumage, heavier markings on breast, conspicuously long legs, and an enormously elongated hind-claw. Moreover, it chiefly frequents swampy grassland bordering *jheels*, etc.—'snipe marshes'.

The Nilgiri Pipit (*Anthus nilghiriensis*) is a common resident at elevations between 5,000 and 7,000 feet in the Nilgiris, Palnis, High Range of Travancore, and other hills of SW. India. It affects the open rolling downs covered with short grass and rock outcrops that are such a feature of the higher portions of these hills. It is somewhat larger than the Sparrow, black-streaked fulvous above, tawny below with narrow, dark streaks on breast and sides. A pale rufous eyebrow and dull white in outer tail feathers may help further in recognition. This, and the Rock-Pipit, are sometimes met with on the same ground, but the latter prefers much more bare and rocky country.

DISTRIBUTION: A widespread species in Africa and Asia. Within our limits Baluchistan, Sind, the Himalayas from Gilgit to Sikkim between 4,000 and 8,000 feet (in summer), Nilgiris, Palnis and other SW. hills (4,000 to 7,000 feet). Three races are recognized on details of colouration and markings. In winter practically all over the Indian Empire (excepting Ceylon), and races then difficult to differentiate.

HABITS: The Rock-Pipit is less gregarious than many others of its tribe and is mostly met with as a solitary bird, or as a member of a widely scattered and loose party. It frequents open rugged grassy hillsides with outcrops of rock, or sparsely scrubbed broken country, and in winter may also commonly be seen in the plains feeding on the ground in standing wheat fields. When flushed in such cover the bird often leaps a few feet up into the air and leisurely hovers and zigzags aimlessly for some moments as if to investigate the cause of disturbance, before descending to perch on a stone or bush or back into the crops, a short distance away. These antics are also indulged in, obviously for pleasure, just before sunset. In the breeding season the males may constantly be seen soaring up a

few feet excitedly and parachuting back to earth. They have no song as
such, but a single note, *tseep*, is repeated at short intervals, sometimes
higher, sometimes lower in key. Otherwise there is nothing distinctive
about the habits or food of this pipit.

NESTING: The season over its summer range as a whole is between
April and July. The nest is of the usual pipit type, a cup of grasses lining
a depression under a tussock or rock on a sparsely scrubbed, open hillside. The eggs—three to five—are indistinguishable from those of the
Upland Pipit, stone-coloured or whitish in ground colour, heavily spotted
and blotched with greyish- or reddish-brown.

THE UPLAND PIPIT

Oreocorys sylvanus Blyth

SIZE: Somewhat larger than the Sparrow.

FIELD CHARACTERS: Very dark brown above; black-streaked creamy
below. Chin and throat white, bordered on either side by a thin black
streak, like a drooping moustache. Tail brown, with white in outside
feathers. All tail feathers noticeably pointed. Sexes alike. Singly on rugged
grassy Himalayan slopes.

Hodgson's Pipit (*Anthus roseatus*) breeds in Kashmir, Garhwal, and
eastward throughout the Himalayas at high elevations. It affects grass-
covered slopes often under open rhododendron and pine forest. In winter
it spreads out over the plains of N. India, Assam and N. Burma, haunting
the wet grassy margins of *jheels*, etc. In summer its throat becomes a
distinctive pinkish-brown. At all seasons it may be distinguished from
other pipits by its bright primrose-yellow axillaries, or underwing
feathers of the armpit region.

DISTRIBUTION: The Himalayas from the Afghan border and Kashmir
to Nepal, between about 4,000 and 10,000 feet elevation.

HABITS: The Upland Pipit is a resident species wherever found and
does not migrate to the plains in winter as other Himalayan-breeding
pipits do. It frequents steep grassy hillsides interspersed with bushes and
broken up by rocky ground, and is also found in open forest of Chir pine
on grass-covered slopes. Here the bird loves to perch rather hunched up
on some rocky outcrop and its long-drawn pleasant, but monotonous,
squeaking or 'tseeping' whistles—*witchee, witchee*, and so on—are the first
to attract the attention of the passer-by to it. In the distance it is

reminiscent of a saw being sharpened with a file! This call-note is repeated three to fifteen times at a stretch, strung out in what is presumably intended to be the bird's song. From time to time the performer flutters a few feet up into the air and descends on outstretched motionless wings back to the same or a nearby perch, singing the while, and recalling to mind the antics of the Red-winged Bush-Lark of the plains.

In its other habits and food it is a typical pipit.

NESTING: The season is mainly May and June. The nest is a pad or rough cup of coarse grass lined with finer grasses. It is concealed in a hollow under a stone, or at the foot of a tuft of grass or weeds in open pine forest or on a bare, rugged hillside. The eggs—three to five—are exact replicas of those of the Rock-Pipit, generally pale grey or buffy-stone in ground colour, covered with numerous freckles and small blotches of grey-brown, reddish-brown or purplish-brown.

THE HORNED LARK

Otocoris alpestris Linnaeus

PLATES 67 AND 71

SIZE: About that of the Bulbul.

FIELD CHARACTERS: Dark-streaked pinkish grey-brown above; white below. White forehead and throat. A broad black gorget or breast band. Bold black and white markings on face. A tuft of black pointed feathers springing like horns from each side of crown. The female is smaller with a broad whitish forehead and less contrasty markings on face. Flocks at high altitudes in Himalayas, near the snows. The large size, the black and white markings on the head, face and breast, and the two black upcurving horns render the identity of this lark unmistakable.

DISTRIBUTION: This species has a wide Palæarctic distribution in N. Africa, Europe and Asia. Within our limits it is found in Baluchistan and the high Himalayas, in Kashmir, Ladakh, Nepal, Sikkim, Tibet, etc. In summer at 10,000 to 15,000 feet elevation or more; in winter slightly lower. Two races are recognized: the large *longirostris* (Kashmir, etc.) and the smaller *elwesi* (Sikkim, E. Tibet, etc.). The latter, moreover, is paler, more pinkish above and less distinctly streaked.

HABITS: It may be questioned if the Horned Lark rightly deserves a place in a book of 'common' hill birds. It is certainly never likely to be found in the neighbourhood of any of the usual Himalayan hill resorts, since it lives at considerably higher altitudes. I include it solely for the

PLATE 59
THE EMERALD DOVE (*see* page 171)
About 3/8 Nat. Size

PLATE 60
THE WHITE-BELLIED OR SNOW-PIGEON (*see* page 172)
About 3/8 Nat. Size

PLATE 61
THE RUFOUS TURTLE-DOVE (*see* page 174)
About 3/8 Nat. Size

PLATE 62
THE WHITE-CRESTED KALEEJ PHEASANT (*see* page 175)
Hen (above). Cock
About 1/8 Nat. Size

benefit of the more enterprising visitor, whose enthusiasm may occasionally lure him off the beaten track in Kashmir and elsewhere to higher levels. For in its accustomed haunts the Horned Lark is far from uncommon, and the general poorness of bird-life there gives it added prominence. It goes about in pairs or small scattered flocks, frequenting the bare hillsides above the limit of trees, dotted with scanty tufts of grass, herbaceous plants and *Artemesia* bushes. The birds feed on the ground amongst the Alpine meadows or on the edge of melting snow patches lying on the slopes, often in company with snow-finches. On the high Tibetan plateau one of the Everest Expeditions found Horned Larks abundant and common about every village, feeding at the refuse heaps on the outskirts and in grass patches and cultivation around along with hill-pigeons, tree-sparrows and accentors. They also used to visit the Base Camp at 16,500 feet and pick up scraps from amongst the tents.

In the breeding season the male has a short, rather loud, but feeble and squeaky, song of disjointed strophes, of rather the volume and quality of a Willow-Warbler's song, resembling in parts also that of the Corn Bunting. It is uttered from a perch on a stone, and this bird does not seem to indulge in a song-flight like the Skylark. Its food consists of seeds as well as insects.

NESTING: The season is from May to July. The nest is a cup-like depression in the ground lined with roots, grasses, goats' hair, vegetable down, etc., under shelter of some tiny bush or grass tuft on a gently sloping hillside. Quite as often as not it is on open stony ground, completely unsheltered against the elements. The eggs—normally two or three—are yellowish-stone or yellowish-grey in ground colour, minutely speckled all over with some shade of brown, sometimes more densely at the broad end.

THE SMALL SKYLARK

Alauda gulgula Franklin

SIZE: That of the Sparrow.

FIELD CHARACTERS: A sober-coloured hen sparrow- or pipit-like bird with dark streaks and pale scaly marks in the brown upper plumage. Underneath pale fulvous with dark streaks on breast. Sexes alike. Pairs or parties—sometimes large flocks—in open country and about cultivation.

Readily differentiated from a pipit by its squatter build and shorter tail, and by the suggestion of a tuft on the crown. Also by the fact that it crouches on the ground when approached instead of running on in spurts. DISTRIBUTION: Wide in S. Asia. Within our limits Baluchistan and the Himalayas from Kashmir to Bhutan. Locally, up to 12,000 feet elevation in summer; down into foothills and adjacent plains in winter. Also practically throughout the Indian Empire. Resident, but also local migrant. Four races mainly concern us, viz., the Kashmir highland race *lhamarum*, the pale NW. Indian *punjaubi*, the darker continental Indian-Assam-Burma *gulgula*, and the larger Nilgiri-Travancore-Ceylon *australis*. HABITS: The Skylark is essentially a bird of grassy meadows, open terraced cultivation and fallow fields in the hills and plains alike, and often found even within the limits of large towns. It is met with running about and feeding on the ground in pairs or loose scattered flocks, often of considerable size in the cold weather. Its diet consists of seeds as well as insects. It has a peculiar fluttering flight.

In spite of its insignificant appearance, the Skylark is a songster of exceptional merit and well-deserved fame. With the approach of the breeding season the males commence their soaring and singing displays. From time to time—shortly after sunrise and in the evenings, but also throughout the day—the bird springs up from his perch on a clod or stone and soars almost vertically upwards on fluttering wings, the legs often dangling below, singing as he rises, higher and higher until almost out of sight. There he remains more or less stationary, hovering on vibrating wings, and continues to pour forth an unbroken stream of spirited, loud, clear and melodious warbling. The performance frequently lasts for over five minutes at a stretch. When it is over, the bird closes his wings and drops like a stone for some distance, then opens them out and flutters a bit, drops lower, and so on by steps until when within a few feet of the ground he shoots off at a tangent and comes to rest near the starting point. Several males may be thus soaring and singing in rivalry at the same time over a meadow or wheatfield, and the air resounds with their full-throated melody. The song is also occasionally uttered from a perch.

NESTING: The season varies somewhat over the different portions of its extensive range, but as a whole falls between February and July. In Travancore and Ceylon, however, they apparently breed in most months of the year. The nest is a cup-like depression in the ground, or a hoof-print, lined with grass, under shelter of a clod or tuft of grass in cultivation or grassland. The eggs—two to four—are normally pale brownish-grey or whitish, spotted and streaked with brown.

THE WHITE-EYE

Zosterops palpebrosa Temm. and Schlegel

PLATE 43

SIZE: Much smaller than the Sparrow.

FIELD CHARACTERS: A tiny, square-tailed bird, greenish-yellow above; bright yellow and greyish-white below. A conspicuous white ring round the eye; and slender, pointed, slightly curved bill. Sexes alike. Parties or flocks in wooded country, gardens, etc.

DISTRIBUTION: Practically throughout the Indian Empire excepting actual deserts. In the Himalayas commonly up to 6,000 feet elevation, and locally up to 8,000 feet. In all the peninsular hills up to their tops. At least six geographical races are recognized within our limits on slight differences of size and shades of colouration.

HABITS: The White-eye, or Spectacle-Bird as it is sometimes called, inhabits well-wooded country and is fond of orchards, groves of trees, and gardens. It is also found in humid evergreen forest. The birds keep in flocks of five to twenty, but occasionally as many as a hundred may be seen together. They are entirely arboreal and spend their time restlessly hunting for food amongst the foliage of lofty trees as well as in bushes, often clinging upside down or sideways like tits to peer into sprigs and buds for insects. But they occasionally descend to the ground to drink or bathe in a garden runnel. The birds constantly utter their feeble, plaintive cheeping or jingling notes, *cheer, cheer*, etc., as they move about the foliage or flit from one tree to another. The flocks break up during the breeding season, but even at this period small feeding parties keep together, the individual pairs detaching themselves off and on for their domestic concerns. The male at this season warbles a pretty little tinkling song, reminiscent of the Verditer Flycatcher's, from some exposed tree-top. Commencing almost inaudibly, the song grows louder, but presently fades out as it began.

Their food consists of tiny insects, spiders, fruits and berries. This is largely supplemented by flower nectar, of which the birds are inordinately fond and for which they may habitually be seen probing into flowers, both wild and cultivated. In the Nilgiris the white brush-like blossoms of the *Eucalyptus* trees always form an irresistible attraction, while *Woodfordia* and *Loranthus* flowers are patronized everywhere.

NESTING: The season is principally from April to July. The nest is a tiny cup of fibres neatly bound with cobwebs—a small replica of the oriole's nest—and similarly slung hammockwise in the fork of some thin

127

twig at the extremity of an outhanging branch. It is placed in a bush or tree between 5 and 10 feet from the ground, but occasionally higher. The normal clutch consists of two or three eggs. In colour they are a beautiful unmarked blue, sometimes with a cap of deeper blue at the broad end.

Both sexes share in building the nest, incubating and tending the young. Incubation takes ten to eleven days and the young leave the nest in a like period.

THE YELLOW-BACKED SUNBIRD

Æthopyga siparaja Raffles

PLATE 43

SIZE: Much smaller than the Sparrow.

FIELD CHARACTERS: A tiny, restless gem of a bird, glistening metallic green, crimson-scarlet, and violet-purple—with bright yellow rump, slender curved bill and long pointed tail. Female dusky olive-green above, dull ashy-green below, with short rounded tail. Pairs, on flowering trees in wooded country and gardens.

Mrs Gould's, or the Simla Yellow-backed Sunbird (*Æ. gouldiae*) is another little jewel distinguished from *siparaja* chiefly by its bright yellow breast.streaked with crimson, and metallic purple-blue throat, crown and tail. The female is sober-coloured brownish and greyish olive-green, with a dull sulphur-yellow rump. It is found in the Himalayas from the Sutlej Valley to extreme East Assam, Manipur, Naga and Chin Hills, etc., between 5,000 and 8,000 feet elevation.

Several other species of Yellow-backed Sunbirds also occur in the Himalayas. The males are all remarkably brilliant plumaged birds with long, pointed tails. The bright yellow rump is their chief uniting feature.

DISTRIBUTION: The Himalayas from about Dharamsala in the west to the NE. frontier. Assam, Burma (to about 7,000 feet elevation), and the Western Ghats (foothills to 5,000 feet) from about Khandesh to the Nilgiris and probably south of Travancore. Over this range at least four races are recognized on details of size and colouration. The Western Ghats race *vigorsi* is somewhat darker and has a patch of metallic violet behind the earcoverts in addition to the usual moustache-like streak. The crimson of its underparts, moreover, is finely streaked with yellow.

HABITS: The Yellow-backed Sunbird frequents forest and scrub jungle, preferably on hillsides or where cut up by overgrown ravines. It also enters hill-station gardens and may commonly be seen on flowering trees and shrubs, e.g. Hibiscus and Canna. The birds go about in pairs flitting tirelessly from flower to flower, hanging upside down and in all manner of acrobatic positions, nervously flicking their wings and probing with their bills for the nectar. A large variety of wild as well as garden flowers are visited in this quest and, along with other sunbirds, they play an important part in cross-pollinating them. Occasionally, a bird will hover in front of a flower for a moment, poised on rapidly vibrating wings like a hawk-moth, and insert its long, tubular tongue into the corolla to suck in the sugary liquid. A male Yellow-back clinging to a brilliant scarlet canna makes a particularly charming picture. In the case of such large flowers, where probing with bill and tongue is impracticable, the birds take a short-cut to the nectar by piercing a tiny hole with their bills at the base of the corolla. Insects and spiders are also eaten. The call notes of this sunbird, uttered as it hunts for food, pivots from side to side on its perch, or flies across from one shrub to another, is a sharp, harsh *chi-chwee*, rather like that of the Black-naped Blue Flycatcher.

NESTING: Over the greater part of its range the season is April to July. The Western Ghats race *vigorsi* breeds from May to October. The nest is a felted pear-shaped purse, usually with a projecting portico over the side-entrance, made of cotton down, rootlets, moss, lichens, etc.—looking like a mass of rubbish and cobwebs caught on a branch. It is suspended from a low bush or exposed roots on a minor landslip or on the out-scoured side of a ravine or stream in forest. The normal clutch is of two or three eggs. They vary greatly in appearance, a common type being white or pale cream, blotched or minutely flecked with some shade of brown, more densely at the broad end.

THE SMALL SUNBIRD

Cinnyris minima Sykes

PLATE 43
SIZE: Much smaller than the Sparrow.
FIELD CHARACTERS: A brilliantly-coloured little sunbird with bright

scarlet-maroon back, metallic dark green crown, and yellow underparts below the breast. Female olive-green above, dull yellow below. Her deep maroon rump is always a tell-tale feature. In non-breeding dress the male becomes like the female, but retains the metallic red lower back in addition to the rump. Pairs, on flowering trees and shrubs in evergreen forest country and gardens.

Confusion between males is only possible with the Purple-rumped Sunbird (*C. zeylonica*), but the *purple*, not red, rump of that species will dispel doubt. Moreover, the respective habitats of the two are totally different, the Purple-rumped being more a species of the plains.

DISTRIBUTION: Ceylon; the Western Ghats, Nilgiris, Palnis, and other hills of SW. India, from near Bombay to South Travancore.

HABITS: The Small Sunbird is restricted to the moist rain-forests of SW. India, and also extends some way into the contiguous semi-evergreen country. It chiefly frequents the foothills region, ascending thence to the highest forest-clad hills. In many localities in the *ghats*—Matheran for example—it is practically the only resident sunbird, and certainly the species most commonly seen. Like sunbirds in general, it lives largely on the nectar of flowers, both wild and cultivated, and it is a common visitor to hill-station gardens in the quest, flitting joyfully amongst the flowering shrubs, and even entering verandahs to investigate the hanging bell-like blossoms of *Fuchsia* and other potted plants. Flowering *Woodfordia* bushes and *Loranthus* clumps are in unfailing attendance, and the birds are extremely partial to flowers of the Coral Tree (*Erythrina*), so abundantly grown for shade in the tea and coffee plantations of S. India. Tiny insects and spiders are also eaten. A single metallic *chik* is constantly repeated as the bird hunts for food among the flower clusters and leaf-buds, clinging on upside down or sideways, or hovering momentarily in front of them. In the breeding season the male utters a squeaky song, *si-si-wee-si-si-siwee*, etc., for five to ten seconds at a stretch with short pauses, and frequently repeated, while he pivots or turns on his perch from side to side.

NESTING: The season in Ceylon is February to April; in Kanara from December to April; about Matheran and Khandala chiefly March to April; while in the Nilgiris it seems to breed in September and October. The nest is a small, neat ball or pouch with a side entrance, made of bright green moss and lichens and draped on the outside with cobwebs and pieces of pith and bark. It is hung from the tip of a horizontal branch of a sapling, or from a 'karvi' or *Strobilanthes* plant amongst undergrowth on a hillside, from 5 to 7 feet up. The eggs—always two—are rather like those of the Yellow-backed sunbirds: white, sparsely speckled all over with reddish, densely round the broad end where a ring is formed. Nest-building is done by the female alone, but the male occasionally accompanies her when she fetches nest material, and sings from a perch in the neighbourhood while she works.

THE LITTLE SPIDER-HUNTER

Arachnothera longirostra Latham

PLATE 43
SIZE: About that of the Sparrow.
FIELD CHARACTERS: A sturdy, oversized short-tailed sunbird, plain olive-green above, yellow below with greyish-white chin and throat. The very long, deeply-curved blackish bill is a conspicuous feature. Sexes alike. Pairs, on flowering trees, in evergreen forest areas.

The Indian Streaked Spider-Hunter (*A. magna*) is slightly larger than the sparrow, with a strongly-curved blackish bill, nearly two inches long, and stout bulbul-like yellow legs and feet. It is olive-yellow above, pale yellowish below, boldly streaked all over with black. It occurs in forest in the Himalayan foothills and up to 6,000 feet elevation, from the Sutlej Valley to E. Assam, and southward thence into Burma. It is fairly common locally, being invariably associated with wild banana plants. It utters a sharp *kikikikik*, reminiscent of the Striped Squirrel.
DISTRIBUTION: Western Ghats from about Belgaum (and probably further north—Khandala?), south through the Nilgiris, Palnis and associated hills to South Travancore. Also Eastern Bengal, Assam and Burma. Over this far-flung range only the one race, *longirostra*, is found.
HABITS: The Little Spider-Hunter is typically a denizen of humid evergreen forest areas. It frequents the low country as well as the hills up to about 5,000 feet elevation. It is usually met with in pairs, and sometimes two or more of these may be seen feeding in company. They keep to the forest, particularly on the edge of glades and clearings, and are inseparable from banana trees whether wild and growing on a hill-side, or cultivated in the proximity of outlying forest homesteads, or adjoining the cooly lines on tea, coffee and cardamom plantations. They are uncommonly fond of the nectar of banana blossoms and visit them regularly at all hours of the day, clinging to the purple bracts of the inflorescence upside down, and probing deep into the flower tubes with their specially adapted bills. Their diet consists largely of flower nectar.

A wide variety of flowers is visited in the quest, including *Loranthus* and *Erythrina*, and the birds doubtless help considerably in cross-fertilizing them. Insects and spiders are also eaten.

The normal call notes, uttered as the birds feed or flit from tree to tree, are a harsh *chee-chee*, rather like those of the Paradise Flycatcher or the Ashy Swallow-Shrike, but somewhat higher pitched and more musical. The song of the male in the breeding season is a metallic, colourless *which-which-which-which*, etc., repeated twice or three times per second and kept up for two minutes or more at a stretch. The volume of sound is slightly bigger than that of the Purple Sunbird.

NESTING: The season in Assam is principally May to August; in SW. India, February to May. The nest is a beautiful compact cup, about four inches deep, made of skeleton leaves, fine soft grass and vegetable down, neatly felted together. It is attached by its rim—like an 'inverted dome' globe of a street lamp—to the underside of a young green plantain, ginger or similar broad leaf by means of threads of vegetable cotton and cobwebs passed through the leaf and neatly knotted on its upper surface. The leaf thus forms the ceiling and roof of the nest. There is a semi-circular entrance hole on one side. The eggs—normally two, but occasionally three—vary from pinkish-white to salmon-pink in ground colour. They are finely but sparsely stippled all over with reddish except at the broad end, where the spots coalesce to form a ring. Both sexes share in building the nest and incubating the eggs.

THE FIRE-BREASTED FLOWERPECKER

Dicaeum ignipectus Blyth

PLATE 43
SIZE: Much smaller than the Sparrow.
FIELD CHARACTERS: A restless, tiny, brilliantly coloured creature, rather like a sunbird, but with shorter bill. Deep metallic bluish-green above, rich buff below with a greenish tinge. The bright crimson breast and the black patch below it are its chief distinguishing marks. Female olive-green above with a contrasting yellowish-green rump; buff below. Singly, on mistletoe clumps, etc., on trees in dense Himalayan forest.

Another brilliant coloured little flowerpecker with a slightly more restricted distribution in the Indian Empire is the Scarlet-backed *Dicaeum cruentatum*. Its whole upper plumage is scarlet-crimson, with glistening

PLATE 63
THE PAINTED BUSH-QUAIL (*see* page 177)
Female (behind).   Male
About 1/2 Nat. Size

PLATE 64
THE CHUKOR (*see* page 180)
About 1/4 Nat. Size

PLATE 65
SCULLY'S WOOD-OWL (*see* page 155)

R. S. P. Bates

PLATE 66
THE WHITE-SPOTTED FANTAIL-FLYCATCHER (*see* page 88)

Author

blue-green on the wings. Eyebrow, sides of head, throat and breast black; rest of underparts buff. The female is olive-brown and buff, with only her rump scarlet-crimson. It is found in the Himalayas (from plains level up to about 4,500 feet) from Nepal to the NE. frontier, Assam, Eastern Bengal, Chittagong and Burma. It frequents fairly open forest, orchards, and groves of trees about cultivation.

DISTRIBUTION: Himalayas from Sutlej Valley to NE. frontier, between 5,000 and 12,000 feet elevation. Also the Assam and Burma hills south to Tenasserim; Siam and parts of China. Only the typical race *ignipectus* is so far recognized within our limits.

HABITS: This lovely little flowerpecker frequents densely forested hills. Like the others of its tribe, it is a purely arboreal species and seldom, if ever, descends to the ground. It keeps mostly to the foliage canopy of the lofty forest trees, hopping tirelessly amongst the orchid clumps and mistletoe-like tree parasites (*Loranthus*) so abundant everywhere, searching for insects and spiders as well as berries. But sometimes it comes down into the underbushes in quest of food. Flower nectar also comprises a considerable proportion of its diet. The single call note *chik* is constantly uttered as the bird hops from twig to twig or flits across from one tree to another. This is varied from time to time by a shrill twittering which has been likened to the noise of rapidly opening and closing a pair of scissors.

NESTING: The season is from March to June. The nest is a beautiful pear-shaped little pouch with a round entrance hole on one side. It is composed chiefly of soft vegetable down compactly felted together in a fabric of considerable thickness, and is sometimes decorated on the outside with caterpillar droppings and scraps of green moss. It is suspended 12 to 20 feet off the ground from the twig of a small tree growing in a ravine in thick forest. The normal clutch consists of two or three eggs, white in colour and unmarked.

THE NILGIRI FLOWERPECKER

Dicaeum concolor concolor Jerdon

SIZE: Much smaller than the Sparrow.

FIELD CHARACTERS: A sobre-coloured flowerpecker dull olive-green above, pale greyish-white below with a faint yellowish tinge. General effect rather like a female sunbird, with short, slender, slightly curved *blackish* bill. Sexes alike. Singly, on *Lorathus* clumps in flower or fruit, in South-Western hills.

Easily confused with this species is Tickell's Flowerpecker (*D. erythro-rhynchos*) found in Ceylon, Assam and Burma, and all India except the arid tracts of the north-west. It occurs chiefly in the plains, but also ascends the Himalayas and peninsular hills to moderate elevations—in the former, locally up to 7,000 feet. It is differentiated from the Nilgiri species by being somewhat paler generally, but primarily by its *flesh*-coloured—not blackish—bill. In habits, food, voice, etc., the two are almost identical.

DISTRIBUTION: Nilgiris, Palnis and associated hill ranges, including those of Mysore and Travancore. Western Ghats possibly north to Khandala. From the foothills to the highest peaks. Other races of this flowerpecker, differing slightly in details of colouration but all possessing the dark bill, are found in the Himalayas from Nepal to Assam (plains level up to 7,000 feet), the hills of Burma and Assam, and eastward beyond our limits.

HABITS: This flowerpecker is particularly common in the Nilgiris and Palnis, but also abundant enough over the rest of its range. It affects well-wooded country both deciduous and evergreen, being found in *sholas* as well as among opener groves of trees in the neighbourhood of hillmen's habitations and about tea and coffee estates. Like its pink-billed cousin it is inseparable from the noxious tree-parasite *Loranthus*. The bird and the plant live together in a sphere of unabashed 'co-prosperity'. The one could not exist without the other. The flowerpecker is dependent for its food almost exclusively on the flower nectar and berries of the parasite; and the parasite in turn depends for its propagation entirely on the bird. The ripe *Loranthus* berries are swallowed whole and the slimy, sticky seeds presently excreted on to an adjoining branch or nearby tree. They soon sprout and drive their roots into the tissues of the host tree, which is deprived of its rightful nourishment, and sucked dry in course of time. Though small in size the bird is great in mischief and is indirectly responsible for considerable damage to orchard and forest trees. The usual call notes are a quick repeated *chik-chik-chik* uttered as the bird incessantly hops about on the *Loranthus* clumps. They are occasionally varied by a series of sharp twittering, which is ostensibly the bird's song.

NESTING: The usual months are February to May. The nest is a pear-shaped purse of felted vegetable down, typical of flowerpeckers of this genus. It is suspended from a twig at a moderate height, in fairly open wooded country or forest. The eggs, usually two, are white and unmarked.

THE SCALY-BELLIED GREEN WOODPECKER

Picus squamatus Gould

PLATE 44

SIZE: About that of the Pigeon.

FIELD CHARACTERS: A typical woodpecker with long, straight, stout, chisel-shaped bill and stiff wedge-shaped tail cross-barred brown and white. Dull green above with yellowish rump; whitish below with black scale-like markings. Top of head and crest crimson in male; black in female, mixed with greyish. Singly or pairs in Himalayan forest, running up trunks and branches of trees in a succession of jerky spurts.

The Little Scaly-bellied Green Woodpecker (*P. vittatus*) is rather similar looking but smaller (Myna +). It is a brighter grass-green above with a prominent bright yellow rump, some orange and a black patch on the nape. The head and crest of male and female differ in the same way as in *squamatus*. The tail is imperfectly barred. It is found in the Himalayas from Kumaon to E. Assam up to 5,000 feet elevation, and locally throughout India east of a line from Ambala to Mt. Abu, hills as well as plains. Also Ceylon and Burma.

The Black-naped Green Woodpecker (*Picus canus*), about the same size as *squamatus*, differs from it in the male having only the fore part of the head crimson, the hind part being black. The female has the forehead and crown black-streaked grey. The underparts are not 'scaly'. Found up to 8,000 feet elevation in the Himalayas west to east; also down into Assam and Burma.

DISTRIBUTION: Baluchistan, Afghanistan and Himalayas from extreme west to Sikkim, between 5,000 and 11,000 feet elevation, with a little seasonal altitudinal movement.

HABITS: Pairs of this fine woodpecker affect forest, both deciduous and evergreen, and also open well-wooded country and orchards. Like others of their kind, the birds are normally seen clinging to the trunks of trees with tail pressed on the bark like the third leg of a tripod. They work their way upwards directly or in spirals, in a series of jerky spurts, tapping with their bills from time to time to stampede insects lurking in the crevices of the bark, or to locate the hidden pupal galleries of boring beetles. The long, worm-like tongue, horny and barbed at the tip, can be shot out far beyond the bill-tip, and enables the grubs to be extracted from their holes. It also eats ants and will occasionally descend to the ground to pick them up, hopping about uncomfortably. Its flight is strong but markedly dipping, consisting of a few rapid noisy flaps followed by a short glide. Besides the loud drumming, produced apparently by rapidly striking the bill on a specially selected 'sounding board', this woodpecker has a clear, far-reaching high-pitched call normally of two notes, but sometimes of only one, and occasionally of three.

NESTING: The season is from mid-April to end of June. The nest-hole is usually cut into the trunk of a large tree 6 to 20 feet—sometimes up to 50 feet—from the ground. It consists of a horizontal tunnel, which turns down at right angles and ends in a widened egg chamber. The normal clutch is of five or six eggs, white, broad ovals.

THE HIMALAYAN PIED WOODPECKER

Dryobates himalayensis Jardine and Selby

PLATE 44

SIZE: About that of the Myna.

FIELD CHARACTERS: A black-and-white streaked, spotted and barred woodpecker with a red patch under tail. Back entirely black with a pure white patch on each shoulder. Crown crimson in male; black in female. Pairs, on tree-trunks in Himalayan oak and fir forest.

The rather similar-looking Brown-fronted Pied Woodpecker (*D. auriceps*) is also common in open oak and mixed forest in the Western Himalayas as far east as Nepal, between 2,000 and 7,000 feet elevation. It is slightly smaller and has the back cross-barred black and white. The crown in the male is golden-brown in front, crimson behind (on occiput). The female lacks the golden brown and crimson on the head.

The Fulvous-breasted Pied Woodpecker (*D. macei*) has a barred back as in *auriceps*, but the entire crown is crimson in male, black in female. It has, moreover, a fulvous breast. It is found in the Himalayas from Murree to East Assam, from the foothills up to about 6,500 feet. Also in Lower Bengal and about the northern end of the Eastern Ghats.

But the commonest pied woodpecker of India as a whole—found from about 2,500 feet in the Himalayas down through practically all the peninsular hills (and plains), as well as in Ceylon, Assam and Burma—is the Yellow-fronted Pied, or Mahratta, Woodpecker (*D. mahrattensis*). It is about the size of the bulbul, spotted black and white with brownish-yellow crown and a scarlet patch on abdomen and vent. The male has a scarlet occipital crest which the female lacks.

DISTRIBUTION: The Himalayas from Afghanistan to Garhwal, between

3,000 and 9,000 feet elevation. Two races are recognized: the Garhwal race *himalayensis*, darker and more rufous below, and the Kashmir *albescens* with the underparts paler and more greyish.

HABITS: This woodpecker affects well-wooded slopes of fir, oak, rhododendron and mixed forest, and is less often seen in opener country and orchards than the Brown-fronted species. It goes about in pairs and has the usual woodpecker habit of scuttling up the trunk and branches of trees in short spurts, tapping on the bark from time to time or digging into its interestices with its strong bill for grubs and insects. It works along the sides and undersurface of the moss-covered branches with great celerity, and occasionally slides down a few spurts in 'reverse gear' to investigate some likely flake of bark it has unwittingly passed by. Its diet also includes fruits and berries, and along with *auriceps* it has been observed habitually to eat quantities of seeds of the Chir pine (*Pinus longifolia*). The birds spend much time and energy in breaking open the cones, months before these are mature enough to open naturally and release the seeds.

NESTING: The principal months are April and May. The nest-hole is bored into a tree-trunk in forest from 6 to 14 feet above the ground. The normal clutch is of four or five eggs. Like all woodpeckers' eggs, they are white in colour and broad ovals in shape.

THE MALABAR GREAT BLACK WOODPECKER

Macropicus javensis hodgsonii Jerdon

PLATE 45

SIZE: About that of the House Crow.

FIELD CHARACTERS: A huge black-and-white woodpecker with crimson cheek-patches, forehead, crown and nuchal crest. In the female the crimson is restricted to the occiput and nape. The white rump and white underside, contrasting with the black of the remaining plumage, form an arresting feature in flight. Singly or pairs, on lofty tree-trunks in *ghat* forest.

A common woodpecker of the South Indian hills (also found throughout the Western Ghats) is Malherbe's Golden-backed (*Chrysocolaptes guttacristatus chersonesus*). It is about the size of the pigeon, golden-olive above with a copper tinge; white below more or less scaled and streaked with black. The large conspicuous crest is crimson in the male; black in the female, with white spots. Cheeks, chin and throat white with five narrow longitudinal stripes. The crimson rump and black tail complete its get-up. It frequents evergreen and moist deciduous forest tracts, chiefly the foothills and up to 6,000 feet elevation or more. It has a loud, discordant, trilling scream. Allied races are found in the Himalayas, Bengal, Assam, Burma and Ceylon.

It must not be confused with the much commoner and widely distributed Golden-backed Woodpecker (*Brachypternus benghalensis*) resident practically throughout the Indian Empire (excepting Burma) from the Himalayan foothills south, and found in fairly dry country at low elevations in all peninsular hills as well as plains. This is readily distinguished from Malherbe's Golden-back by being more golden-yellow above, and by its *black* instead of crimson rump. The crimson of the crest in both male and female is confined to the hind part (occiput) only. Its chin, throat and foreneck are black, spotted and streaked with white.

DISTRIBUTION: Throughout the Western Ghâts from Travancore to their extreme northern limit in the Surat Dangs; foothills and up to 4,000 feet elevation. Two other races occur in Burma, Siam, Malaya, Java, etc., but this bird itself is obviously a race of the Black Woodpecker (*Dryocopus martius*) of Europe.

HABITS: This magnificent woodpecker is confined to evergreen and moist deciduous forest tracts. Cardamom *sholas* and tea and coffee plantations in the South Indian hills with their lofty primary shade trees, and mixed timber and bamboo forest elsewhere, are amongst its favourite haunts. The birds go about in noisy scattered pairs or family parties of three or four, scuttling up and around the large tree-trunks in jerky spurts, tapping the bark and hunting for food in the typical woodpecker manner. Its wild resounding call of a single note *chiank*, evidently uttered by both sexes, is reminiscent of the *chee-ah* of the Oriole, but is louder and more metallic. It is repeated every two or three seconds, three or four times in succession as the bird climbs, or in its flight from one patch of forest to another. Besides this note it has a short ringing laugh of three or four seconds duration uttered on the wing, rather like that of the Malabar Grey Hornbill, also found in much the same habitats. Its loud and heavy tapping on the boughs and drumming are almost as unmistakable as its calls. Its food consists largely of the grubs of woodboring beetles. Its flight is stately and unhurried, with deliberate wing beats.

NESTING: The principal months are January and February. The nesthole is excavated by the birds in rotten tree-trunks between 35 and 50 feet up. The eggs—one to four—are white broad ovals.

THE SPOTTED PICULET

Vivia innominata Burton

PLATE 44
SIZE: Smaller than the Sparrow.
FIELD CHARACTERS: A tiny woodpecker with short, rounded tail; yellowish olive-green above; whitish below with half-moon-shaped black spots. Sides of head and neck whitish, relieved by a dark moustachial streak and a broad band from behind the eye. In the male the forecrown is black and orange; in the female olive like the rest of the upper parts. Pairs, on thin branches of shrubs, etc., usually in the mixed hunting parties of birds.

The Indian Pigmy Woodpecker (*Dryobates nanus*) is another diminutive species not uncommon in Ceylon and over a large part of Northern, Central and Southern India—plains as well as hills, including the Himalayas up to 6,000 feet elevation locally. It is about the size of the sparrow with normal stiff, wedge-shaped woodpecker tail. Blackish-brown above with white cross-bars; brownish-white below with dark, longitudinal streaks. A white stripe from above the eye to the side of the neck is conspicuous. The male has a scarlet streak on either side of the hindcrown, which the female lacks. The birds feed on the smaller topmost end branches of high trees, and on stems and twigs of shrubs and saplings, and are frequently seen in the mixed hunting parties of nuthatches, warblers, flycatchers and other insectivorous birds in forest.
DISTRIBUTION: The Himalayas from Dharamsala to the NE. frontier (foothills and up to 6,000 feet elevation; locally up to 9,000 feet), Assam, Burma and beyond both east and south. Hills of SW. India from Travancore to N. Kanara, and perhaps farther north. Two races chiefly concern us: the Himalayan *innominata* and the Nilgiri *avunculorum*. The former has brighter, orange-tinged upper parts, and paler, greenish head.
HABITS: This minute woodpecker inhabits the moist intermediate zone of vegetation between the deciduous and evergreen types, and is partial to low secondary jungle and tangled brushwood, especially where there is a good sprinkling of bamboo clumps. It is usually seen in pairs, and almost invariably as a member of the mixed hunting parties of small insectivorous birds that rove the forest. Careful scrutiny is necessary to distinguish it from tree-warblers and other similar coloured birds, among which it may easily be overlooked. They are active little birds running jerkily up and down or circling around the thin outer branches of shrubs and small trees, tapping on the bark now and again to stampede lurking

139

insects. Their actions are very like the nuthatches, and like them also they creep along the undersides of branches back downwards, or cling like an acrobat upside down. The normal call-note is described as a sharp, squeaky *spit spit*, frequently repeated. It also drums on rotten wood like other woodpeckers, producing a sonorous *br-r-r-r, br-r-r-r*, repeated persistently at short intervals. Controversy still rages as to whether the 'drumming' of woodpeckers is vocally produced or mechanical. In the case of so small a bird as this the sound produced certainly seems too loud and far-reaching to be solely due to hammering with the bill, but further observation is necessary.

NESTING: The season in the Himalayas is April and May. In Mysore I have taken a laying bird in January. The nest-hole is drilled into the branch or trunk of a sapling, or in a bamboo stem just below a node so as to provide a deep egg chamber—3 to 15 feet from the ground. The normal clutch consists of four white eggs, hard, glossy and blunt oval. Both sexes share in excavating the nest-hole and incubating the eggs.

THE GREAT HIMALAYAN BARBET

Megalaima virens marshallorum Swinhoe

PLATE 46

SIZE: Between the Myna and the Pigeon.

FIELD CHARACTERS: A gaudily-coloured bird with a large ungainly yellow bill. Plumage largely green, with a violet blue-black head and a scarlet patch under the tail. Underparts olive-brown, blue and yellow. Sexes alike. Singly or in parties. Exclusively arboreal.

The Blue-throated Barbet (*Megalaima asiatica*), about the size of the Myna, is chiefly grass-green with a stout greenish-yellow bill. The crown of its head is crimson, intersected by a black cross-band. Sides of head, throat and foreneck blue. A large crimson spot on either side of the foreneck and a small crimson speck near the gape confirm its identity. Its habits are typical of the barbets. This species is found throughout the Lower Himalayas from Dalhousie in the Punjab, eastward to lower Bengal and Assam, and down into Burma, from about plains level to 6,000 feet elevation. Its calls, *kutroo, kutroo*, etc., are rather similar to those of the Large Green Barbet.

DISTRIBUTION: The race *marshallorum*, which chiefly concerns us,

PLATE·67
THE KASHMIR SKYLARK (*see* page 126)

W. T. *Loke*

TURKESTAN ROCK-PIGEONS (*see* page 173)   *Author*

THE INDIAN YELLOW-HEADED WAGTAIL (*see* page 119)   *W. T. Loke*
Female in immature plumage with nest and young

PLATE 68

THE HIMALAYAN RUBYTHROAT (*see* page 61)   *W. T. Loke*
Female approaching nest with food

THE BROWN CRESTED TIT (*see* page 15)   *Author*
At nest

THE COMMON GREY HORNBILL (*see* page 148) *E. H. N. Lowther*
At nest

THE MALABAR PIED HORNBILL (*see* page 148) *E. H. N. Lowther*
At nest

PLATE 70

occurs throughout the Himalayas, west to east. In summer between 4,000 and 9,000 feet; in winter at lower elevations—in the foothills and plains about their base.

HABITS: Summer visitors to Himalayan hill-stations are doubtless far more familiar with the calls of this barbet than with its appearance. Its colouration makes it difficult to observe among the foliage of the tall trees it frequents. The bird is silent in winter, but it regains its voice as soon as the season warms up. Duets and choruses of its plaintive monotonous, far-reaching calls, *mewli, mewli, mewli* (also rendered as *peee-oh*), repeated about thirty times a minute *ad nauseam*, are amongst the commonest bird sounds in the lower Himalayas. To the hillmen of Garhwal it is known as *Mewli*. Another of its common notes is a quick-repeated *gyok-gyok-gyok*.

Its diet, as that of all barbets, consists of fruits and berries, but in winter when these become scarce it is supplemented by insects, including hornets. While ordinarily met with singly or in small parties, the birds band themselves into flocks in winter, often of as many as thirty individuals. Their flight is noisy, swift, strong, and dipping like a woodpecker's, being attained by a few rapid wing flaps followed by a short break.

NESTING: The season is principally April to July; earlier at lower elevations, later higher up. The eggs are laid in deserted woodpecker nest-holes, or in those excavated by the birds themselves. These are usually in upright branches of forest trees at heights of between 10 and 15 feet from the ground—sometimes considerably more. The holes are often 12 to 18 inches deep. The normal clutch is of three or four (sometimes five) pure white eggs, rather blunt ovals in shape.

THE SMALL GREEN BARBET

Megalaima viridis Boddaert

PLATE 46
SIZE: About that of the Myna.
FIELD CHARACTERS: A dumpy, heavy-billed grass-green bird with dark brown crown and nape. Chin and throat whitish. A band running back from the eye and a narrow cheek-stripe dark brown. Breast whitish, streaked with brown. Abdomen and undertail pale green. Small patch

of naked skin around eye, brown and inconspicuous. Sexes alike. Arboreal.

The Green Barbet (*Megalaima zeylonicus*) is a similar but slightly larger species (Myna +) which inhabits for the most part deciduous country, hill as well as plain. It is found in the Western Himalayas, Eastern and Western Ghats and other hills of peninsular India and Ceylon. It may be differentiated from the above by its head, neck, breast and upper back being brownish, streaked with white. Also by the large naked orange-coloured patch round the eye which extends to base of bill. Its loud call: *kor-r-r . . . kutroo, kutroo*, and so on, is almost indistinguishable from the Small Green Barbet's.

A closely related species, the Lineated Barbet (*Megalaima lineatus*), of the same size as the Green, occurs in the Lower Himalayas from about Mussooree to Assam, and in Burma. In this bird the pale shaft stripes are much broader. The bare skin round the eye is deep yellow and less in extent, not reaching to base of bill. Its call is similar to that of the above two.

DISTRIBUTION: Western Ghats from about Khandala (and perhaps farther north) to Cape Comorin, including the Nilgiris and Palnis, etc., and the heavy rainfall portions of the Eastern Ghats (e.g. Shevaroy Hills, Chitteri Range, etc.). Commonest and most abundant between 1,500 and 2,500 feet elevation.

HABITS: Within its range the Small Green Barbet occupies both deciduous and evergreen types of country, but it is most partial to the zone intermediate between the two. It is usually seen in pairs and small parties. Fairly large gatherings will collect on the various wild fig trees when in ripe fruit, whether in forest or in a grove near a village. This barbet is a minor pest in S. Indian coffee plantations and sometimes does considerable damage. The birds swallow large quantities of the ripe 'cherries' and disperse the seeds ('berries') far and wide. As these are voided individually and not in bunches (as by monkeys and jackals) it is not possible or worthwhile to collect them and they just mean so much loss to the grower. Besides fruits and berries, it also eats insects on occasion. Moths and flying termites are taken in the air by launching ungainly sallies after them from a perch. During the hot weather the birds call obstreperously all day long, and sometimes also during moonlit nights. The jungle resounds with their well-known monotonous call, *kor-r-r . . . kutroo, kutroo, kutroo*, reiterated *ad nauseam*. As soon as one bird begins, another in the distance is sure to join in at once and the uneven duet is kept up for a considerable time.

NESTING: The season is a very protracted one, and ranges between February and June. The birds usually excavate their nest-hole themselves. The site for it is a branch or snag at almost any height from the ground. Sometimes a suitable branch has several entrance-holes, presumably cut in successive seasons. The eggs—two to four—are pure white, and the usual rather regular ovals characteristic of the barbets.

THE CUCKOO

Cuculus canorus Linnaeus

SIZE: About that of the Pigeon—somewhat slimmer.

FIELD CHARACTERS: General appearance, pointed wings and speed and manner of flight very hawk-like.

Above dark ashy-grey. Chin, foreneck and breast pale ashy; rest of lower parts white, cross-barred with blackish. Female similar but somewhat browner above with the upper breast pale brownish. Rarely, she is of a very different colouration—mottled chestnut and black, known as the 'hepatic' phase.

Several other cuckoos, confusingly similar to look at, occur in the Himalayas as well as in the peninsular hills (and plains). They can best be differentiated by their calls, heard chiefly during their breeding seasons.

The Indian Cuckoo (*Cuculus micropterus*), of about the same size, is distinguished by a subterminal black band on the tail which *canorus* lacks. It has a distinctive four-noted call rendered variously as *orange-pékoe, cross-word-puzzle, ham-sōta-tha* (Anglo-Indian Hindustani!) repeated *ad nauseam*.

The Himalayan Cuckoo (*Cuculus optatus*), slightly smaller, has a call very like that of the hoopoe, but louder and of four notes instead of three, commencing with a subdued *hook*, thus: *hook . . . po-po-po*.

The Small Cuckoo (*Cuculus poliocephalus*), smaller still (about equal to a small dove), has what Whistler describes as 'a wild screaming note'. It is an unmusical chattering of six notes repeated several times in descending scale. Osmaston syllabifies it as '*That's your smoky pepper*'. This is perhaps the commonest cuckoo about Darjeeling.

The Large and Common Hawk-Cuckoos (*Hierococcyx sparverioides* and *H. varius*) are cross-barred with brown underneath and have a broadly barred tail. They look very like the Shikra Hawk, and are the producers of the much-maligned aggravating 'Brain-fever' screams.

DISTRIBUTION: Found practically throughout the Old World, either as resident or seasonal migrant. Besides the typical race which is the same as in Europe, we have two slightly differing races found within Indian limits, viz., the doubtful Asiatic—*C. c. telephonus* (Himalayas) and the Khasi Hills Cuckoo—*C. c. bakeri* (Assam).

HABITS: The cuckoo inhabits orchards and open cultivated country interspersed with trees. It is a resident in some areas, a marked seasonal migrant in others; but being mostly silent when not breeding its wanderings are not easy to follow. In the Lower Himalayas it arrives in March or April, breeds, and is mostly gone by the middle of July. Its food consists chiefly of hairy caterpillars taken off the branches of trees or on the ground. The call, *cook-koo*, *cook-koo*, repeated a great many times, is familiar to most hot-weather visitors to the hills, especially the Himalayas. It is occasionally varied by *cook-cook-koo* and by a variety of harsh throaty croaks and chuckles, particularly when a male is chasing off a rival. While calling the tail is partly spread and cocked, the wings drooped at the sides and the bird pivots or oscillates lightly from side to side like a clockwork toy. Sometimes the tail is depressed and the rump feathers fluffed out. Occasionally, the call is also uttered on the wing. The female does not say *cook-koo*, but she has a series of peculiar loud notes for which perhaps 'water-bubbling' is the most suggestive description.

NESTING: The 'parasitic' habit of the cuckoo has been well known from ancient times. The female is promiscuous in her sex relations. No nest is built, the eggs being deposited in the nests of a large variety of other birds, mostly much smaller than herself, and then left to be hatched by the dupes. Laughing-thrushes, pipits and warblers are some of the normal fosterers. In colour and markings cuckoos' eggs usually resemble those with which they are laid. The newly-hatched cuckoo possesses a sensitive patch on its back by means of which it manages to heave its rightful companions over the edge of the nest, thereby monopolizing the attention of its foster-parents. Each female cuckoo may lay eighteen to twenty eggs in a single season, perhaps in as many different nests. She apparently lays only in the nests of such species as she herself was nurtured by. The methods of inserting eggs into seemingly inaccessible nests, and many other problems connected with the parasitic habit, are ably discussed in Mr E. C. Stuart Baker's recent book *Cuckoo Problems*, which may be recommended to all bird students in India.

THE SLATY-HEADED PARAKEET

Psittacula himalayana Lesson

SIZE: Slightly larger than the Myna, with a long, pointed tail.

FIELD CHARACTERS: A slender green parakeet with dark slaty head, red shoulder patches, the typical deep hooked bill (red and yellow), and bright yellow tips to the pointed tail feathers. The female has the head a paler grey and she lacks the red shoulder patches. Screaming parties in forest trees.

The Blossom-headed Parakeet (*Psittacula cyanocephala*) is of somewhat smaller size, but of very similar general appearance. It has a bright bluish-red plum-coloured head instead of slaty-grey, and *white* tips to its pointed tail feathers instead of yellow. The female is confusable with the female of the slaty-headed species, but may be differentiated by the white instead of yellow tail tip. The two species frequently occur together up to about 5,000 feet in the Himalayas, the Blossom-head extending also over most of the peninsular hills as well as plains.

DISTRIBUTION: The Himalayas from Kashmir to Assam, between 2,000 and 10,000 feet seasonally, and through South Burma to Tenasserim. Two races are recognized: the Himalayan (*himalayana*), with bright yellow tail-tips, and the Burmese (*finschii*), with dull pinkish-yellow tips and other minor differences.

HABITS: Like the more familiar Blossom-head, this parakeet keeps to well-wooded country and forest, in family parties and small flocks. It seldom bands itself into large flocks as the crop-destroying rose-ringed species of the plains often does. Its food consists chiefly of wild fruits, but the birds occasionally also do some damage in hill orchards. Cones of the Chir pine are commonly eaten. The flight is swift and direct, and usually accompanied by a high-pitched double call-note rather like the interrogative *tooi?-tooi?* of the Blossom-head, but harsher and quite distinctive.

NESTING: This species commonly nests up to about 7,000 feet all along the Himalayas between April and June. The eggs—four to six in number —are the usual round ovals—pure white in colour. They are laid in an unlined chamber at the end of a tunnel (like a woodpecker's nest), in the trunk or branch of a tree at some height from the ground. The tunnel is usually excavated by the birds themselves. They do not normally nest in colonies, but it is not uncommon to find two or three pairs occupying holes in apartment-house fashion in the same tree, or in other trees in close proximity. These parakeets are popular as cage birds, and nestlings are commonly hawked for sale in hill-station bazaars.

145

THE BLUE-WINGED PARAKEET

Psittacula columboides Vigors

PLATE 47

SIZE: About that of the Myna; slenderer, and with a long, graduated pointed tail.

FIELD CHARACTERS: A greyish- or bluish-green (rather than yellowish-green) parakeet, with pinky-grey crown, back and breast, and a brilliant blue-green and black collar. Conspicuous blue wings and tail; the latter tipped yellowish. The female lacks the blue-green collar and the dove-grey back and breast. Small flocks in forest.

DISTRIBUTION: The Western Ghats from about Khandala down to S. Travancore, including the Nilgiris, Palnis and the Mysore, and associated hill ranges. From plains-level to about 5,000 feet elevation.

HABITS: The Blue-winged Parakeet is chiefly a dweller of evergreen hill forest above 1,500 feet, though occasionally it descends lower and even enters deciduous jungle. It feeds on various fruits on the lofty forest trees, not infrequently commits serious ravages on the hillmen's crops of vetches and jowar in *taungya* clearings or *poddus*. The birds are also very fond of flower nectar, and may invariably be seen clambering about the end branches and biting into the blossoms of *Grevillea* and *Erythrina* trees planted for shade in coffee estates. It has a harsh double-noted call reminiscent of the Paradise Flycatcher's, but louder and more penetrating. This is chiefly uttered as the birds dash through the forest, twisting and turning their way through the enormous tree trunks.

Under the name of 'Bababudan Parrot' this species is highly prized as a cage bird by fanciers in Mysore and neighbouring areas. It has acquired spurious reputation as a talking paragon, and is credited with being able to converse with human beings in Arabic! The basis for this widespread belief seems to be the fact that one Babuddin, a holy pilgrim from Mecca who settled on the Bababudan Hills of Mysore about a hundred years ago (and incidentally first introduced coffee-growing from Yemen), kept some local parakeets whom he taught to recite verses from the Koran. These birds were afterwards released or escaped, but they remained in the neighbourhood of the holy man's establishment and were regularly fed by him. They excited the wonderment of the visiting devotees, who carried the tale back with them and suitably garnished and broadcast it far and wide as proof of the saint's miraculous piety!

NESTING: The season ranges between January and March. The nest site is a hole in a tree-trunk in forest at heights between 20 and 100 feet from the ground. Lofty ironwood trees (*Mesua ferrea*) seem to be particularly favoured, although it must take the birds a great deal of time and labour to cut into the hard wood of this species. The normal clutch is of four typical round white parakeet eggs.

THE BLUE-BEARDED BEE-EATER

Alcemerops athertoni Jardine and Selby

PLATE 48
SIZE: About that of the Myna.
FIELD CHARACTERS: A large grass-green bee-eater with light blue forehead, throat and upper breast, and buffy underparts. No pin feathers in tail. Sexes alike. Pairs or small parties in forest and well-wooded country.
DISTRIBUTION: The Himalayas (from foothills up to about 5,000 feet) from about Dehra Dun to East Assam and down through Burma. Western Ghats from Belgaum south to Travancore, Mysore hills, Nilgiris(?) and Palnis. Parts of the Central Provinces (Pachmarhi, Satpuras, etc.), Eastern Ghats (Shevaroy Hills, Chitteri Range, etc., Vizagapatam Ghats). Resident and local migrant.
HABITS: This large and handsome bee-eater is principally a denizen of forest—chiefly evergreen and wet deciduous. It affects hilly country or where cut up by steep-sided ravines densely overgrown with secondary scrub and with a sprinkling of large trees. Pairs or small loose parties keep to the canopy of tall trees, whence they make aerial sallies after flying insects such as bees and wasps, sailing gracefully back to the base after each capture. They are partial to leafless flower-laden Silk Cotton trees for the sake of the insects that visit them. These are taken off the blossoms as well as on the wing. The dipping or undulating flight, seemingly less swift than that of the Small Green Bee-Eater, is very reminiscent of the Himalayan and Green Barbets'. It consists of a few rapid wing beats, followed by a short pause of sailing. Its harsh, guttural call notes—*kor-r-r, kor-r-r*—resemble those that preface the *kutroo, kutroo* calls of the Large Green Barbet, but are deeper in tone. Sometimes these are followed up by other quick-repeated throaty notes, the bill pointing skywards and the bunch of elongated glistening blue throat-feathers—the beard—standing away from the breast. This is what may be called the bird's song.

147

NESTING : The season covering most of its range is February–March to August. The nest is an unlined chamber at the end of a tunnel bored by the birds into the precipitous bank of a forest ravine or landslip, or in the face of an earth-cutting for a hillside contour path. Occupied burrows invariably have a quantity of undigested cast-up insect remains lying outside below the entrance. The eggs—four to six—are pure white, round, and with a fair gloss. They closely resemble the eggs of the White-breasted Kingfisher. Both sexes share in feeding the young.

THE GREAT HORNBILL

Dichoceros bicornis Linnaeus

PLATE 70

SIZE : About that of the Vulture.

FIELD CHARACTERS : A large pied black-and-white bird with an enormous horn-shaped black-and-yellow bill. This is surmounted by a peculiar broad double-peaked helmet. The broad black subterminal band across the white tail, white neck, and largely black underparts, are points to look for. Sexes alike. Singly or pairs in primeval evergreen forest.

Two other hornbills that are sometimes mistaken for this species are: the Malabar Pied (*Anthracoceros coronatus*) and the Large Indian Pied (*A. malabaricus*). Both are of equal size and considerably smaller than the Great, if compared side by side. The helmet above the bill in these two species is narrow and ends in a single point. Their black necks and largely white underparts will further distinguish them from the Great Hornbill. In *coronatus* the outer tail feathers are all white; the helmet compressed and flat-sided. In *malabaricus* the outer tail feathers are black with white tips; the sides of the helmet bulge outwards (convex).

Our two grey hornbills also need to be mentioned here: the Common Grey (*Tockus birostris*) and the Malabar Grey (*Tockus griseus*). They are considerably smaller (about equal to the Kite) and of more or less uniform slaty-grey or slaty-brown colour. The former is widely distributed in the peninsula; the latter confined to the heavy rainfall areas of the Western Ghats. *Birostris* possesses, *griseus* lacks a helmet on top of its bill.

DISTRIBUTION : Western Ghats from about Khandala to South Travancore. Himalayas (from foothills up to about 5,000 feet elevation) from Kumaon to Assam. Burma, and through the Malay Peninsula to Sumatra. Northern birds are larger and will presumably need to be recognized as a separate race.

ELWES' HORNED LARK (*see* page 124)   *Author*
Female on nest

.TIBETAN RAVENS (*see* page 1)   *Author*
Scavenging on nomadic shepherds' camp site

PLATE 71

PLATE 72.
THE HIMALAYAN GRIFFON VULTURE (*see* page 159)

W. T. *Loke*

HABITS: The Great Hornbill frequents heavy evergreen forest country in pairs or small parties of three to five individuals. Large gatherings sometimes collect on wild fig trees to feed in company with other frugivorous birds. Solitary males are commonly met with in the breeding season while their walled-up mates are busy incubating the eggs. Their flight is laboured and noisy, consisting of a few heavy wing beats followed by a short glide. The loud 'hasping' noise produced by the pinions carries a tremendous distance. So do the deep, harsh roars and croaks which the birds utter. The hillsides and forest-clad valleys reverberate with their loud resonant calls: *tok, tok*, and so on. When uttering these, the neck is stretched upwards and the bill points to the sky. The roars are responsible for its Malayali name *Malamōrakki*, which apparently means 'Mountain-Shaker'. Its diet consists of forest fruits of every description, to which reptiles, rodents and large insects are freely added. The morsel is seized in the tips of the mandibles, tossed up in the air and caught in the gullet and swallowed entire.

NESTING: The season is January to March in the south; March-April over the rest of its Indian range. A large, natural hollow is selected in a lofty tree in dense evergreen forest, often 60 feet or more from the ground. Within this, the female imprisons herself, using the flat sides of her great bill as trowel to wall up the entrance with her droppings, which duly harden to the consistency of cement. Only a narrow slit is left, through which the cock assiduously feeds her throughout the period of her incarceration. After the young hatch out, the hen emerges from her self-imposed confinement, the wall is built up again, and thenceforward she assists her mate in feeding the young. While foraging for his incubating wife, the cock is extremely circumspect in his comings and goings to the nest so that it is not easy to locate one. But its presence is often betrayed by the droppings lying on the ground or on bushes underneath the site, squirted out by the young through the feeding window.

The eggs, usually two, are white at first, but become stained to a dirty yellowish brown as incubation proceeds.

All our hornbill species have more or less the same remarkable nesting habits.

THE MALABAR TROGON

Harpactes fasciatus Pennant

PLATE 49
SIZE : About that of the Myna, with a longer tail.

FIELD CHARACTERS: A strikingly coloured bird with a longish, broad and square-ended tail. Male: head, neck and breast blackish brown. Underparts brilliant crimson-pink, with a white gorget dividing them from the breast. Back and upper parts yellowish-brown. The female is duller with the underparts orange-brown instead of crimson.

Pairs in evergreen or wet deciduous jungle.

The male of the allied Red-headed Trogon (*Harpactes erythrocephalus*) differs in having the head, neck and breast deep crimson, and the underparts brighter and lighter crimson. Back and upper parts chiefly rusty-brown. The female has the head, neck and breast dull orange-brown; remainder of underparts crimson as in the male. The white in the outer tail feathers and on the wings of both sexes shows up conspicuously in flight. This trogon replaces the Malabar species in the Eastern Himalayas (between about 1,500 and 5,000 feet elevation, as at Shillong) from Nepal to Assam and down through Burma to Tenasserim.

DISTRIBUTION : The Sahyadris or Western Ghats from West Khandesh to South Travancore (from plains-level up to about 5,000 feet elevation), Nilgiris, Palnis, Mysore hills and associated ranges. Also West Bengal and Chota Nagpur, and south through the Vizagapatam Ghats to about the mouths of the Godavari River.

In Ceylon this race, *malabaricus*, is replaced by the endemic typical *fasciatus*, which is smaller and much greyer on head and neck.

HABITS : This beautiful trogon affects heavily-forested tracts, both evergreen and wet deciduous. In the latter, mixed bamboo jungle forms the favourite habitat. It is usually seen singly or in scattered pairs, sometimes fairly high up in trees or on bamboo culms, but more often in moderate secondary growth or even in low scrub. The birds flit gracefully from branch to branch, or from one tree to another. They turn and twist in the air after winged insects with the agility of the Paradise Flycatcher, and sometimes also pick off their quarry from the trunks and branches. Trogons are shy and retiring birds, and are silent except for some curious low mewing calls which they occasionally utter. These are often the first indication of their presence in a forest patch. They have a knack of always presenting their sober-coloured backs to the observer, and as they perch upright and motionless among the saplings, it is not easy to spot them in passing unless a bird flies. Their food consists largely of beetles and cicadas. They are rather crepuscular, and may frequently be seen hunting till well after evening dusk.

NESTING: The season is principally from February to May. For laying in, the birds normally select natural hollows in tree stumps in heavy forest, as a rule under 20 feet from the ground. But I have seen a nest which was an untidy flimsy platform of rotten twigs, etc., slightly cupped in the centre (rather like a dove's nest), wedged in at a height of about 8 feet between a growing sapling and a sweeping stem of rattan cane. The normal clutch is of two to four eggs, pale ivory white, unspotted and well glossed. Both sexes share in incubation.

THE ALPINE SWIFT

Apus melba Linnaeus

PLATE 50
SIZE: Between the Bulbul and the Myna.
FIELD CHARACTERS: A slim, sooty-brown swift with white underparts and very long narrow wings, bow-shaped in flight. A brown band across the breast provides a good identity mark. Short, square-cut tail (not forked like the swallow's). Sexes alike. Loose parties hurtling at terrific speed about grassy hillsides and precipitous cliffs.

Two other large swifts of about the same size must be distinguished from it: (1) White-throated Spinetail (*Chaetura caudacutus*) and (2) Brown-throated Spinetail (*Chaetura giganteus*). Both are chiefly brown and metallic black. Their tail feathers end in stiff needle-points. In (1) the centre of the back is white; in (2) sandy brown. Both have brown undersides with a white patch under the tail (coverts). In (1) the chin and throat are white; in (2) brown. The White-throated Spinetail occurs throughout the Himalayas; the Brown-throated in the Travancore hills, Nilgiris, Palnis, and associated ranges of South India. They are amongst the world's fastest fliers and estimated to attain well over 150 miles per hour. The sound of their wings as they hurtle through the air can be heard a long distance away.

In general habits they resemble the Alpine Swift, but they nest within the hollow decaying trunks of large trees in forest.

Several smaller swifts are also met with in the hills: (a) the Eastern

Swift (*Micropus apus pekinensis*) is somewhat smaller than the bulbul, and much slimmer, with long, pointed, narrow wings. It is dark brown with a white chin and throat (Himalayas).

(*b*) Blyth's White-rumped Swift (*Micropus pacificus leuconyx*) of the Himalayas and Assam (probably also South Indian hills) is roughly the same size as (*a*). Blackish-brown with some white squamation on the underparts. A conspicuous white rump and whitish chin and throat give it marked resemblance to the smaller House-Swift (*Micropus affinis*) of the plains. But the House-Swift has no white on the rest of its underside. Also its tail is square-cut and not forked as in (*b*). In some localities the House-Swift is also found in the hills—Himalayan as well as peninsular.

Several species of the so-called Edible-nest Swiftlets (*Collocalia*) are found in the Himalayas, as well as in the Nilgiris, Palnis, and associated hill ranges of South India. They are small sooty-brown birds, rather like palm-swifts on the wing, but with square instead of forked tails. Their flight—rapid wing beats—is very reminiscent of a pipistrelle bat's. Usually seen hawking insects in loose scattered 'flocks'.

DISTRIBUTION: Himalayas, and more or less throughout India and Ceylon. Local and irregular. Two races are recognized: the typical South European-Himalayan *melba*, and the darker and smaller peninsular *bakeri*.

HABITS: The seasonal migrations and local wanderings of this magnificent swift are as yet little understood. Its phenomenal speed on the wing enables it to cover such vast distances in the course of its daily round of feeding that the true significance of its sporadic appearances and disappearances is not easy to interpret.

The birds spend the daylight hours in hawking winged insects high up in the air. Cloudy, overcast weather or a shower of rain invariably brings them lower, near the ground Their food consists of hemipterous bugs and other insects captured entirely on the wing. They drink water by skimming along the surface of a forest pool or stream, flying butterfly fashion with wing-tips quivering above the back, and scooping up a droplet from time to time in the bill. In common with other swifts, they have the characteristic habit of 'balling' up in the sky at sunset in a close-packed flock, wheeling and tumbling playfully to the accompaniment of shrill, joyous screaming notes—*chee, chee*, etc.

The birds roost at night in fissures of cliffs and rock scarps, clinging at an angle to the rough surface. On account of the structure of its foot—all four toes directed forwards—a true swift cannot perch in the same way as a swallow.

NESTING: The season in the Himalayas is apparently May and June.

In South India the race *bakeri* nests in December–January. One well-known breeding place is the cliffs flanking the Gersoppa or Jog Falls in Mysore. The nests are built usually in colonies inside fissures of cliffs. It is a half-saucer shaped structure when stuck against a rock face, and a concave pad when placed upon a ledge. It is made of wind-blown feathers and straw collected in the air and agglutinated with the birds' saliva. Mating also takes place in mid-air. The eggs—two to four—are pure white, long, narrow ovals.

THE LONG-TAILED NIGHTJAR

Caprimulgus macrourus Horsfield

PLATE 51

SIZE: Between the Myna and the Pigeon.

FIELD CHARACTERS: A soft-plumaged, long-winged, owl-like bird, brownish-buff mottled with rufous and black, producing a remarkably disruptive pattern. In the hand, the male is distinguishable from other nightjars by a white spot on the first four primary wing-quills, and white tips to the two outermost pairs of tail feathers. In the females these white markings are buff. Legs feathered down to the toes. Singly, squatting on ground in shady nullahs by day; hawking insects in noiseless wandering zigzag flight at dusk.

Two other nightjars are commonly met with on the hills: (1) Franklin's (*Caprimulgus monticolus*) and (2) the Jungle Nightjar (*C. indicus*); the latter in the peninsular hills only, but Franklin's up to about 6,000 feet in the Himalayas as well. They resemble each other superficially and are difficult to differentiate in the field except by their calls.

Franklin's Nightjar utters a loud penetrating *sweesh* or *chweep*, rather like a whip-lash cutting the air, chiefly at evening dusk and dawn. This is delivered both on the wing, and from the ground or a post or tree. The Jungle Nightjar commences calling at dusk and continues more or less throughout the night, especially if moonlit. Its call is a not unpleasant *ūk . . . krūkroo*, repeated monotonously every two seconds or so for half an hour or more at a stretch. This call is sometimes varied by a quick-repeated *chuckoo-chuckoo-chuckoo*, three to twelve times, at the rate of about two calls per second. The series is repeated again and again with a break of a second or two after each run.

DISTRIBUTION: Himalayas (up to about 8,000 feet). from the NWF.

Province to Assam. Peninsular and South Indian hills, with also large tracts of the intervening forested country. Burma and Ceylon. The three races that chiefly concern us are the smaller southern race *atripennis*, the larger N. Indian *albonotatus*, and the pale Burmese *bimaculatus*. The race occupying Ceylon is apparently the typical *macrourus* of Java.

HABITS: This nightjar, like the others, is purely crepuscular and nocturnal. It spends the day squatting among the dry leaves in some shady forest ravine, where its colouring camouflages it perfectly. It emerges at evening dusk, and is on the move all through the night and till shortly before sunrise. Its food consists of moths and beetles, including some very large ones. These are captured on the wing, the bird turning and twisting in their pursuit and dodging the tree trunks and other obstacles in forest with amazing dexterity. They may commonly be seen squatting in the middle of forest roads after dusk, their eyes gleaming ruby in the beam of the oncoming headlights, and are adept at dodging clear when the car is almost upon them.

The call of the Long-tailed Nightjar is a very loud and resonant *chaunk*, aptly likened to the blows of an adze on a wooden plank, or even the sound of felling a tree. It is repeated any number of times from one to fifty, at the rate of about one a second. It is usually uttered from up in a bare branch with the bird crouching along it—not perched crosswise. During the hot weather these calls continue incessantly throughout the night, especially in moonlight.

NESTING: The season in N. India is March to May, continuing to about August in the south. A favourite site is in a deep shady nullah, preferably in forest. No nest is made, the eggs—normally two—being laid on the bare earth or on the fallen dry leaves. The eggs are rather larger than those of the other nightjars. They vary in ground colour from pale salmon or buff to pinkish-grey, and are blotched with pale purplish and blackish-brown.

THE FOREST EAGLE-OWL

Huhua nipalensis Hodgson

PLATES 52 AND 65

SIZE: About that of the Pariah Kite, but heavier built.

FIELD CHARACTERS: A large dark brown owl with two black horn-like tufts or aigrettes above its head. Underparts tawny-white barred with blackish-brown. Eyes *brown* instead of the usual bright yellow. Legs feathered to toes. Sexes alike. Singly, or pairs, in deep forest.

This species must not be confused with the commoner Great Horned Owl (*Bubo bubo*) of opener country in which the general colouration is buff and brown, and the eyes bright lemon yellow. The Dusky Eagle-Owl (*Bubo coromandus*) is similar to the Great Horned, but greyish-brown; while the Brown Fish-Owl differs from all three in its bare unfeathered legs.

Another large owl commonly met with, singly or in pairs, in wooded ravines in Kashmir and the NW. Himalayas (up to about 11,000 feet elevation) is Scully's Wood-Owl (*Strix aluco biddulphi*). It is distinguished by its large, round head being without 'horns' or aigrettes, and by a well-developed whitish saucer-like facial disc. It is pale grey-brown above, streaked and barred with dark brown and mottled with whitish. Underparts white, close-barred on chin and throat; streaked and narrowly cross-barred on the remainder. Eyes dark brown like the Forest Eagle-Owl's. Its usual call, mellow and not unpleasant, is described by Osmaston as *hoo . . . hoo . . . hoo-oo-oo-oo*, with an interval of about four seconds between first and second *hoo* and about half a second between the second *hoo* and the final rolling note. According to Bates it is *hoo* (interval) *hoo* (shorter interval) *hoo-ho-ho-hoo*, the final *hoo* being somewhat drawn out. A loud *quack* is also sometimes heard, as well as a soft *koo* rather similar to a pigeon's.

A similar owl, often mistaken for Scully's, is the Himalayan Wood-Owl (*Strix nivicola*). It differs chiefly in being a darker brown above with no dark longitudinal streaks, but only transverse barring. It is found between about 4,000 and 11,000 feet from about Murree across to Eastern Assam, and beyond. Its usual call is a mellow *twit . . . too-hoo*. The initial *twit* is more or less undertone and only audible when close at hand. The accent is on the *too*, and the call tails off in the final *hoo*. It is repeated at half-minute intervals. Both these owls breed between February and May, laying two or three roundish white eggs in the hollow of an ancient tree or in the fissure of a rock cliff, without any proper nest.

DISTRIBUTION: Himalayas from about Kumaon eastwards to Assam and hills of Central Burma. Nilgiris, Travancore, Mysore, and associated hill ranges of South India. Ceylon.

HABITS: The Forest Eagle-Owl spends the day-time dozing in some large tree in deep forest or *sholas*. At evening dusk it moves up to the edge of clearings in quest of food. It is a bold and powerful creature, and will overpower large birds such as junglefowl and peafowl, pouncing on them while they are roosting for the night up in trees or bamboo brakes.

It is said to kill jackal, young barking deer and hares, but also eats lizards, snakes and fish. Jerdon describes its cry as 'a low, deep and far-sounding moaning hoot'. To this owl are also attributed the blood-curdling shrieks as of a woman in grief sometimes heard at night in forest, and which have earned it the name of 'Devil Bird'. The real identity of the Devil Bird, however, is still a subject of controversy, some people claiming this title for the Crested Hawk-Eagle.

NESTING: The season in the Himalayas is February–March; in Travancore December–January. But the bird apparently breeds in other months as well. The single white egg is laid in the hollow of an ancient tree or in the disused stick nest of an eagle; sometimes on the bare ground, or in a cave or horizontal fissure in a rock-scarp. Apparently it does not ever build a nest.

THE SPOTTED SCOPS OWL

Otus spilocephalus Blyth

PLATE 53

SIZE: Same as of the familiar Spotted Owlet of the plains; about that of the Myna.

FIELD CHARACTERS: A dainty little owl of rufous-brown plumage, vermiculated with black and speckled with white or buff; with well developed aigrettes or ear-tufts. Legs fully feathered. Singly or pairs in Himalayan hill forest.

The Collared Scops Owl (*Otis bakkamoena*), divided into a number of geographical races on minor differences of size and colouration, occurs practically throughout India, Burma and Ceylon—plains as well as hills. All along the Himalayas, east to west, and Assam hills up to 7,000 or 8,000 feet elevation; in the Nilgiris and other South Indian ranges, and Ceylon to 4,000 or 5,000 feet. In general appearance it is very like the Spotted Scops, but differs from it chiefly in having a distinct pale collar on the hindneck. Its call is unmistakable: a mellow, interrogative *wüt?* repeated at intervals of three seconds or so. It usually commences soon after dusk and continues monotonously for long stretches, off and on, throughout moonlit nights, particularly in the hot weather. At this season is also heard a peculiar chattering occasionally uttered in between the ordinary calling.

DISTRIBUTION: The Himalayas from about Murree in the west, to east

Assam and Manipur. Also Chittagong Hill Tracts and NE. Burma. Two races are recognized: the paler and greyer West Himalayan *huttoni*, and the more rufous-brown East Himalayan *spilocephalus*. They meet about the western boundary of Nepal.

HABITS : The Spotted Scops Owl is more or less confined to the hill-oak, pine and deodar forests, normally between 2,000 and 7,000 feet elevation. It is purely nocturnal and its double bell-like whistling calls are often the only indication of its presence in a locality. The bird begins to call at evening twilight. The call is a metallic plaintive double whistle with the tone of the jangling of mule bells. There is a half second's pause between the two notes: *phew . . . phew*. This call is repeated at intervals of a few seconds for over long stretches of time, throughout the night. The bird can easily be decoyed by an imitation of its call.

Its food consists principally of beetles and other insects. Mice are also eaten.

NESTING : The season is between April and June. Holes in the trunks and boughs of trees at moderate heights, either natural or those excavated by woodpeckers, barbets or parakeets are used. The normal clutch consists of three or four white roundish eggs.

THE HIMALAYAN BARRED OWLET

Glaucidium cuculoides Vigors

PLATE 53

SIZE : Slightly less than the Pigeon. Larger than the Spotted Owlet of the plains.

FIELD CHARACTERS : A dark brown owlet, closely barred with whitish above and below, with longitudinal striations on abdomen. A white patch on throat. Sexes alike. Singly or pairs, in trees on wooded hillsides, etc. Largely diurnal.

The jolly little Collared Pigmy Owlet (*Glaucidium brodiei*), though less closely or completely barred and with a distinct rufous collar on hindneck, is a passable miniature of it. It is about the size of the bulbul, but squatter and with shorter tail. It extends throughout the Himalayas up to about 7,000 feet elevation, in two races: the paler Western *brodiei* and the darker Eastern *tubiger*. The boundary between them lies about W. Nepal. It also continues down to Burma, Malaya and China. It is active in bright sunshine as well as during the night. Its pleasant whistling call:*Toot*

. . . *toottoot* . . . *toot*, repeated every few seconds, is a familiar nocturnal sound at most Himalayan hill-stations.

The Barred Jungle Owlet (*Glaucidium radiatum*) is similar to the Himalayan, but smaller (about equal to the Spotted Owlet), and with abdomen transversely barred, not longitudinally striated. It also occurs in the lower Himalayan ranges up to about 4,000 feet, but principally inhabits the peninsula to the south, excepting Sind, Punjab and Rajputana. Two races are recognized: the greyish-brown *radiatum*, and the more rufous Malabar race *malabaricum*. A third race, *castanonotum*, distinguished by its chestnut back and longitudinally streaked abdomen, is peculiar to the Wet and Hill Zones of Ceylon; the Indian *radiatum* also occurs in the drier portions of that island.

This Barred Owlet is very partial to mixed teak and bamboo forest in hilly, broken country, being almost invariably coincident everywhere with the Racket-tailed Drongo. It also frequents evergreen jungle. It is on the move both during day-time and at night. Its call is quite pleasant and has rather the tone-quality of the distant crow of the Grey Junglecock. It begins with a loud *koo-koo-koo-koo* (or *kāo*), and is followed up by *koo-kūk* . . . *koo-kūk* . . . *koo-kūk*, repeated four or five times. The initial notes are loud but slow; each succeeding *koo-kūk* faster and less loud, and the call fades off and ends abruptly. Duets and irregular choruses of birds calling from different points in the jungle are commonly heard throughout moonlit nights, and they are particularly vocal on cloudy, overcast days also. Another call occasionally heard is a pleasant bubbling, something like *woioioioioi* . . . *kēēk*, of the tone-quality of the Koel's. The final *kēēk* is in quite a different and much higher key.

It breeds from February to May, laying three or four white round eggs in holes in forest trees.

DISTRIBUTION: Throughout the Himalayas (up to 7,000 or 8,000 feet) from about Murree in the west, to E. Assam. Also Burma and beyond, east and south. Two races concern us: the West Himalayan *cuculoides*—dark brown with heavily barred underparts—and the East Himalayan-Burmese *rufescens*—rufous brown above, with more longitudinal streaks on abdomen.

HABITS: A common and familiar resident of Himalayan hill-oak and horse-chestnut forests, and one of the most diurnal of the owls, often hunting in broad sunshine. Its food consists of beetles, grasshoppers and other insects, as well as lizards, mice and small birds. The flight, in common with that of the other owlets described, is dipping—at times almost 'saw-edged'—the result of rapid wing strokes followed by a pause with closed wings in which the bird dives obliquely. The ordinary call of this owl, though quite different from that of the Barred Jungle species, resembles it in a general way. Whistler describes it as 'a rising crescendo of harsh squawks which sound as if the bird was trying to rise to some great effort, and then end suddenly and unexpectedly'.

It has a variety of loud croaks and chuckles besides.

NESTING: The principal months are March to May. The normal clutch of three or four eggs is laid in natural hollows of large trees in forest. They are white in colour and of the usual round shape of owl's eggs.

THE HIMALAYAN GRIFFON VULTURE

Gyps himalayensis Hume

PLATE 72

SIZE: Enormous. Practically the largest bird in the Himalayas.

FIELD CHARACTERS: An unmistakable vulture with the usual long, naked, scrawny neck and unfeathered bald head. Old birds sandy white or pale khaki; immature chocolate-brown. In overhead aspect the large size, pale underside, black tail, black trailing edges of the broad wings, together with the 'splayed-fingers' tips, are diagnostic. Sexes alike. Gatherings at animal carcases, or individual birds soaring at great heights.

Another vulture commonly seen in Kashmir and the NW. Himalayas is the Fulvous or Indian Griffon (*Gyps fulvus*), only somewhat smaller than the Himalayan. The adult is a rich fulvous or cinnamon brown, but often also quite pale. Small numbers are found about Mt. Abu and trickle eastwards to Assam. Southward they extend to the Deccan. It breeds in small colonies on ledges of cliffs in Kashmir, around Quetta, and probably also in the Kirthar Range of Sind. February to April.

The vultures normally met with in the hills (and plains) of peninsular India are chiefly the White-backed or Bengal (*Pseudogyps bengalensis*)— also in the Himalayas up to about 4,000 feet—and the Long-billed Vulture (*Gyps indicus*). At rest the adult White-back is easily identified by its blackish-brown plumage and white back. When overhead, a broad whitish band along the underside of the wings provides a good recognition mark. The sub-adult is more or less uniform dark brown and lacks the white markings. In this stage it is easily confused with the Long-billed Vulture. Young birds of the Himalayan Griffon, the Fulvous, the White-backed and the Long-billed Vultures are all chocolate-brown and extremely difficult to tell apart.

The White-backed Vulture nests in large trees; the Long-billed on cliffs.

DISTRIBUTION: The Himalayas from extreme west to about Bhutan, normally between 4,000 and 8,000 feet. North to Tibet and Turkestan.

HABITS: The Himalayan Griffon is a purely mountain-dwelling species and is not found in the plains. It quarters the heavens at tremendous heights, sailing majestically over mountain-top and valley on motionless outspread wings. Like the other vultures it lives entirely on carrion. Small numbers gather to feed on dead pack animals that have fallen by the wayside along the beaten trade routes and mountain passes. They also frequent the neighbourhood of mountain villages and hill-stations where the dead domestic animals dumped on the outskirts provide them with sustenance. The gatherings are usually far smaller than what are met with in the plains, but the feasts are nevertheless accompanied by all the customary jostling and screeching, and tugging and prancing with stiffly craned necks, that attends these ghoulish funeral rites elsewhere.

NESTING: The usual months are January to March or April. The nest is a rough untidy pad of sticks and rubbish placed on the ledge of a cliff. The birds often breed in small colonies in favourite sites, which are resorted to year after year. The old nests are reconditioned by adding to the ragged remains of the preceding season. Only a single egg is laid, usually unmarked white, but sometimes handsomely blotched with pale reddish to deep reddish-brown.

THE LÄMMERGEIER OR BEARDED VULTURE

Gypaëtus barbatus Linnaeus

SIZE: Very large. Wing span (about 9 feet from tip to tip) exceeding that of the Himalayan Griffon, but bird itself of somewhat slenderer build.

FIELD CHARACTERS: A large eagle-like bird without the disgusting naked neck and head of the true vulture. Deep silvery grey and black above, streaked with white; pale rusty-white below. Head and neck creamy or rusty white. A tuft of black feathers—the beard—pendant under the chin and conspicuous in profile. Legs fully feathered. Young birds may be recognized by their very dark plumage and almost black head. Sexes alike.

In overhead flight the longish wedge-shaped tail and the comparatively narrow and pointed wings differentiate it straightaway from a
vulture. Seen singly, sailing majestically over valleys and mountain-sides.
The only other bird of prey whose tail looks wedge-shaped in flight is
the White Scavenger Vulture (*Neophron percnopterus*) met with about most
hill-stations, Himalayan as well as peninsular. But it is much smaller,
being the size of the Pariah Kite, dirty white with a yellow face when
adult. The black flight quills form the broad trailing edge of the wing in
overhead aspect. Young birds are dark brown.

DISTRIBUTION: The race *hemachalanus* is found in the mountains of
Afghanistan, Baluchistan and Sind, and through the Himalayas from
extreme north-west right across to Bhutan, normally between 4,000 and
13,000 feet. One of the Everest Expeditions observed it at 24,000 to
25,000 feet. Birds breeding in the North Cachar Hills apparently belong
to the paler and larger Central Asian race *altaicus* (*vide* Stuart Baker).

HABITS: This majestic bird, commonly miscalled 'Golden Eagle', is
quite abundant in the Himalayas. It is seen quartering the open hillsides
and valleys, gliding effortlessly on outspread wings, sometimes quite low
near the ground, at others a mere speck in the heavens. As it sails past
on a level with the observer on a mountain-top, bill pointing below and
eyes intently scanning the countryside, its absurd little black goatee
stands out in clear profile. A fairly loud *trrrr* sound (produced by the
primaries?) is heard in the sailing flight, and sometimes also a loud
droning as of some gigantic wasp, when the bird is close overhead.

In many respects the Lämmergeier is midway between the eagles and
the true vultures. Its general appearance is certainly far more noble than
any vulture's, though its compressed bill is typically vulturine. Its talons,
too, are blunt and short, and ill-adapted for striking down live prey.
Nevertheless, it can lift and carry things in its claws as no true vulture
can. It walks on the ground with a dignified eagle-like gait and can take
off without the preliminary run necessary for a 'regulation' vulture.

It is a scavenger pure and simple, and commonly seen feeding on
wayside carcases and at village refuse dumps in company with griffons,
neophrons, ravens and crows. It keeps to the neighbourhood of hill-
stations and cantonments where it swoops to pick up scraps from the
ground in the manner of the Pariah Kite. In spite of frequent allegations,
it has never been known to attack live animals. Its method of smashing
bones is well known. The bird carries a large bone in its claws up to a
height of 200 or 300 feet and drops it on rocks below. This is repeated
again and again, if necessary, until the bone splinters, whereupon the

bird alights to pick up and swallow the pieces. It is a very silent bird, and only rarely utters a squeal.

NESTING: The season is from December to February–March. The Lämmergeier breeds at elevations between 4,500 and 8,000 feet—sometimes higher. The nest is a huge collection of sticks, to which is added quantities of miscellaneous rubbish such as sheep's wool, fragments of the hairy skins of mammals, and large bones. It is usually built on some inaccessible ledge, or in a cave in a cliff-face. The same site is used year after year. One or two eggs are laid. In colour they are some pale tone of greyish rusty, blotched and spotted with various shades of deeper red. Occasionally, very dark red eggs occur. A pair indulge in a great deal of aerial interplay as the breeding season approaches, tumbling, chasing, and mock-fighting with each other in spectacular fashion.

THE SHAHIN FALCON

Falco peregrinus peregrinator Sundeval

PLATE 54

SIZE: Somewhat larger than the House Crow.

FIELD CHARACTERS: A broad-shouldered, compact, streamlined bird of prey, slaty-blue above with black head; pinkish and rusty-red below strongly cross-barred with black. A dark moustachial or cheek stripe on either side of throat. Long, pointed wings and swift direct flight. Sexes alike, but female larger. Singly or pairs on and about cliffs.

The Eastern Peregrine Falcon (*Falco peregrinus calidus*), a visitor from Northern Asia, is commonly seen in the vicinity of duck-shooting tanks and *jheels* in winter. It differs from the Shahin in having the head dark slaty instead of black, and very little red on the underside, which is largely white.

The smaller Central Asian Hobby (*Falco subbuteo centralasiae*), also breeding in the Himalayas, is found in winter in the peninsula along with the somewhat darker immigrant European form (*F. s. subbuteo*). It is about the size of a dove, slaty-grey above, whitish and rust-coloured below. In general aspect it is a very good miniature of the Peregrine, but has the breast longitudinally streaked instead of transversely barred, as in that falcon. In its pointed wings, streamlined contours and swift flight also, it closely resembles the Peregrine. Its food consists of dragonflies, locusts and other large insects, and small birds captured on the wing.

On seizing a dragonfly near the ground the Hobby rises in the air to some height, slowly sailing round in circles and devouring the prey held in its claws.

The Indian Hobby (*Falco severus rufipedoides*) differs from it in colouration more or less in the same way as the Shahin differs from the Peregrine. Its head is blackish, upper parts slaty-grey. Underneath more rusty red, with unstreaked breast. It breeds in the Himalayas from Kumaon to Western Assam, and spreads over the peninsula in winter. It possibly also breeds in some of our south-western peninsular hills.

The Kestrel (*Falco tinnunculus*) is another small falcon often met with in the hills. It is pale brick-red above with a grey head; whitish below with longitudinal dark streaks and arrow-head marks. Graduated grey tail with broad black band across tip. Female rufous above, including head, cross barred with blackish. The bird is best known for its spectacular habit of hovering stationary in the air as it scans the ground below for mice, lizards and insects which form its food. The typical race *tinnunculus* breeds in the Western Himalayas between 2,500 and 7,000 feet elevation and spreads out over the peninsula in winter. The Indian race *objurgatus* breeds in the Nilgiris and other hills of South-Western India. In this race both sexes are a richer red above and very rufous below.

DISTRIBUTION: The Shahin is eminently a bird of steep rugged hills. Pairs keep to favourite crags, which serve as foraging bases for miles of the surrounding country. Its flight is extremely swift and direct—a few rapid beats of the long pointed wings followed by a motionless glide at tremendous speed. Chukor, partridges and pigeons comprise the major portion of its food, but other game birds, including large species like pheasants and junglefowl, are also hunted. From its tactical circling high up in the air the Shahin hurls itself obliquely on its quarry, wings pressed in at the sides, literally a bolt from the blue. The victim is struck in mid-air with the powerful hindclaw, which rips open its back. If of large size the quarry is allowed to fall to earth, whence it is subsequently retrieved. If of manageable proportions it is borne away in the falcon's stride hanging limp from its talons. The tearing swish of the lightning stoop, and the spectacular manner in which the whole manœuvre is executed leaves the observer spell-bound with fascination.

In the breeding season pairs indulge in playful stooping at each other around their nesting cliff with incredible velocity, and go through a variety of remarkable aerobatics, 'looping-the-loop', and mock fighting.

NESTING: In the Himalayas the Shahin breeds principally from March to May. In the peninsular and South Indian hills January and February appear to be the favoured months. The nest is a stick platform, sometimes compactly built and lined with wool and grass; at other times scanty, unlined, and even practically non-existent. It is placed on a ledge or in a niche in the face of a cliff, usually in accessible situations. The full clutch is of three or four eggs. They vary from pale stone to pale brick-red in ground colour and are marked in varying degree with a few bold blotches or numerous small ones of brick-red or reddish-brown.

THE HIMALAYAN GOLDEN EAGLE

Aquila chrysaëtos hodgsoni Ticehurst

PLATE 55

SIZE : About that of the Vulture.

FIELD CHARACTERS : A very large and powerful eagle deep chocolate-brown with golden or tawny-rufous hindcrown, nape and hindneck. Some light rufous-brown on thighs, under the tail and on shoulders of wings. In soaring flight the broad wings held in a wide open V above the back (as in the King Vulture or the Black Eagle), and ending in upturned widely-splayed 'fingers', make it distinctive. Young birds are glossy brownish-black, with tawny head and neck. In flight a white patch in the centre of the wing, and the white tail with a broad blackish terminal band, are revealing features.

Sexes alike. Singly or pairs in rugged high Himalayan country.

A bird that is often mistaken for the Golden is the adult Imperial Eagle (*Aquila heliaca*); but this has a much lighter tawny-coloured head. It is seen in the Himalayas only while on spring and autumn migration, between its breeding grounds in SE. Europe and Central Asia, and its winter quarters in the North Indian plains (south to the Deccan). In soaring flight the tail of the Imperial Eagle is relatively shorter and its wings broader than the Golden Eagle's. Moreover, its slow and heavy vulture-like flight, with wings held in a straight line with the body, contrasts strongly with the light and graceful sailing—wings above body level in a wide V—which characterizes the Golden Eagle.

In the distance, when size differences are not so obvious, perhaps the only bird with which the Golden Eagle on the wing can be confused is the Black Eagle (p. 166). Fortunately, the two species are rarely found in the same locality.

In the hand the Golden Eagle can always be told from every other species by its enormous and powerful hindclaw, measuring between 2½ and 4 inches round the curve.

DISTRIBUTION: The Himalayan race *hodgsoni* (= *daphanea*)—larger and paler than the typical *chrysaëtos* of Europe—inhabits Central Asia and the Himalayas from Afghanistan and Baluchistan to East Assam. It is resident from about snow-line down to 7,000 feet or so, and seldom found lower, even in winter.

HABITS: This regal bird dwells in rugged mountainous country with nullahs and sparse open scrub. Although not abundant anywhere in the Himalayas it is perhaps less uncommon than is generally supposed. It keeps to its remote mountain fastnesses and is unlikely to be met with in the neighbourhood of the usual hill-stations. The alleged 'Golden Eagles' of Mussooree and Simla are in reality Bearded Vultures so miscalled. Pairs hold sway over extensive feeding territories. These are occupied throughout the year for many years in succession.

The Golden Eagle's method of hunting is very falcon-like; it sometimes chases down the quarry at speed, but usually stoops at it from a height with terrific velocity. It strikes with the powerful hindclaw, virtually ripping open the largest prey. Pairs often hunt in concert, one bird driving and harrying while the other stoops from above and strikes down the game. Their food consists of Chukor, Snowcock and Monal, and such other pheasants as venture out on the open sparsely scrubbed mountainsides. In some localities crows appear to form the principal item on their menu. Foxes and Martens are often carried off, as well as lambs of Burhel and fawns of Musk Deer. Carrion is seldom, if ever, touched.

Its call is said to be like the yelping of a dog.

NESTING: The season commences in March or April. The nest is a huge platform of sticks lined with leafy branches, usually placed on a ledge of rock. Sometimes it is built in a stunted juniper or other tree growing out of and overhanging a sheer cliff.

Two eggs are laid, sometimes unmarked white, but usually blotched with rufous brown. As in many other eagles, only one of these is normally hatched out, or only a single young reaches maturity. The environs of an eyrie are usually littered with remains of the birds and mammals brought in for the young.

THE BLACK EAGLE

Ictinaëtus malayensis Temm. and Laug.

PLATE 56

SIZE : Larger than the Pariah Kite.

FIELD CHARACTERS : A dark brownish-black eagle whose closed wing tips, when at rest, reach to the end of its tail. On the wing its black plumage, narrowly grey-barred tail and bright chrome-yellow legs and feet, set off by the dark underparts, are diagnostic. The bright yellow cere and a white patch under the eye are clearly seen at close range. The underside of the wing is dark with a light area on the primaries.

The tail is relatively longer than in the Tawny and most other eagles. At a distance in sailing flight the outlines are rather like the Golden Eagle's, viz., broad wings held above the line of the back in a wide V and ending in upturned 'splayed fingers'. Sexes alike. Singly, sailing over forested hillsides and ravines.

The Crested Hawk-Eagle (*Spizaëtus cirrhatus*), though also not a purely hill bird, needs to be mentioned as it is commonly met with about many hill-stations. It occurs in two races, from the base of the Himalayas to Travancore and Ceylon, and from Eastern Punjab to Western Bengal. It is somewhat larger than the Pariah Kite, brown above, white below, with narrow black longitudinal streaks on throat, and broad chocolate streaks on breast. Its most prominent feature, however, is a long crest of a few black feathers which stick out jauntily behind its head. It frequents forest and hunts hare, peafowl and junglefowl by pouncing on them from above. It perches upright and motionless on the horizontal branch of a tree at the edge of a forest clearing or glade, not so much concealed by the foliage as backed and obliterated by it, waiting for its prey to emerge into the open. It has a loud high-pitched cry: *ki-ki-ki-ki-ki-ki-ki-ki-keee*, beginning short, rising in a crescendo and ending off in a scream. In overhead flight its relatively long and narrow tail, and rounded silvery white wings narrowly barred with black, are suggestive clues to its identity. This eagle is co-suspect with the Forest Eagle-Owl as being the unidentified 'Devil Bird'—producer of the oft-described ghoulish nocturnal screams in forest.

A superficially similar crested species, Hodgson's Hawk-Eagle (*Spizaëtus nipalensis nipalensis*), occurs throughout the Himalayas from Hazara in the west to Eastern Assam, between about 2,000 and 8,000 feet elevation. It straggles into the forested hills of the central peninsula in winter. A second race, Legge's Hawk-Eagle (*Spizaëtus n. kelaarti*), occipies the Nilgiris and other hill ranges of Mysore, Malabar and Travancore and extends into Ceylon. Both these are very destructive to game. In the hand *nipalensis* may be distinguished from *cirrhatus* by its somewhat larger size and by the feathering on its legs running down beyond the first joint of the middle toe instead of ending just above its base.

Bonelli's Hawk-Eagle (*Hieraëtus fasciatus*) is a species that is likely at one time or another to confound the visitor to the hills, though also by no means restricted to the highlands. It is found practically throughout India from at least 7,000 feet in the Himalayas south to Ceylon. It is a comparatively slender-built, uncrested eagle; dark umber-brown above, white below with blackish longitudinal streaks when adult. In overhead aspect the silvery white body and dark brown wings with greyish patches and streaks are revealing. From underneath, a young bird in flight appears dark-streaked brick-red with patchy grey-and-brown wings. The relatively long tail, and wings held in an open V above the level of the back, and their upturned 'splayed finger' tips, give it rather the silhouette of a Black Eagle. It lives largely on game birds and crows.

DISTRIBUTION: Himalayas (up to about 6,000 feet) from Chamba State in the Punjab to Eastern Assam, Bengal and Chota Nagpur. Peninsular India from about the latitude of Baroda south through the Sahyadris (or Western Ghats) to Cape Comorin, and Ceylon; east to the Mahadeo Hills in Central Provinces, and Bastar State. Rare straggler in Burma.

HABITS: The Black Eagle is a forest-loving species, and partial to hilly evergreen country. It sails gracefully and deliberately on outstretched motionless wings in and out along the contours of wooded hills, and circles above the tree tops in forested ravines, quartering the slopes and scanning the bushes for birds' nests and living prey. When opportunity offers it suddenly checks itself and drops on the quarry in the manner of a harrier. Its food consists of frogs, lizards and large insects. Birds, small as well as large, like pheasants and junglefowl, are also killed when they come within the range of its hunting technique. It is reputed to be a confirmed robber of birds' nests, searching for them meticulously as it sails past bushes, and taking both eggs and young.

It is a quiet bird on the whole and no regular call appears to have been recorded.

NESTING: The season in South India is chiefly between November and March; in the north it apparently begins a couple of months later. The nest is a neat and compact platform of twigs built high up in lofty trees in evergreen forest, usually hidden by the foliage. A single handsome

egg is normally laid—sometimes two. It varies from whitish to pinkish in ground colour, densely and finely stippled with pale brick-red. The birds are bold and determined in the defence of their nest.

THE KOKLA OR
WEDGE-TAILED GREEN PIGEON

Sphenocercus sphenurus Gould

PLATE 57

SIZE : About that of the familiar Blue Rock.

FIELD CHARACTERS : A yellowish-green pigeon with varying amount of maroon on the middle of the back and scapulars. Chin and throat yellow. Breast pale orange-pink. Tail comparatively long and graduated. A prominent yellow bar in the wing. Bare bluish skin round eyes; bluish bill; red legs. The female lacks the maroon patch on the back. Flocks in fruiting forest trees.

The Pin-tailed Green Pigeon (*Sphenocercus apicaudatus*) differs from the above in having a long, pointed tail, like a parakeet's. The male has no maroon patch on the back; the female is merely a duller edition of her mate. Two yellow wing-bars 'and cinnamon-coloured undertail coverts confirm its identity. It occurs in the Himalayas from Kumaon eastwards to Assam, and down through Manipur and Burma to Tenasserim.

Several other species of Green Pigeon are found within Indian limits. The commonest two to be met with in the hills (and plains) of peninsular India are:

1. The Common Green Pigeon (*Crocopus phoenicopterus*), a stout yellowish-olive, green and ashy-grey bird with a lilac patch on the shoulders and a conspicuous yellow bar on the blackish wings. In contrast with all other Indian Green Pigeons it has *yellow* legs instead of red. It is split up into three races: the grey-bellied North-India-Assam *phoenicopterus*, the yellow-bellied South-India-Ceylon *chlorigaster*, and the Burmese *viridifrons* with yellow forehead.

2. The Grey-fronted Green Pigeon (*Dendrophassa pompadora affinis*) of the southern Sahyadris (W. Ghats), Nilgiris, Palnis, and associated hill ranges. Smaller in size than the Common Green Pigeon, and also yellowish-green, but with grey forehead and crown. Purplish maroon-chestnut back; two yellow bars on the wings. In the female the maroon on the back is absent.

DISTRIBUTION: Himalayas (up to 8,000 feet in summer) from Murree in the west to Assam, and down through Burma and Shan States to Tenasserim.

HABITS: The Wedge-tailed Green Pigeon is essentially a bird of broad-leafed Himalayan hill forests. Like all other green pigeons, it is an exclusively fruit-eating species and subject to local movements and migrations governed by its food supply—the ripening season and abundance of the various fruits and berries on which it lives. Thus in winter it is found at lower elevations, and seen about many hill-stations only in summer.

This species usually keeps in smaller numbers than many of its congeners, and flocks of over fifteen are rare. Their flight is noisy, swift and strong. They give good sport with a variety of difficult shots as they flash through the forest trees, and are good eating.

The birds clamber about the fruit-laden twigs upside down and side-ways with the celerity of a squirrel, stretching out like acrobats for berries beyond normal reach. Their colouration obliterates them so effectively in the surrounding foliage that only the movement of one bird here and another there gives away their presence. The number that will fly out of a leafy tree when a shot is fired is often quite amazing.

The beautiful calls of this pigeon, from which it gets its Hindustani name *Kokla*, consist of a large number of mellow musical whistling notes. They have been rendered by one observer as: *Ko-kla-koi-oi-oi-oi, oilli, illio-kla,* and so on. On account of its sweet 'song' it is in great demand as a cage bird. But it otherwise makes an uninteresting pet, and is quarrelsome in mixed aviaries.

NESTING: The season is April to June, in some cases continuing on till July–August. The nest is the characteristic flimsy twig structure of all pigeons. It is built high up in some tall leafy tree in forest. Two white eggs form the full clutch, almost invariably. Both sexes take part in incubation and feeding the young.

THE NILGIRI WOOD-PIGEON

Columba elphinstonii Sykes

PLATE 58
SIZE: Larger than the Blue Rock-Pigeon. About that of the Jungle Crow.
FIELD CHARACTERS: A large pigeon with grey head, and a black-and-

white 'chessboard' on either side of neck. Upper parts reddish-brown with a glistening sheen of metallic purple and green; underparts grey. Sexes alike. Singly, pairs or small parties in forest.

The Ceylon Wood-Pigeon (*Columba torringtonii*) with top of head and underparts lilac instead of grey, and upper parts blackish-slate, replaces this species in the Central Hill Zone of Ceylon, from about 2,500 feet up.

Jerdon's Imperial Pigeon (*Ducula badia cuprea*) is of about the same size and general appearance, but lacks the white-spotted black patches ('chessboards') on sides of neck. Dull olive-brown above; pale greyish-lilac head and underparts. It inhabits the hills of South-West India up to about 4,000 feet elevation—Nilgiris, Palnis, Mysore and Travancore hills, and associated ranges—where it is met with in twos and threes in evergreen forest. Its call is a deep, rather mournful, booming crescendo, *ūk-ook . . . ook*. It flies with leisurely wing-beats like the crow. The male has a remarkable and spectacular display in the breeding season consisting of nose-diving and other aerobatics reminiscent of the Blue Jay. Three slightly differing races of this pigeon are found along the Himalayas from W. Nepal to Assam, and south through Burma to the Malay Peninsula and Sumatra.

DISTRIBUTION: The Sahyadris or Western Ghats from about Mahableshwar to the extreme south. Also Nilgiris, Palnis, and associated hill ranges.

HABITS: The Nilgiri Wood-Pigeon inhabits evergreen forested hills from about their base up to the highest *sholas*, and is usually met with singly or in pairs; occasionally in small parties of four or five. It keeps to the tall trees and seldom descends to the ground. The densely wooded ravines or *sholas*, so characteristic of the Nilgiris and associated hill ranges, are its favourite haunts. Its food consists mainly of a variety of wild fruits, and the birds are subject to a certain amount of local movements coinciding with the ripening season and availability of their food supply. Its call, chiefly heard in the early morning, is said to be a soft and pleasing *coo*; but it is a very silent bird on the whole.

NESTING: The season is principally between April and June, from about 4,000 feet elevation upwards. The nest is the characteristic flimsy platform of twigs normally placed in a moderate-sized sapling in a *shola*, but sometimes quite high up in a tall tree. Only a single white egg is laid.

THE EMERALD OR BRONZE-WINGED DOVE

Chalcophaps indica Linnaeus

PLATE 59

SIZE: Slightly larger than the Myna.

FIELD CHARACTERS: A brownish-pink dove with glistening emerald bronze-green upper parts (excluding tail), and conspicuous white forehead and eyebrows. In flight the chestnut undersides of wings are characteristic. Sexes alike. Singly or pairs in forest.

The Green Imperial Pigeon (*Muscadivora aenea*) is introduced here because of its rather similar colour scheme. In size it is considerably larger—about equal to the Jungle Crow. The underparts are paler (greyish-pink) than in the Emerald Dove; the upperparts (including tail) bright metallic green with a bronze or copper lustre.

It occurs in parts of the Eastern Himalayas, and much of the forested country of the Eastern and Western Ghats as well as the central plateau. It is found both in the plains and hills up to 6,000 feet elevation or more. Two races chiefly concern us: the smaller *pusilla* of Ceylon and South India, arbitrarily restricted by the 20th N. latitude, and the larger *sylvatica* of the country north of this, including the Eastern Himalayas. They grade into each other imperceptibly.

This is a large, purely arboreal, frugivorous forest pigeon, and lives largely on figs of the various species of *Ficus*. Its call is distinctive. It consists of deep notes something like *wuck-woor-woor-woor-woor*, ending in a peculiar prolonged rolling which I have likened to a mocking or jeering laugh. The call has a curious ventriloquistic character.

DISTRIBUTION: The typical race of the Emerald Dove *indica* occurs in the Sahyadris and their outliers, from the Tapti River to the extreme south of the peninsula, including the Nilgiris, Palnis, Shevaroys, and associated hills, as well as the Travancore and Mysore ranges. Himalayas from Kumaon to East Assam. Bengal, Bihar, Orissa, etc. Burma, with the exception of the central dry zone.

The island of Ceylon is occupied by the smaller endemic race *robinsoni*.

HABITS: This lovely little dove is a dweller of well-wooded country, plain as well as hill, but seldom ascends to over 5,000 feet elevation. It is particularly fond of foothills broken up by wooded ravines and clothed with scrub and bamboo jungle. The bird may be seen singly or in pairs walking about and picking seeds on cart tracks through forest, or in shaded tea and coffee plantations. When disturbed it flies off with rapid wing-beats at great speed for some distance along the path before turning off into the jungle. On tea and coffee plantations and the like, the birds frequently come to grief by dashing themselves against the whitewashed walls of cooly lines and bungalows, no doubt mistaking these for openings in the shrubbery.

Although berries are occasionally eaten, its staple diet consists of seeds which are gleaned on the ground in the normal manner of doves. Termites are also eaten at times.

The call of this dove is a soft, deep and very low *hoon*, with a nasal ending. It is quite an intriguing sound when heard for the first time, and takes some effort before it can be reconciled with the producer!

NESTING: The season varies according to locality, and since the bird often has more than one brood in succession, it is much prolonged. The principal months in South India are January and February; in the Lower Himalayas, March to May. In Ceylon it is said to breed between January and October. The nest is the usual flimsy twig structure typical of the pigeons and doves, although in this case it is slightly more compact. It is built on a sapling or in a bamboo clump, 5 to 10 feet from the ground. The eggs—almost invariably two—are creamy-yellow to 'white coffee' in colour, and elliptical in shape.

THE WHITE-BELLIED OR SNOW-PIGEON

Columba leuconota Vigors

PLATES 60 AND 68

SIZE: About that of the Blue Rock-Pigeon.

FIELD CHARACTERS: The parti-coloured plumage reminds one of a domestic pigeon. In flight, seen from above, the black tail with a narrow white subterminal cross-bar, white rump patch, brown back, blackish head and three dark bars on the grey wings are conspicuous. When overhead, the white body and blackish head are revealing. In the distance the white underside, black head and rapid wing-beats are curiously reminiscent of the Cotton Teal. Sexes alike. Flocks on high Himalayan cliffs or about upland cultivation.

The Blue Rock-Pigeon (*Columba livia*), too well known to need description, is also found in the Himalayas (up to about 5,000 feet elevation), the peninsular hills and Ceylon. Also in the drier parts of Burma. The South Indian race *intermedia* has the back uniform bluish-grey; in the North

Indian *neglecta* the lower back is much paler and contrasts with the dark back. Its call notes are also well known—a deep *gootr-goo, gootr-goo,* etc.

The Turkestan Rock-Pigeon (*Columba rupestris*) is really a bird of beyond our northern limits—Tibet, Turkestan, etc.—but it occurs on our fringe in Gilgit and the higher parts of Kashmir between 11,000 and 15,000 feet. It differs from the Blue Rock in being a much paler grey with almost whitish underparts. A pure white rump-patch and a broad white bar across the tail confirm its identity. Its call is a high-pitched, quick-repeated, rolling *gūt-gūt-gūt-gūt*, etc., reminiscent of the jeering 'laugh' of the Green Imperial Pigeon (p. 171).

DISTRIBUTION: The Himalayas, from Afghanistan to Sikkim, are occupied by the Western race *leuconota*. The Tibetan race *gradaria*, differing in minor details of colouration, occurs in SE. Tibet, Yunnan, etc., mostly beyond our borders.

HABITS: The Snow-Pigeon is essentially a bird of the high Himalayas, seldom met with at elevations under 5,000 feet, even in winter. In summer it keeps mostly between 10,000 and 14,000 feet up. Its habits differ little from those of its familiar cousin, the Blue Rock. It lives in colonies on cliffs and flies out to feed in the terraced cultivation in neighbouring upland valleys. The flocks often contain up to fifty or one hundred birds with sometimes an admixture of Blue Rocks. They also feed on the edge of melting snow patches, and it is amazing how obliterating their plumage is in such environment. Their food consists of barley and other grain and seeds. When gleaning in the fields the birds walk about briskly, the flock keeping together in a compact bunch. Their flight is strong and direct as of the Blue Rock. Flocks flying against the gigantic cliffs look like midges by comparison, and the birds make a pretty picture as they sail gracefully round a prominence before settling on the ledges.

Its call has been described as 'a repeated croak, not unlike a hiccough'. It is very different from the normal *coo* of a pigeon.

NESTING: The season is May to July. Snow-Pigeons nest in colonies—sometimes very large ones—on ledges and in crevices of rocky cliffs, at elevations between 10,000 and 15,000 feet. The nests are the usual flimsy platforms of sticks. The full clutch is of two white eggs, which in size and appearance are indistinguishable from those of the Blue Rock-Pigeon.

THE RUFOUS TURTLE-DOVE

Streptopelia orientalis Latham

PLATE 61

SIZE: Slightly smaller than the Blue Rock-Pigeon.

FIELD CHARACTERS: A large pinkish-brown, dove with scale-like rust-coloured pattern on upper parts, and a grey-spotted black patch ('chessboard') on either side of hindneck. The broad white-fringed bluish-grey tail, usually well expanded fanwise, contrasts strongly with the rufous wings when the bird is flying away from the observer, or when alighting on a perch. Sexes alike. Pairs or small flocks in open forest.

DISTRIBUTION: Himalayas (up to about 12,000 feet, or even somewhat higher) from Kashmir to Assam, and beyond our limits both west and north-east. Also Burma, south to Tenasserim. Rare straggler into Ceylon. Practically throughout peninsular India (plain and hill), except the arid portions of Sind and Rajputana.

Three races concern us: (1) the highly migratory West-Himalayan *meena* with pale underparts, much white on belly, white undertail coverts and white tips to tail feathers; (2) the likewise migratory East-Himalayan *agricola*, very richly coloured with the white portions of (1) replaced by grey; and (3) the more or less resident peninsular race *erythrocephalus* distinguished by the much richer vinous-red tone of its plumage, above and below.

The boundary between (1) and (2) is about Western Nepal. In winter both wander south into the range of (3) and are then liable to produce some confusion in the identification of the races.

HABITS: The Rufous Turtle-Dove is a dweller of well-wooded country and light forest. It is common about most Himalayan hill-stations in summer, where pairs or parties may be met with gleaning on shady paths, and often in the neighbourhood of outhouses and bungalows. Its hoarse, mournful *goor . . . gŭr-grŭgroo* is one of the more familiar bird voices there. The final *groo* is especially mournful and uttered as with pulling in of breath.

Everywhere this dove is fond of shady glades and cart-tracks through open bamboo and mixed forest, and a pair or small party may commonly be seen walking about quietly and feeding along these. When disturbed, the birds scatter and settle in trees. They also frequent the regular *paraos* or stations on country roads where bullock carts halt and unyoke for rest during the mid-day heat, picking up the rice and other grain dropped from the sacks.

174

Like other doves, it is a thirsty bird and drinks regularly in the mornings and evenings, and also in the early afternoon.

Though usually rather tame and confiding about hill-stations, I have always found it shy and difficult to approach in outlying forest tracts. Its flight is swift and pigeon-like. At a distance the stouter build and relatively shorter tail give it more the lines of a pigeon than a dove.

NESTING: The season varies according to locality, being more defined only in the northern portions of its range. In the Himalayas, May to July are the principal months. At lower elevations, and in peninsular India, it may be found nesting in practically all seasons of the year, and often raises two or more broods in succession. The nest is the usual flimsy platform of twigs, built in trees or bushes, or up in a bamboo clump (usually under 20 feet from the ground) in fairly open forest. The normal clutch invariably consists of two white eggs of the typical oval shape of pigeons' eggs.

THE WHITE-CRESTED KALEEJ PHEASANT

Gennaeus hamiltoni Griffith and Pidgeon

PLATE 62

SIZE: About that of the domestic fowl.

FIELD CHARACTERS: Male black above, glossed with steel blue, with a whitish rump, long white lying-down crest and bare scarlet patch round the eyes. Underparts chiefly brownish-grey. Tail long, of glossy black sickle-shaped pointed feathers. Female chiefly reddish-brown with pale scaly markings, brown crest and scarlet eye-patch.

Pairs or family parties in Himalayan forest.

Several other species of pheasants are found in the Himalayas, of which the Koklas, Cheer and Monal need mention.

The Koklas (*Ceriornis macrolophus*)—one of the group of medium-tailed Himalayan pheasants—is of about the same size, without the unfeathered scarlet eye-patch. The cock is grey above, streaked blackish; chestnut below. A brown lying-down crest between two long metallic green horn-like tufts jutting out behind its metallic green head is its most outstanding feature. A white patch on either side of the head is also prominent. The tail is reddish-brown and pointed, but not curved and drooping as in the Kaleej. The hen is mottled black and brown with buff streaks above; buff with black streaks below, and has a conspicuous white throat.

She lacks the metallic green face of the cock and also the 'horns'. Her crest is short and pale coloured.

The Koklas, in several races, is found on steep forested hillsides, locally between 6,000 and 14,000 feet elevation, in the mountains of Afghanistan and the NW. Frontier, and in the Himalayas from Kashmir to Western Nepal. The crow of the cock, from which the bird gets its local name, is a loud, ringing, *kok-kok-kok . . . kokrās* (or *pukrās*). In the distance it is not unlike the crow of the Red Junglecock in a general way.

The Cheer (*Catreus wallichii*) is a long-tailed West Himalayan pheasant, rather like the hen English pheasant to look at. It is buffy-white and rusty-brown, barred above and mottled below with black. The long, narrow, pointed 'pheasant tail' broadly barred buff and brownish-black, the narrow-pointed lying-down crest, and the bright scarlet patch round the eyes confirm its identity. The hen is similar, but smaller in size and with a shorter tail.

Keeps in small coveys of five or six on precipitous hillsides or ravines covered with tall grass, scrub and oak forest. Shoots or hurls itself headlong downhill when first disturbed. Extreme skulker, and difficult to flush a second time without dogs or until almost trampled on. The loud crow of the cock, heard early morning and at evening dusk, has been well rendered as *chĭr-a-pĭr, chĭr-a-pĭr, chĭr, chĭr, chĭrwa, chĭrwa*, and so on. As the bird sails across a ravine on open motionless wings it reminds one in a curious way of the Common Babbler (*Argya caudata*), which is a passable miniature of it.

The Monal or Impeyan Pheasant (*Lophophorus impejanus*) is a large, dumpy bird, rather ungainly for a pheasant, with a short, broad and square-cut tail. The brilliant metallic green head and crest (of wire-like spatula-tipped feathers), the glistening purple upper parts, white patch on back, cinnamon coloured tail and velvety black breast, render the cock unmistakable. The hen is a plain looking brown bird, mottled and streaked dark and pale, with a white throat and short crest of normal feathers. It occurs in the mountains of Afghanistan and in the Himalayas from Kashmir right across to extreme NE. Assam, at elevations between 6,000 and 14,000 feet, according to season.

Frequents high oak, rhododendron and deodar forest. Also seen near open sheep-grazing slopes and precipitous hillsides with grass and weeds growing on the narrow ledges. Digs with powerful bill for tubers and seeds on alpine pastures. Also eats berries, shoots and insects. A very silent bird on the whole, with apparently no regular crow, but an occasional whistling chuckle.

DISTRIBUTION: The White-crested Kaleej is found in the Western

Himalayas from Kashmir to Nepal, from the foothills up to about 10,000 feet elevation.

Several closely allied species represent it in the Eastern Himalayas, Assam and Burma.

No true pheasants occur in peninsular India or Ceylon, their place there being filled by the Red, Grey and Ceylon Junglefowls.

HABITS: The Kaleej inhabits all types of Himalayan forest with heavy undergrowth of bushes and bracken, and is partial to the neighbourhood of water. Pairs or small family parties come into the open to feed in the mornings and afternoons on *kutcha* forest tracks and firelines, and also in freshly-sown terraced fields on the hillsides. In foothills country the birds often associate with Red Junglefowl.

As with its relations, the diet is mainly vegetarian, consisting of shoots, tubers and berries. But insects and small reptiles are also readily eaten. The cock has a loud crow described as a 'whistling chuckle or chirrup'. When flushed it produces a variety of guineapig-like squeaks and chuckles.

NESTING: The season ranges, according to altitude, between March and June. The nest is usually little more than a crude collection of leaves and rubbish in a shallow scrape in the ground. It is placed under the shelter of an overhanging tuft of grass or stone, in a patch of jungle. The normal clutch consists of six to nine eggs, exactly like those of the domestic fowl—creamy-white to reddish-buff in colour.

THE PAINTED BUSH-QUAIL

Cryptoplectron erythrorhynchum Sykes

PLATE 63

SIZE: That of the Quail.

FIELD CHARACTERS: A brightly coloured quail with conspicuous deep red bill and legs. Male, olive-brown above, finely streaked with white and spotted with black; underparts chestnut mottled with black-and-white on flanks. Pure white throat, bordered by narrow, black loop. A narrow white band running backward from forecrown down sides of blackish head to nape. The female lacks the white throat and head stripe; her underparts are brick-red.

Coveys in broken grassland at edge of jungle.

DISTRIBUTION: The typical race *erythrorhynchum* occupies the Sahyadris

(Western Ghats) from about Khandala south to Travancore, including the Cardamom Hills, Nilgiris, Palnis, hills of Mysore, and associated ranges. Also the Shevaroys. The paler and smaller race *blewitti* occurs in the Central Provinces to the north and east of the range of the foregoing, stretching to Bihar and Orissa.

HABITS: The Painted Bush-Quail inhabits tall grass in broken foothills country, and thin scrub on open stony hillsides, especially on the edge of *sholas* and jungle, commonly between 2,000 and 7,000 feet elevation. Coveys of six to ten birds are normally met with. In the mornings and evenings the birds come out into opener patches to feed, and may then be seen dusting themselves on the sides of *kutcha* paths and cart-tracks.

Their habits do not differ from those of their better known cousins, the Rock and Jungle Bush-Quails. When flushed a covey scatters, but the birds soon begin calling to one another and work their way back through the undergrowth to re-unite. The call, something like that of the Jungle Bush-Quail yet different, is a soft whistling of about two seconds' duration repeated every couple of seconds or so. According to one observer (Primrose) it rises 'gradually till it reaches a certain pitch, which note is repeated a few times, and then dies down rather more rapidly'. The call uttered by the cock in the breeding season is rendered as *kirikee, kirikee,* and so on. It is said to be easy to imitate, and by this means the birds can apparently be decoyed without difficulty.

When flushed the bird utters a short whistle like the Grey Quail as it flies off low above the grass to tumble headlong into the undergrowth again after fifty or a hundred yards. Its food consists of grain and grass seeds for the most part, but white ants and other small insects are also eaten.

NESTING: The season is not well defined and varies locally to include practically every month of the year. The eggs—four to seven—are laid in a hollow scratched in the ground and thinly grass-lined, under a bush or rock in long grass or a scrub patch at the edge of forest. They are very like the eggs of the Jungle Bush-Quail—creamy-white to pale buff—but somewhat larger and deeper coloured.

THE COMMON HILL-PARTRIDGE

Arborophila torqueola Valenciennes

SIZE: About that of the Grey Partridge.

FIELD CHARACTERS: A dumpy, short-tailed partridge, olive-brown above, mottled with black and chestnut, and with a bright chestnut cap. A patch of bare crimson skin round the eye. Chin and throat black, with a white moustachial streak. Breast grey with a white band separating it from the black throat. Rest of underparts grey and white, with some chestnut on the flanks. In the hen the crown is brown, streaked with black; chin and throat rufous spotted with black; breast-band chestnut instead of white. Her breast is brownish.

Pairs or family parties in Himalayan forest.

The Rufous-throated Hill-Partridge (*Arborophila rufogularis*), in several local races, is also common in the Himalayas from Garhwal to Eastern Assam, between 4,000 and 8,000 feet elevation, and down through Manipur, Arakan, and the Burmese hills to Tenasserim. In some areas both species are found. Male and female are nearly alike and resemble the female of *A. torqueola*: i.e. they have olive-brown crown and bright rufous chin and throat. But the breast is slaty-grey (not brownish) and separated from the throat by a black band. Rest of lower parts grey; the flanks being slaty, spotted and streaked with deep chestnut and white.

DISTRIBUTION: The Himalayas from Chamba, Kulu and the Kangra Valley in the west to extreme east of Assam; also Naga, Chin and Kachin Hills. Divided into three races differing from each other in details and colouration.

HABITS: This beautiful partridge is essentially a bird of evergreen hill forest, found locally and seasonally at elevations between 5,000 and 10,000 feet. It is usually met with in family parties of six or seven, rummaging among the mulch and humus beneath dense forest of oak and laurel. It loves steepish broken hillsides covered with an undergrowth of ringal, grass, raspberry and other shrubs. The birds seem to prefer broad-leafed forest to conifers. When disturbed they trust to their agile legs for escape. Once flushed, however, they fly with considerable speed and dexterity in and out through the maze of tree trunks, often alighting up in a branch well hidden by the foliage. They roost at night in trees sitting all huddled together along a branch like babblers.

The mellow whistling call of this partridge is quite unlike that of any other game bird, and highly intriguing when heard for the first time. It is a low, rather mournful whistle of about 1½ seconds duration, repeated at regular intervals of three seconds or so, reminding one of the intake whistle of a schoolboy just learning. Occasionally, this is varied by a two- or three-noted call repeated three or four times, ascending in scale and tempo and ending abruptly. The birds answer one another from different parts of the forest and are particularly vocal in the evenings.

Its diet consists of seeds, shoots, berries and other vegetable matter, to which insects are freely added.

NESTING : The season is chiefly from April to June. The nest is merely a scrape in the ground, or a natural hollow, in dense ringal or scrub undergrowth—sometimes with the surrounding grass bending over to form a rough dome. The eggs—normally three to five—are pure white, with a fine texture, and well glossed.

THE CHUKOR

Alectoris graeca Meisner

PLATE 64

SIZE : Larger than the Partridge.

FIELD CHARACTERS : A large, plump, pinkish grey-brown partridge with conspicuous rib-like bars on flanks in buff, black and chestnut. A black band running across forehead through the eyes and down sides of neck to meet in a gorget or necklace on the upper breast. This black necklace, combined with the prominent white chin and throat enclosed within it, are unmistakable pointers to its identity. Bill and legs crimson. Female somewhat smaller and lacking the blunt leg-spurs of the cock.

Coveys on high open hillsides.

The Seesee Partridge (*Ammoperdix griseigularis*) is smaller in size— between the Quail and the Partridge—grey and sandy coloured, with orange-yellow legs and bill. It is a bird of the bare stony hills (up to about 7,000 feet elevation) of the Punjab, Sind and Baluchistan, extending westward beyond our limits. Its double whistling call is responsible for its local name 'Seesee' and its wings also produce a peculiar whistling sound in flight.

The Himalayan Snowcock (*Tetraogallus himalayensis*) is met with in the high Himalayas, chiefly between 9,000 and 18,000 feet—higher in summer, lower in winter—from NW. Kashmir to Garhwal, and else- where beyond our limits. It inhabits alpine pastures and rocky hillsides above the limit of tree growth, living on tubers and tender shoots and grass at the margin of the melting snows. It looks like a giant edition of the Grey Partridge (as large as a peahen minus tail) with mixed grey, white, chestnut and black plumage. When alarmed and running uphill, as it habitually does with a waddling goose-like gait, it jerks its tail up in the manner of a moorhen, revealing the white undertail coverts. The call of the cock, uttered from an exposed mound or ridge, is a loud, prolonged penetrating whistle of several notes with rather the cadence of the Common Green Pigeon's.

DISTRIBUTION: Throughout the mountainous country of the north-west, Baluchistan and Sind. Kashmir, Ladakh and the Western Himalayas east to Garhwal. It also extends beyond our limits in the north-west and north. Three races are recognized on minor differences of size and shades of colouration.

HABITS: The Chukor is eminently a mountain partridge living on barren rocky slopes, and in ravines, sparsely dotted with stunted grass and bushes. In winter it comes down to elevations of 4,000 or 5,000 feet, but reascends with the advance of summer to 15,000 or 16,000 feet. It commonly keeps to the neighbourhood of terraced wheat fields on the hillsides, and also works its way down to feed in the cultivated montane valleys. Parties of four or five birds are usually met with, but coveys of up to fifty and more are not uncommon in late autumn. Their diet consists of grain, tender shoots of grass and food crops, and insects. A quantity of grit is invariably swallowed with the food. Cocks call chiefly early in the mornings and late in the evenings, and are particularly challenging during the breeding season. The call, uttered from some exposed rock or eminence, is a rattling, gamey *kāk-kāk-kāk, kāwāk-kāk, kāwāk-kāk, kāwāk-kāk,* and so on, and sounds something between that of the Grey Partridge and of the Guineafowl.

Chukor are fast and strong fliers; they afford excellent sport when driven and are very good eating. By nature of the terrain they inhabit, chukor-shooting entails strenuous work for the shikari. When flushed, a covey scatters, the birds sticking to the contours of the hillside wherever possible and invariably flying downhill with great velocity.

If taken young, Chukor become very tame, moving freely about the house, following the inmates, and boldly attacking strangers and stray dogs. Cocks are highly pugnacious. They are kept for fighting purposes in NW. India, and considerable sums of money change hands over the bouts.

NESTING: The season ranges, according to altitude, between April and June—even later. The nest is merely a hollow scratched in the ground under shelter of a rock or bush, or at the base of a grass tussock, on rugged hillsides. Sometimes it is roughly lined with leaves and rubbish; at others practically without lining. The normal clutch is of seven to twelve eggs, but up to twenty have been found in a single nest. They are a pale yellowish or greyish-stone colour ranging to 'white coffee', with light reddish freckles scattered all over the surface.

THE WOODCOCK

Scolopax rusticola Linnaeus

SIZE: About that of the Partridge.

FIELD CHARACTERS: An outsize snipe; brownish with black and rufous markings forming a highly obliterative or camouflaging pattern. Long, slender, straight bill and comparatively short legs. Sexes alike. singly on damp or marshy patches in hill forest.

DISTRIBUTION: Kashmir, and the Himalayas generally east to west, between 8,000 and 12,000 feet elevation. Also beyond our limits in Europe and North Asia, east to Japan. Winter visitor to the Nilgiris, Palnis, hills of Travancore and Mysore, and other South Indian ranges. Occasional visitor to the central hill zone of Ceylon.

HABITS: The Woodcock is quite a common bird in parts of the Himalayas. It frequents fir and mixed forest with dense scrubby undergrowth in places where the ground is moist or waterlogged, as in the neighbourhood of streams. It is largely crepuscular and nocturnal, and unless specially flushed in day-time is seldom on the move till evening dusk and after sunrise. It probes deep into the mud for its food, which consists largely of worms and grubs. Its eyes are placed far behind the normal position in birds—literally at the back of its head—presumably to protect it from the attacks of predatory foes while it is busy feeding. Its flight is rather sluggish, very like that of the Painted Snipe, but it is expert at turning, twisting and dodging its way through the tree trunks. In spite of its large size, therefore, it needs considerable quickness and straight shooting to bring the bird to bag. In flight the bill is carried pointing characteristically downwards.

In the breeding season the male (?) may be observed at dusk and dawn flapping slowly across open glades, uttering a bat-like squeak at intervals, the significance of which is not clear.

Woodcock begin to arrive in the Nilgiris in October and reach the peak of their abundance in December–January. By the end of March they have all departed again. This species is one of those that normally perform their migratory journeys between the Himalayas and the Nilgiris in a single hop of at least 1,500 miles. Records of stragglers found in the intervening country are exceedingly rare. In their winter quarters in the South Indian hills, Woodcock frequent moist spots in *sholas* between 5,000 and 7,000 feet altitude or so. Their presence in any locality can be detected by the honeycomb-like beak holes they leave in the soft mud where they have been probing for food.

NESTING: Woodcock breed in the Himalayas. The season varies with altitude, and is mainly between April and July. The nest is a depression in the ground with a bed of dry leaves for the eggs. It is well concealed among bracken and other undergrowth, preferably near a stream in forest. Four eggs comprise a normal clutch. They are broad ovals, pale clay to deep buff in colour, marked with pale reddish-brown and grey blotches.

A curious habit of the Woodcock, which has been reliably observed, is its transporting its chicks when in danger, one after another, to a place of safety, carrying them pressed between its thighs and breast, dangling below the parent as it flies.

INDEX

(Italics indicate species described in brief only)